BASIC INTENT
AND THERAPEUTIC APPROACH
OF CARL R. ROGERS

BASIC INTENT
AND THERAPEUTIC APPROACH
OF CARL R. ROGERS

A STUDY OF HIS VIEW OF MAN
IN RELATION TO HIS VIEW OF THERAPY, PERSONALITY
AND INTERPERSONAL RELATIONS.

HARRY ALBERT VAN BELLE

WEDGE PUBLISHING FOUNDATION
TORONTO ONT., CANADA
1980

Printed by
ACADEMY PRESS LTD.
BURNABY, B.C., CANADA

WEDGE PUBLISHING FOUNDATION
229 COLLEGE STREET
TORONTO, ONTARIO, CANADA
M5T 1R4

I.S.B.N.: 0-88906-109-2

to Jenny

112423

Acknowledgements

No one ever writes a book strictly by himself. It is a cooperative effort involving the contributions of many people other than the author. I too am keenly aware that without the help of so many others I could not have written this book. I gratefully acknowledge my debt to them all. I want to make special mention of some, whose input and efforts were crucial to the creation of this book.

First, I want to thank Dr. Carl R. Rogers for responding so graciously to the steady stream of experimental chapters which I sent his way. His encouraging letters and conversations were a constant source of inspiration to continue. Perhaps I can best express my appreciation to him by saying that I always felt received by him in my analysis of his work.

Three persons have given almost as much of their time to this book as I have. I want to thank Prof. Dr. H.R. Wijngaarden for his sustained efforts to help me think my own thoughts. He truly gave me the freedom to learn. I am especially happy that throughout our many discussions I could become his friend. I thank Prof. Dr. C. Sanders and Prof. Dr. J. VanderHoeven for the many hours they spent critically evaluating the manuscript. Their critique and insight have been invaluable to me.

I thank the staff of the Institute for Christian Studies for the things they have taught me. They will recognize a kinship between their views and the perspective of this book.

No one has had a greater impact on my life than Dr. H.E. Runner. To him I owe the insight that life is integral. He gave direction to my life. I thank him for it.

Finally, how can I possibly thank the members of my family? To receive as much love as I have received from them over the years is a very humbling experience. Thank you Alicia, Terry and David for tiptoeing through the house all these years while "daddy was writing his book". I love each of you dearly. I could not have written this book without the self-giving support and dedication of my wife. Throughout these years of preparation, Jenny, you have been my loyal partner for better or worse and I love you for it. I think it is rather unfair that your contribution to this book is not recognized more visibly. If I had my way I would place your name next to mine on the cover of this book, where it belongs. But, since convention does not allow me to do this, I dedicate this book to you.

TABLE OF CONTENTS

CHAPTER ONE:
DELINEATION OF THE PROBLEMATICS

CHAPTER TWO:
CULTURAL-HISTORICAL INFLUENCES ON THE DEVELOPMENT OF CARL ROGERS' THOUGHT

CHAPTER THREE:

ROGERS' VIEW OF THERAPY, PERSONALITY AND INTER-PERSONAL RELATIONS

CHAPTER FOUR:

ROGERS' VIEW OF MAN AND ITS IMPLICATIONS FOR THERAPY

CHAPTER FIVE:

CRITICAL EVALUATION OF ROGERS' VIEW OF MAN IN RELATION TO PSYCHOTHERAPY, PERSONALITY AND INTERPERSONAL RELATIONS

CHAPTER ONE:

DELINEATION OF THE PROBLEMATICS

I. PSYCHOTHERAPY: ONE EVENT, MANY INTERPRETATIONS

In order to practice psychotherapy one needs to know what it is all about. For this, a thorough acquaintance with existing views of psychotherapy would seem to be a first requirement. By means of an intensive study of past and present approaches the student can come to know much about the subject. However, considering the diversity of viewpoints in psychotherapy, he may also come to think that he will never know what psychotherapy is all about.

A. Conflicting Totality Views of Psychotherapy

The variety of approaches which he encounters during his study is considerable. Implicitly or explicitly each approach pretends to speak about the whole of psychotherapy. Each pretends to define the ''nature'' of psychotherapy. Each pretends to describe what psychotherapy is all about. Some authors may indeed present their views as applying only to some parts of it, and acknowledge that other viewpoints are more applicable to other parts. But this involves them in yet another, hidden, more total view of psychotherapy in terms of which they can distinguish those parts to which their views are applicable from those to which they are not. In short, no matter how we turn it, each worked-out view of therapy intends to be a total view.

This in itself would present no problem if, in speaking about the *one* activity of psychotherapy, therapists had offered similar, or at least mutually consistent, views as to its character. In actuality, however, the viewpoints are often so diverse as to be opposed to one another.[1] All this leaves the student with the unenviable task of having to account for, and somehow reconcile these differences, as he seeks to obtain an understanding of the nature of psychotherapy.

In view of the unitary character of psychotherapy, it seems impossible that there be many divergent, or even opposing interpretations of the same event. Yet there are, and we must learn to deal with them if we are to learn from

1

them. So the question becomes: How can we learn from existing approaches what psychotherapy is all about, without getting lost in this diversity of interpretation? This question forms the background of all my deliberations in this dissertation.

B. Some Attempts at Unity

There are some easy ways of obtaining a unified view of therapy. One can simply write off this diversity of interpretation on grounds that it amounts to no more than a reflection of the pre-scientific state of current psychotherapy, and count on science to eventually bring about the unity of conception that psychotherapy seems to need. But this "living in the future" does little for one's present practice as a therapist, since there is as yet no such unified scientific view of therapy available. One can further ignore the diversity on grounds that it is "theoretical" only, and that in practice all therapists do more or less the same thing. However, close scrutiny of therapeutic practice is likely to show that in actual fact therapists very much practice what they preach.

Another way of dealing with the diversity is to discard all the divergent elements of the existing interpretations, and retain all those elements which they have in common. These common elements can then subsequently be combined to form a sort of common-denominator view of psychotherapy. Finally, one could come to a unified view, by simply recognizing only one of the existing views as the right approach to psychotherapy, and relegate all the others to the realm of pseudo-psychotherapy.

However, the trouble with all of these attempts at unity is that each of them entails that the authors of these existing views are less competent as interpreters of their experience than we are. For this is implied, if we claim to know which parts of the existing interpretations describe the nature of psychotherapy and which parts do not. But this will hardly do, if we are to learn what the nature of psychotherapy is, *from* these existing views.

C. Schoolformation and Extra-Therapeutic Considerations

Another solution comes to mind. Perhaps psychotherapy itself is so diverse that each of us can only see parts of it, but never the whole of it. This would mean the existing interpretations are as diverse as they are because psychotherapy is *not* unitary, but rather a highly complex, multifaceted phenomenon. This seems like an appealing solution, but it does not explain why so many approaches continue to say what psychotherapy is *all* about, and that in a manner that coflicts with what other views have to say about it. If psychotherapeutic systems can never be more than *approaches* to psychotherapy, why then do they so readily present themselves as *totality* views of psychotherapy?

This leads to the possibility that extra-therapeutic considerations may somehow play a role in what we have come to know as "schoolformation" in psychotherapy. Broadly speaking, psychotherapy is a human relationship in which one person attempts to help one or more other persons with their personal or relational problems. This implies that next to a view of therapy, one also needs a view of personality, of interpersonal relations and finally also a view of man. This is partially recognized by therapists when next to their approach to therapy, they also explicitly formulate a view of personality and of interpersonal relations. Much less frequently recognized or explicated is the fact that to do psychotherapy one also needs to have some kind of understanding of who man is. Psychotherapy being a *human* activity, persons being *human* beings, and interpersonal relations being *human* relations, none of these can be understood without some sort of view of man, or anthropology. A view of man is what a view of each of these has in common. An anthropology is that in which these three cohere. In it they find their unity.

II. INDEPTH STUDY OF THE RELATION BETWEEN PSYCHOTHERAPY AND ANTHROPOLOGY

In the interest of learning, therefore, how extra-therapeutic considerations influence the diversity of interpretation found *in* psychotherapy, it seems profitable to me to investigate the relation between psychotherapy and anthropology in the various approaches to psychotherapy. Quite possibly a comparative study of their respective anthropologies might show that there is less divergency on that level, and this would considerably alleviate the burden of the student in coming to know the unity of psychotherapy. The question thus becomes: How can we go about doing this? Psychotherapists seldom explicate their view of man. Most frequently, it is tacitly understood by them in the formulation of their view of psychotherapy. Their anthropology would thus have to be distilled from their writings via a process of inference. This in turn would seem to call for an indepth study of at least the major schools of psychotherapy prior to our being able to study their respective anthropologies comparatively.

Such an indepth study would start with a scrutiny of a given author's views on psychotherapy, personality and interpersonal relations and from the various hints distributed in his writings one would subsequently have to piece together his basic view of man which, because it is basic, would coincide with his basic intent in therapy. Or to put it more broadly, such an indepth study would first have to study the history and the systematics of a given approach to therapy, personality and interpersonal relations. That is, it would have to describe how these came into being and how they hang together conceptionally. Only thereafter could we explicate the view of man implied in it. Once this had been accomplished we would be in a position to review the relation between its anthropology and its psychotherapy as also to evaluate the relative merit of its anthropology *for* its psychotherapy. If this were done for all major approaches to psychotherapy we might find that what appears to be irreconcilable differences on the level of psychotherapy prove to be much less so on the level of anthropology.

A. Central Hypothesis of this Study

In this dissertation I intend to begin the investigation of the relation between psychotherapy and anthropology, by making an indepth study of the views of Carl Rogers, who is the originator of one such major approach to psychotherapy, namely that of client-centred therapy. The general hypothesis to be investigated might be formulated as follows: *There is an anthropological basis to Rogers' writings which comes to expression in his views on psychotherapy, personality and interpersonal relations. Knowledge of the former will increase our insight into the latter.*

B. Methodological Criterion

Before I outline in some detail how I intend to go about demonstrating this hypothesis, one more preliminary remark is in order. In indepth studies, the danger of devaluating the competency of the person under study to interpret his own experience is as great as in comparative studies. Thus in explicating his largely tacit view of man, I may, for the sake of cognitive closure, endow Rogers with an anthropology to which he does not in fact adhere, or I may invest him with a basic intent that he does not in fact have. In order to avoid that danger I intend to study, understand and present his views as much as I am able from out of his own "frame of reference". Thus in explicating Rogers' view of man I will attempt to be as "Rogerian" as I can be, with the understanding that if I were to study the views of Freud, I would attempt to be as "Freudian" as I could be, and if it were the views of Jung that I was studying I would be as "Jungian" as I could be.

An additional value of this empathic method of investigation is that it forms a practical test of Rogers' view of how we come to significant knowledge. According to Rogers, when we have empathically understood another person's private, personal world from the inside out, we have thereby also gained general knowledge, since he believes that what is the most personal is at the same time most general.[2] In adopting this approach as a method of investigating his views on psychotherapy I will, therefore, also learn how valuable an empathic understanding of his views will be for my coming to know the nature of psychotherapy.

Given this method of investigation, Rogers' response to my work will obviously be crucial in determining its success. Thus a major criterion for judging the worth of my description of Rogers' views will be the extent to which he can recognize himself in it.[3]

C. Outline of Dissertation Program

This brings me to the proposed outline of my dissertation. In chapter two I will give a biographical description of Rogers' early life and career. Its chief purpose is to show how the central theme of his life work originated within the cultural-historical situation in which he found himself. In this chapter I hope to demonstrate how Rogers' "non-directive" approach to therapy, (as it was then called), shows many important similarities to the central themes of the American culture in which it was forged. I will further show how, in developing his central theme, Rogers not only provided psychotherapy with some important new insights, but also offered some new solutions to the cultural problems of his time. Thus chapter two will describe how, historically speaking, client-centered therapy, (or person-centered therapy as it was later called), came into being and in doing so it will offer some reasons for its popularity.

A "central theme" is not the same as an approach to therapy or a view of personality or interpersonal relations. Thus chapter three will describe how this central notion came to work itself out in Rogers' views on these three areas of human life. It intends to be an exhaustive, systematic description of Rogers' view of therapy, personality and interpersonal relations. Its contents will form the raw materials for my description of his anthropology in chapter four.

My intention in chapter four will be to integrate the whole of Rogers' thinking into one systematic, unified description of his basic intent or anthropological commitment. The contextual implications of his anthropology for his psychotherapeutic approach will also be discussed. This will allow me to describe his therapeutic approach in terms of his anthropology.

Finally, in chapter five I will attempt to critically evaluate Rogers' view of man in relation to psychotherapy, personality and interpersonal relations.

CHAPTER TWO:

CULTURAL-HISTORICAL INFLUENCES ON THE DEVELOPMENT OF CARL ROGERS' THOUGHT

I. INTRODUCTION

The central purpose of this second chapter is to present a biographical sketch of Rogers' early life and career, based on autobiographical data found throughout his writings.

In pursuing this purpose, however, I will consciously seek to go beyond the mere enumeration of biographical facts. In addition I will attempt to highlight the significance of these facts for the development of Rogers' thought. I will do this by placing the biographical data gleaned from his writings in their cultural-historical context.

Thus, the overall attempt of this chapter is to understand, as concretely as possible, the man Rogers as a person embedded in a particular cultural climate and living at a particular time of historical development. In that manner this chapter will serve as an introduction to the more systematic presentation of his views in later chapters.

Because of its introductory character, this chapter will deal exclusively with the first part of Rogers' life. It will focus on the factors that influenced the development of his thought up until the time when his client-centered approach to psychotherapy had taken on a more or less definite shape. The third, more systematic chapter, will deal with the changes in his system, once it had come to be established.

More concretely now, this chapter will present, particularly, the early Rogers as an American, who grew up just after the turn of the century in a Protestant home milieu. He had a rather unusual combination of educational experiences, through which he came in close contact with the dominant cultural issues of his time. Subsequent to this he chose a vocation, in which he brought some of the pervading cultural themes of that time to specific expression. This is as far as I intend to go in my first chapter.

In order to achieve my aim in this chapter, it will be necessary to elaborate from time to time on the cultural-historical meaning of the biographical data that are presented. But it should be clearly understood that these cultural-historical elaborations are in no way meant to add anything to the biographical data obtained from Rogers' own writings. Rather, their purpose is to enrich the meaning of these data, such that by means of these elaborations the data will obtain more concrete significance for the reader.

Neither do they intend to deny the uniqueness of Rogers' many contributions to human knowledge and culture in general. On the contrary, I give these elaborations in the conviction that the uniqueness of Rogers' contributions can only be gauged concretely in comparison with the cultural-historical context in which he lived.

A major advantage of presenting Rogers' thoughts and deeds in the context of the dominant cultural themes of his time is that it may give body to a remark Rogers himself has made recently regarding the pervasive cultural impact of his work, this notwithstanding the fact that most of his work had been done in the relatively minor area of psychotherapy. After expressing surprise about this phenomenon, he suggests that is was perhaps due to the fact that . . . "without knowing it, (he) *had expressed an idea whose time had come*".[1]

By highlighting the cultural-historical background of Rogers' work, this chapter will hopefully make the meaning of this remark more concrete to the reader.

II. EARLY YEARS: FAMILY INFLUENCE

Carl Ransom Rogers was born on January 8, 1902, as the middle child in a family of six children, five of whom were boys. He lived most of his childhood years in the suburbs of Chicago, one of America's larger metropoleis.[2]

Rogers' recollection of his family is that of a rather cohesive, yet non-communicative family when it came to personal feelings and private thoughts. It was a family, furthermore, in which each member adhered as a matter of course to a set of unspoken regulations, instituted and maintained by subtly controlling, but also loving parents. These regulations were mostly prohibitive in character, aimed against certain behaviours, such as smoking, drinking and card playing, in which one was understood *not* to indulge, as a member of that family. It was also understood without saying by all, that their family was somehow different from the other families living in the area. This made for very little close social contact by the children with those outside of the immediate family circle.

Both his parents had received higher education, but they were down-to-earth in character, to the point of being anti-intellectual. They revered the work ethic. They were Protestant in their religion and within that context, fundamentalistic[3] rather than liberal in their convictions.

As it seems to Rogers, his mother became increasingly fundamentalistic over the years. Two of the "biblical" phrases used in the family prayers stand out in Rogers' mind as being particularly characteristic of her religion. These were: "Come out from among them and be ye separate", and "All our righteousness is as filthy rags in Thy sight, oh Lord". The first seems to have been her religious basis for limiting the social interaction of the family members with those outside the family.[4] The second expressed her conviction of man's basic inferiority, such that even at his best, man is not good enough.

In anticipation of later discussions, it is interesting to note that the convictions which his mother held on these points, and with which in extension, Rogers himself complied without thinking during his childhood, are in sharp contrast with the convictions which the mature Rogers held on these matters.

Whereas his mother seemed to have insisted on a separation of persons on the basis of religious creed, Rogers' adult life is characterized by what he himself calls an . . . "obsession with communication"[5] between all kinds of people, regardless of creedal or other differences. In fact, he elevates the recognition of and the respect for the inherent individual separateness of each person to a position, where it becomes the condition *sine qua non* for genuine interpersonal communication. The very principle which for his mother increasingly became the basis for dissassociation from others, leads with the mature Rogers to the closest communication possible between persons.

Secondly, whereas his mother seems to have been convinced that man is inherently evil, the pervasive conviction of Rogers' work is undoubtedly the inherent goodness of man.

These differences in basic conviction were not simply personal differences between Rogers and his mother, nor were they restricted to his family. As will become increasingly clear throughout this chapter, they reflect the religio-cultural differences of that period of American history.

As a child, Rogers himself was a dreamy youngster, who had a tendency to withdraw into fantasy and who incessantly read everything he could lay his hands on. This was contrary to the family convention, which held that reading was a leisure pastime, in which one could only indulge *after* working hours. He was also a bit of a loner throughout his elementary and highschool days. By his own admission, (p.376), he remained so throughout the rest of his life.

Rogers' father was self-employed, hardworking and successful in his business to the point where he was able to buy himself a hobby farm, some thirty miles west of Chicago. When Rogers was twelve, the family left the suburbs and took up permanent residence on the farm.

This was ostensibly done so that his father could thereby engage more fully in his hobby of running the farm by the latest scientific methods in agriculture. In actual fact, Rogers suspects that the move was made in order to shield the growing children from the evil temptations, that were presumed to be about in the city suburbs.

At any rate, the move was to Rogers' liking. On the farm, more than anywhere else, he acquired his lifelong fascination with the nature and growth of living things. There too, via books on experimental agriculture and the application of their contents in actual experiments, he acquired the deep admiration for and skill in experimentation and the scientific method. This was to remain with him for the rest of his life.[6]

With that kind of background and interest, it was almost a foregone conclusion that he should take up the study of agriculture in college, when in 1919 he reached the college age.

III. COLLEGE YEARS: PARTICIPATION IN THE Y.M.C.A.

It also went without saying that he should go to the University of Wisconsin, since all of the older family members, including his parents, had studied there. For the same reason, while at the university, he found lodging at the Y.M.C.A. (the Young Men's Christian Association) dormitory, since his older brother stayed there as well.

At the Y.M.C.A. Rogers joined a group of students in his field, which met each Sunday morning for bible study and discussion, resulting in all kinds of social service activities. Rogers mentions one such service he took upon himself, the leadership of a Boys Club. The friendship and companionship, the fellowship, the trust and closeness that developed between the members of this group was an extremely important experience for the young Rogers. Here, for the first time in his life was a group outside his family, of which he could feel a part, with which he could emotionally identify. Largely through the influence of his activities at the Y.M.C.A. Rogers made the decision in his second year at the university to change his vocational choice from agriculture to "religious work".

A. Protestant Evangelism and the "Religious Work" of the Y.M.C.A.

To place that decision in its proper setting some historical background on the Y.M.C.A. program is needed.

The Y.M.C.A. was an organization that had originated in Great Britain earlier, was imported into the U.S.A., and first instituted in Boston in 1851. It was one of the more successful ways in which Protestant churches of America attempted to stem the erosion of religion in the large urban centers of the U.S.A. It was social service oriented, interdenominational in character and particularly intended as an evangelistic outreach of the churches to the young men in the big cities. By means of all kinds of social services to them, the Y.M.C.A. attempted to bring them (back) into regular church life.[7]

It described itself as —

> a social organization of those in whom the love of Christ has produced love to men; who shall meet the young stranger as he enters our city, take him by the hand, direct him to a boarding house where he may find a quiet home pervaded with Christian influences, introduce him to the church and

Sabbath school, bring him to the Rooms of the Association, and in every way throw around him good influences, so that he may feel that he is not a stranger, but that noble and Christian spirits care for his soul.[8]

Prayer meetings, Bible classes, a reading room, an employment bureau, and a lodging house register were the principal features of the program.[9] However, the organization soon expanded to extend its outreach to many other groups in the cities, such as immigrants and other disadvantaged. This latter service was by and large performed by the very young men it originally focussed on as objects of its evangelization efforts.[10] In that sense, once a young man had been taken in by the Y.M.C.A., he soon found himself participating in the "religious work" of the Association, and Rogers was no exception. The pattern of this religious work was always the same: evangelization through social service.[11]

It is difficult for us, living in a post-protestant era of history, to fully appreciate the cultural impact which evangelization efforts like the Y.M.C.A. program and others by Protestantism had on Nineteenth Century America.

This was not the effort of a small minority in some out of the way part of the nation, but a total, concerted drive by people in the main stream of American Culture to "churchify" the people and rescue the nation from immorality.[12] In terms of the scope of its cultural impact it is comparable to the impact in our century of the sexual revolution of the fifties, the civil rights and counterculture movement of the sixties, and the Women's Liberation movement of the seventies. Religious work of all kinds was immensely popular during the nineteenth century, and also very successful in its results.

To be sure, Protestantism had been a dominant religious and cultural force in the U.S.A. from its beginning. But by the middle of the nineteenth century it had, by means of its evangelistic action, established undisputed sway over almost all aspects of the national life.[13] So much so was this the case that by the end of the nineteenth century it was redundant to speak of Protestant America, since Protestantism and America were practically synonymous.[14]

During the latter part of the nineteenth century, the name of Dwight L. Moody was frequently associated with the Y.M.C.A. program. He was a business man, who had been led to see the importance of the Y.M.C.A. work during one of the "businessmen revival meetings", a branch program of the "Y". He subsequently decided to devote all his time and business talents to the promotion of this type of work.[15]

Largely under his leadership, another type of "religious work" was instigated and made to prosper. This was the work of the Student Christian Movement (also called the Student Volunteer Movement) on the college campuses. Its aim was to recruit the best minds and most promising young students into the evangelization efforts of the Protestant churches. Its specific focus was foreign mission service, and it recruited its staff principally through mass rallies. As a result, thousands of students pledged themselves to "the evangelization of the world in this generation".[16]

During the Christmas vacation of his sophomore year, Rogers attended such a mass rally, which resulted in his decision to switch from agriculture to religious (or "Christian") work as the choice of his life's vocation. However, he did not want to go into the field of foreign mission, but rather into some sort of Christian leadership position at home.

B. Social Service, Means or End of "Religious Work"? A Shift

It should be noted at this point, that with respect to the types of evangelistic outreach as the Y.M.C.A. program, and others, there occurred a shift of emphasis and thinking within Protestantism, already in the latter decade of the nineteenth century. This shift had certainly completed itself by the time that Rogers became involved. Originally the social service and humanitarian efforts were very much intended as *means* toward the conversion of persons to Protestantism. But by Rogers' time they had become the *end*, the goal of "religious work".[17]

Foreign missions also increasingly became the transmission of all that was good in the American culture (which, as we have seen, had become decisively shaped by Protestantism) to nations and peoples abroad who were not so privileged, rather than the inculcation of the specific faith of the Protestant religion. Hence it is understandable that Rogers compares the Student Volunteer Movement with the modern Peace Corps, which expressed similar sentiments.

This shift could take place because Protestantism had increasingly begun to identify itself with democratic American culture in general. Thus, for example, it also had little difficulty supporting the American involvement in World War I. From the point of view of Protestantism of the first decades of the Twentieth Century there was little or not contradiction between the latter national effort "to make the world safe for democracy",[18] and its own peculiar effort "to evangelize the world in one generation".

This shift in emphasis by the churches to humanitarian service occurred particularly in the Liberal wing of Protestantism. It began to increasingly view church agencies as social service agencies for the promotion of humanitarian ends. In terms of this aim they became practically indistinguishable from other community agencies of this kind by roughly 1930.[19]

C. Effect of the China Trip on Rogers

Rogers came particularly in contact with this type of thinking in his junior year at college, when he made a six month journey to China as one of the ten U.S. student delegates to attend a World Student Christian Federation conference in Peking.

Much of this journey was made by ship. Because of its leisurely pace this allowed for prolonged and stimulating conversational contact by Rogers with such national and world reknown leaders of the Y.M.C.A. as John R. Mott, Kenneth Latourette and David Porter. In addition, he met with many foreign representatives of the Y.M.C.A. who, in Rogers' words, were "highly cultured, and well informed individuals'', and who were ''not at all the evangelical missionary types'' with which he was familiar. Rogers learned a great deal from them and was ''rapidly becoming much more liberal in religion and politics''.

As he discovered on his return to the U.S.A., this change of thinking implied a severing of ''the intellectual and religious ties'' with his family. He especially became aware of this on the return trip. As a result of conversations with Dr. Henry Sharman, ''a student of the sayings of Jesus'', he came to the conclusion that ''Jesus was a man like other men - not divine!''. Then it also became obvious to him that in an emotional sense he could never return home.

Rogers seems to have experienced this change in him as a liberation and a growth toward personal independence. He himself puts it this way:

Due to this six month trip I had been able freely, and with no sense of defiance or guilt, to think my own thoughts, come to my own conclusions, and to take the stand I believed in. This process had achieved a real direction and assurance — which never wavered — before I had any inkling that it constituted rebellion from home. From the date of this trip, my goals, values, aims and philosophy have been my own and very divergent from the views which my parents held and which I had held up to this point. Psychologically, it was a most important period of declaring my independence from my family.

When Rogers had made the decision, prior to his China trip, to go into religious work, he had switched his major area of study at the university from agriculture to history. He had felt that knowledge of history would better prepare him for the ministry. In his study of history, he was influenced by a number of gifted teachers. One paper which he wrote for professor George Sellery on ''The source of authority in Martin Luther'', stands out in Rogers' mind as particularly significant. In it he formulated for the first time the thesis . . . ''that man's ultimate reliance is upon his own experience'', a theme that stayed with him and became prominent in his writings in his later years.

In 1924 he graduated from Wisconsin with a B.A. degree in history, one year later than the rest of his classmates. The latter was partly due to the six month trip to China, and partly due to a stomach ailment, resulting from a duodenal ulcer. It had troubled Rogers ever since he was fifteen and he attributes it to the gently suppressive family atmosphere of his childhood.

IV. YEARS IN NEW YORK: UNION THEOLOGICAL
   SEMINARY

Subsequent to his graduation, Rogers got married and left for New York with his wife Helen, whom he had known from his childhood, to take up seminary training in preparation for the ministry.

His father offered to finance his entire education, provided that he would choose to attend Princeton Seminary, which at that time was the center of fundamentalistic thinking. Instead Rogers chose to go to Union Theological Seminary, "because it was the most liberal in the country and an intellectual leader in religious work". This was quite a decision to make for a newly married man, midstream in his educational career. For, even though Rogers, who had always been a top student, had little difficulty obtaining a good scholarship through which to finance his studies, by far the easier road would have been to accept his father's offer. That Rogers did not do so, shows how ready he was to act upon his newly formed convictions, in independence from his family background.

A. Influence of Liberalistic Protestantism

For Rogers the two years at Union Theological Seminary were very rewarding. As far as he was concerned, they gave him "the best philosophical training" he could have gotten anywhere.[20]

What impressed him most was the pervasive atmosphere of free independent thinking at Union. Rogers recalls one seminar in particular on religious and philosophical issues which moved him a long way toward a philosophy of life of his own. This seminar was started on the initiative of the students themselves and completely controlled by them. In it they set out to explore questions and doubts that they themselves had, to see where these would lead them. In thinking their way through these questions, most of the seminar participants, with Rogers among them, thought themselves right out of religious work.

For Rogers this meant that he could no longer see himself working in a profession which he would *have to* profess a prescribed set of beliefs as a condition for employment. His own views had changed tremendously, and it seemed likely to him that they would continue to change. Hence, he began to look around for a field in which he could be sure his freedom of thought would not be limited, and he found it in psychology.

There is little doubt that Rogers experienced this whole development of his thought, including his decision to leave religious work, as a process of gaining independence from an externally imposed point of view. Little did he seem to realize that his development away from one view of life implied the selection of, or at least a development towards another view of life which, if practiced with any degree of seriousness, would in time demand equally stringent adherence.

However this be, the development of Rogers' thinking away from the point of view that characterized his home life, culminating in the decision to leave religious work in exchange for another profession, did not occur in a vacuum. In the very least, it was facilitated by the trend in Liberalistic Protestantism of his day. Via its New Theology of Incarnation the latter had invested culture and the social process itself with redemptive tendencies,[21] and had thereby made the distinction between the church and the rest of culture meaningless. By implication it had also eradicated the distinctive meaning of religious work as opposed to social service.

The main theme of Liberalistic Protestantism in Rogers' time was its affirmation of ''humanity''.[22] It believed in the basic goodness rather than the sinfulness of man, and focussed its affirmation of ''humanity'' in a concern for human beings. Humanitarian services were propagated for their own sake rather than as means towards evangelization.[23] This view stood in sharp contrast to the fundamentalistic emphasis in American Protestantism. It strongly insisted on the sinfulness of men and maintained the earlier equation of the primacy of evangelism with a passion.

B. From ''Religious Work'' to Humanitarian Service

With Rogers himself, humanitarian service, working with individuals, clearly took precedence. His strong interest in helping people was again shown in that after he had rejected religious work as a vocation, he did not revert to his earlier interest of agriculture. Instead he chose a field of study that later would lead him to become a psychotherapist (a move not uncommon among ex-seminarians).

Rogers' interest in psychology was never academic. It was, and always remained, an applied interest for him, a means for helping the individual. His applied interest in psychology made it secondary to the general task of helping individuals. This may partially explain a phenomenon that always puzzled Rogers a bit, namely, that proportionately speaking his impact has been greater in areas outside the boundaries of psychology than among psychologists themselves.[24]

In this respect, his experience ran parallel to that of another great American thinker of his time, John Dewey, who, at least initially met with the same fate in the area of philosophy, for roughly the same reasons.[25] Many parallels could be drawn between Rogers and Dewey. This is not surprising, as we shall see presently, since in several ways Rogers was exposed to the influence of Dewey's thinking already early in his career, and Dewey's writings in turn expressed the general cultural mood of America in Rogers' time.

V. YEARS AT TEACHERS COLLEGE: DEWEY'S INFLUENCE

The purpose of this chapter, it will be remembered, is to sketch the cultural-historical influences on the development of Rogers' thought. Up until now, these influences had been very much tied in with the religio-cultural background of Protestantism, particularly as expressed in the conflict of its fundamentalistic and its liberalistic wing. It is this background which initially led Rogers into religious work and subsequently out of it.

15

A. Influence of the Wider Cultural-Historical Climate

Once into psychology, the wider cultural background, which had not been absent in his earlier development, but which was filtered through Protestantism, now began to play a more direct role in his thinking. This occurred particularly as he moved from Union Theological Seminary to take up studies in educational and clinical psychology at Teachers College, Columbia University. It continued during his early practical experience.

In this larger cultural-historical climate, the problem of the freedom of the "individual" versus conformity to "society", or some other external system was significantly dominant. In general abstract terms, this was the dilemma between following a prescribed course of action or pursuing one's individual choice of action as a way of life. It is this problem which from now on takes on direct significance in Rogers' thinking and professionally culminates in the development of his "non-directive" approach to psychotherapy.

To be sure, this problem had been operative in Rogers' thought prior to this point. In some sense it could be said to characterize his entire life from beginning to end. One only has to recall the manner in which he experienced the required uniformity of conduct that was part of his home life. Moreover, the resolution of this problem in favor of individual choice can be said to be the motive behind his decision to leave religious work. Yet, the direct manner in which this problem took charge of his life and intellectual development from here on down, was decidedly different from what it had been earlier.

Earlier the problem to be decided by Rogers had been one of "evangelization versus humanitarian help". With that problem resolved, Rogers now begins to ask *how* one was to help the individual. For Rogers the answer to this question was very much tied up with the above-mentioned wider, cultural dilemma which, for the sake of ease in description, I shall label as "individualism versus conformity."[26]

B. Historical Development of the Problem of "Individualism Versus Conformity"

For this reason too I believe it to be necessary to sketch, very schematically, the history of this problem, beginning at the founding of the U.S.A. and culminating in a description of the manner in which, in Rogers' days, the upcoming philosophy of Pragmatism attempted to resolve it.

Hopefully, my description will serve to demonstrate the pervasiveness of this problem in the American mind, and show that in being preoccupied with it, Rogers is very much an American. I would further suggest that the success of his work is in no small measure due to the fact that he placed a problem of this cultural magnitude central to his therapeutic approach. In the course of my sketch, I will also find occassion to elaborate rather extensively on the philosophy of Pragmatism. Hopefully this will bring the formative influence of especially Dewey's Pragmatism on Rogers' early thought into clearer focus.

1. formulation of the problem in early American history

Originally, America was a nation of Protest-ants, both in the ecclesiastical, and literal sense of the word. It was founded mostly by religious exiles from England, who in broad terms were Calvinistic in their outlook on life.[27] Within this camp, again roughly speaking, two factions were evident from the start — that of the Puritans who, with their emphasis on the "objectively revealed Will of God" stressed submission to law and order, and that of the Wesleyan Evangelicals who, with their emphasis on the personal religious conversion experience, stressed the free will of man, viewing negatively the "outward conformity to law" in human life.[28]

As could be expected from a nation founded by Protest-ants, it was this latter strain that predominated throughout its history, insofar as it was time and again held up as the ideal. Thus, for example, the New Evangelicalism within the churches of the late eighteenth century, and the Revivalism of the early nineteenth century led to the remarkable growth of Protestantism, *not* by placing the nation under the *ipse dixit* of the Law of God, but by appealing with gentle persuasion, to the ability of each individual to freely choose for "religion and morality". Thereby it was able to exercise its remarkable formative influence on the broader American cultural scene of the nineteenth century as well.[29] It could do this, because it appealed to what was fundamental to the thinking of every American, be he church member or not.

It was part of the democratic spirit that was shaping the nation in the eighteen hundreds to place the emphasis on the "individual" and his freedom in choosing a course of action, or forming a society. So much so had this become part of the American mind by Rogers' time that John Dewey could assert with confidence:

"Society is composed of individuals; this obvious and basic fact no philosophy, whatever its pretentions to novelty, can question or alter".[30]

This primacy of the "individual" over "society", ecclesiastical, political or otherwise, was rooted in the common conviction that all men ought to be treated as equal, — equal in the sight of God, equal before one's peers, and most of all equal with respect to the opportunities for development of resources, be they natural or human.[31]

Undergirding that conviction, there lay the peculiarly American optimism regarding the human individual: that, if allowed to follow his free conscience in matters of religion, he would rightly worship God; that, if respected as one among equals by society, he would acquit himself as a responsible member of that society; and that, if given equal opportunity for self betterment, each individual would naturally make the most of that opportunity.

Based on these convictions regarding the equality of all men, interhuman relations in the American culture tended to exhibit a number of characteristics peculiar to these notions. There is first of all an extraordinary sensitivity to, and concern for, the views and feelings of others. This is based on the argument that if the other is one's equal in every way, then, in relation to oneself, his views and feelings are as important as one's own.[32] Not only is this characteristic operative in the American culture with respect to religion or politics, but also in areas of marriage, family, and economic life. Wives, husbands, children and workers are first and foremost viewed as "individuals" and must be respected as such.[33]

Secondly, there is a general aversion to authoritarianism and an affirmation of permissiveness with repect to each other. This is based on the conviction that if the other is left to do his thing, he is more likely than not to do it right.[34]

Finally, the notion of equality comes to its clearest expression in interhuman relations, when it concerns the equality of opportunity for self-development. In the American culture the notion of equality never meant that all men are equal in terms of *acquired* possessions, status or learning. It is understood by all that, whether by fortune or sheer hard work, some persons will acquire more of these than others. However, it is equally understood by all that interhuman relations are not to be based on what any of the participants had acquired, but rather on his or her *potential for* such acquisition. For example, it is no sin, in the eyes of an American, that one citizen should acquire a higher social or economic status than another. However, if he were to pull rank on the basis of such acquired status, in relation to the other, he would be considered to be committing a violation against the dignity of the other as individual. His behavior would be interpreted as showing a lack of respect for the other's potential for self-development.[35]

Admittedly, the above characteristics are not always and everywhere actually practiced, but they are nevertheless consistently held up as the ideal.[36] *Ideally speaking,* therefore, interhuman relations in the American culture are basically *unconditional* in their intention. As we will see towards the end of this chapter, and even more fully in the third chapter, each of the above notions regarding persons, or interpersonal relations, can be found back almost verbatim as central notions in the writings of Carl Rogers. Specifically in his view of therapy, he, perhaps more than any other therapist, brought the central cultural notion of the primacy of the individual to specific expression in what was to become known as the client-centered approach to psychotherapy.

This American faith in the capacity of the individual for self-help was not entirely without base in the American experience. It had proved itself over and over in the early frontier days, when pioneers were often forced to settle in outlying areas and fend for themselves in total isolation from the support of social institutions that had already been established in the more settled areas of the land. It could even be said that, in absence of any social support to fall back on, the pioneer had to individually create his own societal structures in addition to providing himself and his kin with food and shelter. Thus in almost every way, a person at the frontier depended on his own individual resources and initiative, and for all that, he did admirably well. Little wonder then, that the primacy of the "individual" over his membership in a larger whole, of whatever description, became a particularly valued notion in the U.S.A.[37]

Nevertheless, such larger wholes did exist and brought with them issues that were peculiar to their functioning to be decided upon together. Yet given the above value pattern, there appeared to be only one way of resolving those social issues which extended beyond the individual's *individual* concern, and were *common* to all. In the absence of the superior judgment of any one person over another, all people are equally equipped to decide issues of common, or public concern, and thus only a quantitative expression of public decisions is attainable.

In this manner, public opinion came to be the sum of the individual opinions and took the form of majority rule. Again, the majority did not only rule in matters related to politics and citizenry. Democratic equalitarianism was never merely a way of running the country for Americans. Rather, it is their way of life. Thus the majority ruled in matters of public taste, religion, education, morals and ideals as well.

As a result of all this, there arose in the course of American history a curious juxtaposition of private and public opinion.[38] With respect to the former, the individual ruled supreme, and with respect to the latter, majority rule held sway. However, this formulation did little to resolve the age old dilemma of individualism versus conformity. For it will be immediately obvious that this duality was fraught with danger for the individual, in that the majority could readily threaten his freedom to choose his own course of action. This danger had become all the more real, since now the individual was bound to *voluntarily* conform to public opinion, rather than as a result of external compulsion. For, since the individual had himself contributed to the formation of public opinion, he felt morally obliged to conform to it.[39]

At the same time, however, once it had been established, public opinion could easily come to run counter to the course of action which the individual was prescribing for himself. Thus, this inner compulsion to conform to a democratically established, public pattern, could in time become as oppressive for the individual's self-realization as any form of external oppression ever had been. In that context, Toqueville's phrase "the tyranny of the majority"[40] and James Bryce's phrase, "the fatalism of the multitude"[41] were very appropriate descriptions of this danger. In Rogers' time, David Riesman referred to this same danger by calling it "other directedness".[42]

That danger, to put it as starkly as possible, meant that as a result of conforming to public opinion, the individual could lose confidence in his own capacity for self-realization, which was tantamount to losing faith in the basic motive of the American culture.

2. the solution of Dewey's Pragmatism

It was to this problem that American Pragmatism, especially in the person of John Dewey, addressed itself prophetically. Dewey's solution to this problem whether by design or by accident of his Pragmatistic philosophy, was simple: Make every established opinion and institution inherently subject to future reconstruction, and make the individual the agent of this continual renewal.[43] Thus the genius of the Pragmatist solution to the dilemma in which the American culture found itself round the turn of the century, consisted in the fact that it performed a marriage between public and private opinion, in such a way that both would receive their *relative* due in American life.

2.1 the interactive relation between the "individual" and "society"

Dewey first of all asserted the notion that all things, events, and conditions at any level of complexity exists only in perpetual development. But he combined this with the notion that individuals had the capacity to perpetually *improve upon* things, events and conditions as they existed at any given stage of development. He held that conditions were subject to change, but argued that whether this change would in fact be an improvement depended upon the extent to which individuals would interact with the conditions to bring about the desired change.[44] Thus, this pragmatistic formulation reaffirmed the relative importance of private and public opinion in the American culture by prescribing the perpetual reconstructing interaction of the individual with the existing social conditions as a way of life.

Dewey performed this feat by making change, more specifically, growth, a central notion in his philosophy. In emphasizing change rather than rest as the basic characteristic of reality, he, and other pragmatists, not only took issue with the notion which had been prevalent in philosophy for millennia, to the effect that there exists an unchanging ideal pattern of social intercourse, and a natural rational-moral order unto which it was the business of human life to aspire.[45] But thereby he also took issue with the Newtonian view of the physical world as a static deterministic world[46] and with the sensationalistic, elementaristic notion that consciousness consists of the association of discrete mental elements.[47]

In combating these notions, and others akin to them, by positing that reality is dynamic rather than static, Dewey was greatly aided by the theory of evolution. The latter had made its inroads into American culture already decades before the appearance of Pragmatism as a cultural force. The theory of organic evolution, orienting itself to the biological sciences, saw growth, that is the coming into being and development of species of organisms, as occurring, not in accordance with some inner principle that was presumed to be inherent to each species, but rather as a result of the organisms' perpetually adaptive responses to the everchanging demands of their environments.[48]

American Pragmatism accepted this notion of growth as the mainstay of its systematics. We find it particularly expressed in Dewey's instrumentalism or experimentalism as it is better called.

Dewey starts with the principle that reality is basically a set of interactions between nondescript entities. In time, clusters of such interactions tend to separate and organize themselves into dynamic wholes or organisms. Motivated by a drive to enhance their own organization, these interact as wholes with their environments for that purpose. That is, they adapt their internal organization and outward action to these environments and adapt their environments to their needs so as to secure maximum possibility of survival.

This interactive (later better called transactive) process, Dewey characterized as growth. He saw it as the fundamental characteristic of *all* that has continuous existence, (including physical, living and human existence as well as the existence of individuals and societies).[49]

It explained, for Dewey, the characteristics of the various kingdoms (rocks, plants, animals, and human beings) and their relations. It did this by defining these as increasingly higher (meaning both improved and more complex) levels of organized interaction with their environment, in a manner that had the higher levels emerging from the lower. This entailed, for Dewey, that the lower levels of organization would become the means, the instruments, the environments, the experimental material in interaction with which higher levels of interaction were formed.[50]

It also explained for Dewey what went on at the highest level of interaction that human beings could possibly attain, the level of the social. There, established mores, habits, opinions, and social institutions were to be the givens with which individuals could experiment. By trying out hypotheses of improved (that is more growth promoting) ways of living (together), they could learn which ways of living would "work" (that is, they could discover which would eliminate the obstacles to growth in the existing life styles).[51]

2.2 Dewey's Solution is a compromise

We are now in a position to summarize in sufficient detail one aspect of the Pragmatist solution as championed by Dewey to the problem of the "individual versus society". It holds that social conditions, existing at any time are first and foremost the results of past experimentation on, and reconstruction of, previously existing entities of this kind. Moreover, by the same reasoning, they are material for future experimentation and reconstruction by individuals, acting alone or together. The sole criterion in terms of which this process is to occur is the improved growth of individuals. In that sense American Pragmatism views present styles of living (together) as experimental realities, in terms of being both the product of past experimentation and the material for future experimentation in the direction of improved individual growth.

Nevertheless, with respect to the basic motive of the American culture, this solution was a compromise. It was a solution that gave both the individual and the social conditions their *relative* due, but not one which maintained the *absolute* primacy of the individual. Earlier, the relationship between individuality and conformity, between the "individual" and "society", between private and public opinion had always been experienced as *paradoxical* in the American mind. Moreover, the resolution of this paradox had always been accomplished in favor of the individual. With the ascent of especially Dewey's pragmatism, this relation became *interactive*.[52]

Furthermore, it should not escape our notice that this pragmatistic solution to the problem brought with it a subtle change in the meaning of the notion of "self-realization". Earlier "self-realization" had been understood as being synonymous with "individuality". Now it became synonymous with "change", "improvement", "growth".

As I see it, Dewey's solution had effectively freed the individual from the stranglehold of tradition. That is, it freed the present from the past. This it accomplished by holding that present conditions are always to some degree problematic and must change or rather improve. More specifically, it held that if the present does not change, it *becomes* problematic, such that it is the past *in* the present that is problematic. In that sense, life for Dewey is perpetually experimental, a never ending exercise in problem solving. The past *qua* problem, in the present conditions, is the material for this experimentation, and control over present conditions is maintained only through its perpetual renewal and reconstruction by individuals.

However, by this formulation Dewey in effect ties individuality to time and activity and makes it wholly dependent on them.[53] That is to say, for Dewey one *is* not an individual first and foremost, as it were by birthright, as was previously argued, but one only *becomes* an individual insofar as one is actively involved in improving things as they are. There is no room in Pragmatism for doing things "the same way" for an extended period of time even when this is one's individual choice. For such a choice represents stagnation and consequently the opposite of self-realization.

Due to criticisms by others on this point, Dewey himself came to realize later in his life that this formulation, which largely stems from his earlier development, could, contrary to his intentions, condemn the individual to a life of excessive change. Thus, he later begins to emphasize more and more the *consumatory* phases of the reconstruction process.[54] This emphasis represents the other aspect of the pragmatist solution to the problem.

The settled, the results of experimentation and reconstruction, now also get their due. Thus, in order to counteract the undesirable side effects of excessive cultural change[55], Dewey felt constrained in his later life to emphasize more the established (which, since the individual was seen as the exclusive agent of innovation, was at the same time the social, the common) rather than the changing.

However, it is clear that *this* emphasis reignites with full force the old controversy regarding the relationship of the individual to the existing social conditions. That is, this emphasis on *results,* could once again threaten individual freedom. Thus the full pragmatistic solution to the problem of "individualism versus conformity" is at best a balance solution, based on the primacy of interactive growth, rather than on the primacy of individuality.

I have gone on at length to develop the views of the pragmatist Dewey in the foregoing pages because of the pervasiveness of his influence on all phases of American life. One simply does not understand the cultural-historical mood of early twentieth century American if one bypasses his impact on the nation.[56] This pervasiveness of Dewey's impact on American culture also forms the basis for our suggestion that his influence on Rogers' thought went far beyond the several books which the latter may have read on, or courses he may have taken in, Pragmatistic philosophy.[57]

C. Rogers' Academic Contact with Dewey's Pragmatism Through Kilpatrick

We have now dealt with the problem of individualism versus conformity and its development through pragmatism in sufficient detail, to take up the further development of Rogers' career and thinking, starting with his stay at Teachers College (T.C.), Columbia University. It was at T.C. that Rogers experienced his first, (and as far as we know, his only) *academic* contact with Dewey's Pragmatism.

Pragmatism was wholly unlike most other philosophies, which first tend to become known in academic circles, and only much later receive popular assent. Although a formidable *philosophical* movement in its own right as was recognized later, Pragmatism initially gained more acceptance in areas outside of philosophy and science. Its initial impact was on the practice of living, rather than on the theory of science.

Largely through the efforts of John Dewey, it was beginning to exercise great influence on American childhood education around the time when Rogers left Union Theological Seminary for T.C. to take up studies in clinical and educational psychology.

Dewey himself had taught at T.C.[58], and had made a number of devoted followers among the faculty. One such disciple of his educational views was William H. Kilpatrick. The latter is himself well known in education circles as the originator of the ''project method''[59], a teaching technique wholly in line with Dewey's educational philosophy. With him Rogers took a course in Educational Philosophy while he was still at the seminary. This course was largely Deweyan in content.

It was Rogers' contact with Kilpatrick at T.C. that structured and consolidated the more pervasive influence of Dewey's Pragmatism, which Rogers experienced in the American culture everywhere. It also laid ground work for his views on education, which later in his life came to practical expression in his own unique approach to education. Of Dewey's educational philosophy, Rogers says in his autobiograpy: ''It has been influential in my thought ever since''.

To be sure, Dewey's influence on Rogers was not restricted to his views on education only. As Idomir[60] has shown extensively, there is in many respects basic philosophic compatibility between Rogers' later developed client-centered counseling and Dewey's Pragmatism. Elsewhere[61], Rogers quotes Dewey with what he himself calls ''fundamental agreement'', when the latter states that:

''Science has made its way by releasing, not by suppressing, the elements of variation, of invention and innovation, of novel creation in individuals.''

Next to sharing Dewey's belief in such basics as the process character of reality and the importance of growth in human life, Rogers was perhaps most attracted to Dewey for the accent which the latter placed on the individual as the agent of innovation.

D. Other Influences on Rogers at Teachers College

Rogers also underwent other influences during his time at T.C., influences which were more specific to psychology. From Leta Hollingworth he learned the clinical approach to psychology. Inspired by her warmth, and guided by her skill, Rogers learned to work with individual children in terms of their emotions and personality dynamics. He was further exposed to this clinical approach during his internship at the newly formed Institute of Child Guidance of New York, where the dominant approach was Freudian.

If Rogers was appreciative of these experiences, he was less enthralled with the decidedly experimental approach to psychology at T.C. Its overall emphasis following Thorndike was on measurement and statistics. In sharp contrast to the clinical approach, it scorned such things as emotions and personality dynamics. As Rogers puts it: ''Freud was a dirty word at T.C.''

Thus, during his training Rogers was exposed to both the experimental and the clinical approach in psychology, and he experienced the tension between these two acutely. This was perhaps his first major confrontation with the dilemma concerning the relation between person and science, between the subjective and the objective. In his later life he tried his utmost to resolve this dilemma. But he finally had to resign himself to it (although not unhappily so, p. 379) as a paradox, saying that it was a matter of ''and — and'' rather than ''either — or''. For all that he was in good company. Earlier, William James, in his *''Principles''*, had come to the same conclusion.[62]

The Freudianism of the Institute where Rogers did his internship was not dogmatic, but eclectic in character and as such showed the influence of Pragmatism on its operation. A central notion of Pragmatism has always been that the meaning of any idea lies beyond itself, in the consequence it engenders in practice.[63] Thus therapeutic theories, too, receive their meaning from the effects they generate in therapeutic practice. Whether a therapeutic approach is meaningful is in this view wholly determined by its outcome, by whether it ''works''. From this vantage point, therapeutic approaches become ''techniques'', i.e. ways of obtaining effect, and therapy as a whole becomes the application of such techniques for the purpose of obtaining results.[64]

Eclecticism in American psychotherapy illustrates this pragmatistic notion of therapy.[65] It tends to take any number of existing therapeutic approaches and it converts these into therapeutic techniques. That is to say, it tends to take any number of these approaches, which could be so divergent as to be opposed to each other in their intent, and utilizes these in therapy as tentative, hypothetical ways of intervening in a person's life, united only by the selective principle of effectivity.

Because of the eclecticism of the Institute, Rogers was exposed to all kinds of psychoanalytic, psychiatric and psychological thinking during his internship. As an educational experience Rogers found the eclectic approach of the Institute very helpful, and at least during his early career he adopted this model as his therapeutic *modus operandi*.

VI. ROCHESTER AND OHIO YEARS: EARLY THERAPEUTIC PRACTICE AND ACADEMIC CAREER

After completing his internship, Rogers took a position with the Rochester Society for the Prevention of Cruelty to Children. There he functioned as a psychologist in its Child Study Department. He was to remain at Rochester for the next twelve years. During those years, Rogers immersed himself completely into the practice of providing psychological services. His clients were mostly the delinquent and underprivileged children and their parents, which were sent to his department for study and treatment by the courts and other community agencies. His work consisted by and large of diagnosis and planning for treatment, but he also carried on some "treatment interviews", as psychotherapy was then called. His only criterion in doing all this was: "Does it work?", "Is it effective?".

Thus, initially Rogers worked very much within the Pragmatistic conception of therapy. In his practice we see him busy applying every conceivable therapeutic technique or manipulation on the market to the juveniles and their environments, in order to resolve their delinquency problems. Such techniques included a change of environment and/or institutional placement for the juvenile, as well as the modification of his environment as treatment possibilities. There also were the treatment interview techniques and "deeper therapies" as the equivalents of modern counseling and psychotherapeutic techniques. The choice of any of these was usually decided on the basis of an elaborate diagnostic workup on the individual in question. Yet the criterion was always the same, and the predominant concern regarding any technique was always that it would "work".

Over the years Rogers became quite an expert in dealing with problems of child delinquency. A full description of those techniques which he came to consider most effective, is found in his first major publication, *The Clinical Treatment of the Problem Child.*[66]

A. The Effect of Pragmatism on Rogers' Rejection of Therapeutic Dogma

Rogers' adherence to this pragmatistic notion of therapy was very important for the development of his thought. This becomes evident when we consider that from the outset Clinical Psychology and psychotherapy were inseparably connected with Freudian Psychoanalysis. The latter was so much *the* authority in these fields in Rogers' days, that it was viewed as being virtually synonymous with therapeutic treatment. Thus for one to reject psychoanalysis was tantamount to rejecting therapeutic treatment outright. Yet, throughout his work Rogers time and again came to conclude differently about the value of psychoanalytic theory, as is illustrated by the following example.

Following the lead of one psychoanalytic theory, which held that delinquency is often based upon sexual conflict, Rogers had been working with a youthful pyromaniac, incarcerated in a detention home. The boy had an unaccountable desire to set fires, which he seemed unable to control. After a lengthy period of therapy Rogers was finally able to trace his desire back to his sexual impulses regarding masturbation, thus presumably "solving" the boy's problem. However, contrary to the predicted outcome, the youth again reverted to his fire setting behavior shortly after his discharge from the detention home. This incident impressed Rogers with the possibility "that there were mistakes in the authoritative teaching and that there was still new knowledge to discover" (p. 358).

Rogers himself bases this conclusion on the fact that his *experience* did not bear out the *prediction*. However, this by itself can hardly be the ground for the particular conclusion that Rogers drew, since by itself experience is ambiguous and the *attitude,* with which one approaches one's experience, will contribute considerably to the conclusions that are drawn on the basis of it. Had Rogers been a dogmatic, rather than an eclectic Freudian in his attitude, he might have questioned his own therapeutic ability or his own interpretation on the basis of the same experience, rather than the authoritative teachings of psychoanalysis. That he did not do so, seems largely due to the fact that he was principally guided by the pragmatistic notion of effectivity in doing psychotherapy. This allowed him to convert existing therapeutic dogma into tentative therapeutic techniques and at the same time allowed him to discard any technique that proved to be ineffective in practice. Thus in the course of his practice Rogers discarded many such techniques and retained only those which yielded the desired effects. This latter group of techniques ultimately found its way into the above-mentioned publication.

However, in keeping with the pragmatistic spirit, Rogers did not consider this publication (nor for that matter anything else he ever wrote)[67] his final word on therapy. He fully expected his views to keep changing upon the discovery of more effective techniques as a result of further experience and experimentation. Already in this, his first book, one can detect an undercurrent of dissatisfaction with the techniques it enumerates. Whereas the effects of their application were real enough, they were not found to be always and everywhere applicable. Moreover, when they were applicable, their effects tended to be superficial and not lasting over longer periods of time.

B. Major Shift: from Experimentalism to Non-Directivity

At this point the direction of Rogers' thinking took what is perhaps the most important turn of his life. Rather than restricting himself to discarding these techniques in favor of more effective techniques, as would be consistent with a pragmatistic stance, Rogers came in time to doubt the very notion of technical control itself as a way of doing therapy. He began to question whether it was therapeutically appropriate to apply techniques to persons, particularly in a therapy which has as its expressed goal the growth, the self-realization of the persons to whom such techniques are applied. As Rogers discovered in his practice, expert manipulatory control is therapeutically ineffective when applied to people.[68]

He recounts one instance that particularly brought this fact home to him. He had been working with a highly intelligent mother, concentrating the session with her on her relationship to her son, whom she found very difficult to handle. As far as Rogers was concerned the problem was clearly that of her early rejection of the boy, but over the many interviews that he had with her he was unable to help her to that insight. Finally, he gave up and suggested that they terminate the contacts. Whereupon the mother requested therapy for herself, and when this was granted she proceeded to relate, in a much more genuine fashion, where she herself experienced the problem areas in her life. As a result, real therapy began and was ultimately highly successful — for her and her son.

This incident, among others, helped Rogers . . . "to experience the fact . . . that it is the *client* who knows what hurts, what direction to go, what problems are crucial and what experiences have been deeply buried"(p. 359).

As a result of experiences such as this, Rogers resolved henceforth . . . "to rely upon the client for the direction of movement in the (therapeutic) process"(p. 359). Thus his therapeutic approach became increasingly non-directive.

C. Beyond a Pragmatistic View of Therapy

By embracing the non-directive principle in therapy, Rogers' thinking took a significant step beyond Pragmatism. For the pragmatistic conception of therapy implied that the therapeutic process was to be *experimental* in charac-ter. That is to say, to every new individual case previously proven established techniques were to be applied with the aim of determining to what extent these were effective for the client *now* in therapy. At the same time, the response of the client to these established techniques served to validate existing therapeutic methods or showed where these methods needed modification. In this manner the techniques were understood to remain in tune with the everchanging population of clients. As the result of this interaction between the individual preferences of a particular client and the established techniques deemed more or less applicable to any client, two kinds of improvement were hypothesized to be the likely result. The client was likely to improve through the beneficial application of proven techniques, and simultaneously, the established tech-niques were likely to improve through their application to individual clients.

The kinship of this therapeutic method to the "scientific method" operative in most modern empirical sciences, will be obvious. This is not surprising since Dewey saw the "scientific method" as *the* paradigm for successful living, everywhere. The pragmatistic notion of therapy was merely the specific application, within therapy, of the pragmatistic view of human life in general.

This view of life saw the interaction of the "established" with the "new", of the "common" with the "individual", as the royal road to pro-gressive change in life's every area, including therapy. For Dewey the scien-tific method was of the essence of human life. To put it another way, earlier we saw that Dewey resolved the problem of "individualism versus conformity" by marrying the "individual" to "society". I can now say that it was the scientific method that performed the ceremony. *Both* the "individual" and "society", both the "new" and the "established" are relativized by Dewey, to this basic experimental, instrumental (later "transactional") movement of human life.

However, the manner in which this interaction takes place in therapy, should not escape our notice. In this interaction process, it is always the therapist, as the representative of the established and the common, who supplies the techniques and the hypotheses. With respect to the techniques, the activity of the client, as a representative of the novel and the individual, is entirely restricted to giving confirming or corrective feedback. This therapeutic paradigm thus tends to retard the improvement of both the client and the techniques. It retards the improvement of the client because it does not free therapy from being a situation where one person (the therapist) attempts to solve the *personal* problems of another (the client). At a minimum this hampers the individual development of the client, which is the goal of both the pragmatistic and the Rogerian approach to therapy. Second, it also retards the improvement of established techniques since in the pragmatistic view of therapy, the client's response can only *modify* or *reject* existing techniques, but it can never be the source of *radically new ones*.

With his non-directive innovation, Rogers went beyond Pragmatism in this sense, that he insisted that the individual client become the sole source of hypotheses with respect to what was to occur in the therapeutic process.

The revolutionary character of this move on Rogers' part becomes clearer to us when we contrast his newly developed approach with the dogmatic approach to psychotherapy. In the latter approach the client is clearly identified as the patient, who will obtain therapeutic relief only insofar as he *adapts* himself to the expertise of the therapist, which at least for the purpose of therapy is considered to be beyond question.

Admittedly, Pragmatism had modified this model, by insisting that both the input of the therapist and the client are involved in whatever improvement occurs in therapy. However, Rogers goes much further and totally reverses this model by insisting that therapy can only be successful to the measure that the therapist adapts himself to the client. In Rogers' view, it is the client who must take the lead and it is the therapist who must follow, if therapeutic improvement is to occur. As with pragmatism, this principle has reference with Rogers, to both the improvement of the client and the socalled therapeutic techniques. For therapy, Rogers' move from experimentalism to non-directivity meant ultimately that science was removed from its position of being the sole guide in the therapeutic process to be replaced by the individual client as its guide. Anyone acquainted with Rogers' life work, knows that this in no way meant a repudiation of science. Rather, Rogers wanted thereby to make science the servant of the individual rather than its master.

Rogers' claim that he came to his change from experimentalism to non-directiveness (ultimately client-centeredness) on the basis of his therapeutic experience has more to say for itself than his earlier assertion that he changed from dogmatism to pragmatism on the same experiential basis.

This is so first of all, because his non-directive approach comes much closer to realizing the goal of the self-realization of the individual, which it shared with the pragmatistic conception of therapy. But more importantly, both therapeutic approaches served people of a nation whose major value was the primacy of the individual and such people are likely to resist the controlling efforts of therapeutic experts as much as they earlier resisted the ecclesiastical control of the clergy, or the democratic will of the majority. Thus the most likely feedback one was to receive from the client's responses in therapy based on the pragmatistic paradigm, was resistance to the techniques being applied. And since resistance is the opposite of therapeutic change, the client was not likely to show great improvement on that basis, as Rogers experienced. Furthermore, with respect to the techniques the client's responses were more likely to result in their *rejection* rather than their *modification*.

Thus the client population itself was likely to be a big factor in experientially demonstrating the need for an alternative to the pragmatistic approach to therapy. Nevertheless, here too, Rogers needed to make a basic change in his attitude toward man before he could liberate therapy from the pragmatistic impasse, via his nondirective alternative. It was only because he reaffirmed the primacy of the individual that his experience could show him that the non-directive approach to therapy was more productive than the experimentalism he formerly adhered to.

Rogers' non-directivity/client-centeredness in therapy represents a specific expression of a general rule for human life, dominant in American culture. It holds that the "common" adapt itself to the "unique", that the "old" adapt itself to the "new", and that "society" adapt itself to the "individual". Thus, as we shall see in the conclusion of this chapter, the revolutionary import of his innovation is not restricted to therapy only, but extends itself to every area of American life.

In moving toward non-directivity in therapy Rogers was clinically aided a great deal by the relatively new approach of "relationship therapy", which based itself on the views of Otto Rank, a renegade Freudian, who stressed the centrality of the will as an expression of the positive, unifying, growing, creative aspects of the individual in his movement toward independence. For therapy, as the mobilization of this will, this, according to Rank, entailed that the therapeutic process was to be flexible, adaptable, individual and patient-centered, and further that every relationship between patient and therapist should be a unique and creative process, in which the patient, not the therapist, needed to point the way to his particular method of achieving self-determination and self-direction.[69]

Strengthened by these insights and additional supporting therapeutic experiences, Rogers proceeded to develop his unique brand of non-directive therapy in his practice at Rochester and also later, when he left Rochester, to take up a teaching position at Ohio State University.

It was in teaching the graduate students there what he had learned about treatment and counseling that he increasingly felt the need for a more systematic formulation of his approach to therapy. Thus, after an initial attempt to crystalize his views in a paper which he presented at the University of Minnesota in December 1940, he gave the first fully systematized description of non-directive therapy in his book — *Counseling and Psychotherapy*, published in 1942.[70]

For the most part, this book was still a negative description of the counselor's role, concentrating on what the counselor or therapist, (for Rogers these are interchangeable) ought to refrain from doing, as also the term "*non*-directive" indicates. Nevertheless it contains many of the basic insights which later came to positive expression in his "client-centered" approach to therapy.

As we would expect, and as we will see in more detail in the following chapter, Rogers continued to change his views subsequent to the publication of his book. He also continued to be influenced by others (notably by Kierkegaard, Buber and Polanyi). None of these changes were fundamental, however. Neither did any of these outside influences, even though they were often enriching and sometimes even corrective, materially change the basic position at which Rogers' thinking had arrived in 1942. By that time Rogers had come to a definite position. Subsequent to that, he himself began to shape the cultural environment which previously was instrumental in the development of his approach.

VII. CONCLUSION: THE REVOLUTIONARY IMPACT OF ROGERS' "IDEA"

We have followed the development of Rogers' thoughts throughout the period of his early life, of his educational experiences and his early career, up until the time when he "expressed an idea whose time had come". That idea essentially expressed the primacy of the individual in human life, now not as an ideal but as a program, first as a therapeutic program and finally as a social program. The idea itself was by no means new, as we have seen, but the manner and time in which Rogers expressed it can be said to be truly revolutionary, so much so that it makes Dewey's earlier attempt to do the same look decidedly conservative.

In order to catch the revolutionary import of this idea we must understand the immediate cultural-historical context in which Rogers expressed it.

The American nation was founded, we saw, in protest against external ecclesiastical control. This resulted in an emphasis on voluntary, free individual choice in matters of religion. This emphasis in time extended itself to other areas of American life as well. Finally, it became culturally established as the central motive of democratic equalitarianism, stressing individual decision in matter of private, and majority rule in matters of public concern.

It was Pragmatism's role in American history to free the individual from the control of tradition even when this tradition had been democratically established, and could therefore require the *voluntary* submission from the individual. Dewey did this by stressing the dynamic character of life, and by making the established traditions and institutions themselves subject to perpetual reconstruction, in accordance with the scientific method. Thus,

Dewey rescued the present from the control of the past by means of the scientific method as a way of living for individuals.

This nevertheless still left the individual under the control of science, and compared with the innovative creative power of the individual, (a notion to which both Dewey and Rogers subscribed, and which in fact is a core element in the American mind), science is basically conservative.

It is conservative because it demands *public* formulation, and implementation of innovative ideas and actions. The hallmark of science, with which it stands or falls is that it be *public,* that what two or more are able to observe and agree on that they see, is more likely to be correct, than what one believes he sees.

Taken out of its scientific context (where this rule properly belongs) and applied as a sociological principle to all of life, it means that public opinion must certify private opinion, that individual ideas and action are to be legitimatized by "society". However, unless it is asserted that "society" has an independent standard of judgment, inherent in itself, an idea which goes contrary to the very tenor of American culture which always held that society derives its authority strictly from the individuals it contains, this view can only mean that what is *already established,* restricts what is *newly proposed.*

Thus, the scientific method as a way of living, is conservative in this sense that, whereas change is possible and in fact inherent in its life style, no *radical* change can ever take place. Only so much change and improvement or growth is possible in a Pragmatistic society as the presently established life styles and institutions will bear.

A. "Society Should Free the Individual"

In contrast to this, Rogers expressed an idea which freed the individual from the domination of any agency outside of himself. It was this idea which earned him the name of "quiet revolutionary".[72] Dewey had always insisted that the individual express his ideas and actions in social, public terms of established opinion. Rogers, however, called upon society, upon the public, upon established opinions and institutions, to understand, respect and facilitate individual ideas and actions *as such,* and not as derivatives of public, established opinion, which are dependent for their validity on the certification of society.

Doing this would guarantee both the freedom of the individual for self-development and growth, and the inevitable renovation of established opinions and institutions in that direction, *more radically* than the pragmatistic notion could ever hope to attain.

To put it as succinctly as possible, whereas Dewey called upon the individual to free society, the revolutionary import of Rogers' idea consisted in this, that he called upon society to free the individual.

In expressing this idea Rogers, as it were, bypassed Pragmatism in reverse and picked up a cultural notion of longstanding in American history, i.e., that of the primacy of the individual. In doing so, he came closer to what moved the hearts of the American people than Dewey ever did, and this would also seem to account for the phenomenal public acceptance of his non-directive principle, referred to earlier.

This does not mean, however, that Rogers rejected Pragmatism outright. On the contrary, Rogers' theories contain many important pragmatistic notions, and as we will see in a later chapter his structural view of man is practically indistinguishable from the one espoused by Pragmatism. Rather, coming to the American cultural scene *after* Pragmatism in historical time, Rogers' insistence on the unreserved, unconditional respect for the individual, as *the agent of innovation and change, radicalized* Pragmatism as a philosophy of social reconstruction.

A detailed, systematic description of the implications of this notion for psychotherapy, for personality, and ultimately for interpersonal relations everywhere, will be the subject of our next chapter.

CHAPTER THREE:

ROGERS' VIEW OF THERAPY, PERSONALITY AND INTER-PERSONAL RELATIONS

I. INTRODUCTION

A. Basic Notions and Constant Development: an Apparent Contradiction

This chapter will contain a systematic presentation of Carl Rogers' view of therapy, personality and interpersonal relations. His thinking in each of these areas shows a number of characteristics, which superficially seem to contradict each other. First of all, Rogers operates with only a handful of basic notions which he develops relatively early in his career and maintains consistently throughout the years. At the same time, there is evidence of a considerable development of his views in his writings, and nigh well all of his views are presented by him as highly tentative formulations.

However, the contradiction is only apparent, and for the most part without basis in fact. This becomes clearer when we realize first of all that, whatever development occurs in Rogers' thinking, it is never more than one of different emphases around a common theme. Subsequent to the publication of his *Counseling and Psychotherapy,* there are no dramatic turnabouts in his thinking of the kind that characterized his earlier development.

Moreover, the tentativeness with which he presents his formulations is entirely in line with the content of his views on therapy and life. for Rogers, life is at best a flowing, changing process where nothing ever stays the same. So, it would be unthinkable for him to present his views as the last word on therapy, personality or interpersonal relations. Another reason for his caution in this respect is his desire to keep his views as close to their experiential and experimental base as possible. For Rogers, theories and views are always theories and views *about* experience. They discover order *in* experience. For that reason also, they are secondary to experience and subject to change whenever experience changes. The one area in which Rogers speaks with any degree of definity is the area of therapy. It is the area in which he has the most experience and did the most research. For that reason also he returns to it time and again when dealing with the topics of personality and interpersonal relations.

33

B. Problems of Systematic Review

The noticeable development of Rogers' thinking, together with his strong desire to base all his views experientially and experimentally can present some problems for a systematic review of his views.

To take the matter of the experiential base of his theories first, this raises the problem of the order in which the three topics under discussion in this chapter ought to be treated. For example, once Rogers has described the orderly process of change that occurs in persons during therapy, he asks what kind of individual would account for the possibility of such a change and thus he develops his theory of personality. Similarly, once he has described the conditions of the therapeutic relationship which facilitate this change, he asks what view of interpersonal relations would account for these conditions. This would seem to mean that his theory of personality and of interpersonal relations are more basic than his view of therapy, since they represent an account of how therapy is possible. Thus a description of either one would have to systematically *precede* a description of therapy. This would also seem to be the reason why so many systematic reviews of therapy begin with the author's view of personality (less frequently with his view of interpersonal relations) in order to subsequently derive his view of therapy systematically from it.[1]

Now, the problem is that for both historic and systematic reasons such a procedure would be incorrect in Rogers' case. It is incorrect for historic reasons, because Rogers did not have a theory of personality, or interpersonal relations, when he developed his theory of therapy. In fact, historically speaking, he rather derived the former from the latter. The same holds true systematically. Theory is of secondary importance as compared with experience for Rogers, as we saw. Theory is no more than "a network of gossamer threads to contain solid facts"[2], and because for him therapy is tied most closely to experience, he clearly identifies his views on personality and interpersonal relations as *extrapolations* of the therapeutic experience. Thus on the one hand, his theories of personality and interpersonal relations would need to be described first because they give an account of the "raw stuffs" of the therapeutic experience. On the other hand, they would have to be described last, because they are experientially secondary to the raw stuffs of therapy which forms their base.[3]

Another problem relates to the fact that Rogers' views seem to be in perpetual development throughout his life. In each of the areas under discussion, Rogers has given some very clear and concise formulation of his views about this area. However, such formulations are always tied to a particular phase of his development. Thus his most succinct, and logically clear formulations in a given area of experience are by their very nature not representative of the whole of his thinking in this area.

These two difficulties are not insurmountable, however. With respect as to which topic to discuss first, I can simply follow the historical development of Rogers' thinking and thus present his views on therapy first, to be followed by his views on personality and interpersonal relations. As to the second problem, I can do justice to both the development and logical clarity of his thinking by simply recording his successive formulations of a given area, whenever that seems to be called for.

C. Order of Presentation.

In view of the above consideration, I hope to describe Rogers' views in the areas of therapy, personality, and interpersonal relations in the following manner.

Since Rogers' view of therapy is part of my focus in this dissertation, and also because of the historical and systematic consideration described above, I will begin with a presentation of Rogers' views on therapy. This presentation will first of all consist of a detailed description of the development of his thinking about therapy. It will pick up where we left off in the last chapter, and begin with his view as it is found in *Counseling and Psychotherapy*. Following this, it will concentrate most heavily on his description of therapy in *Client-Centered Therapy*, and end with some elaborations on this view as they are found in his book *On Becoming a Person*. In this section no special attempt will be made to define the terms utilized in the description. Its main focus will be on concrete developmental description, rather than exact abstract definition.[4]

A description of two compact formulations of therapy, given by Rogers at successive stages of his development [5] will complete my review of Rogers' views on therapy. After a description of Rogers' view of therapy there follows a description of his view of personality and interpersonal relations.

My own purpose for also including Rogers' view of personality and interpersonal relations in this chapter is two-fold. First, Rogers' description of these two areas clarifies, to a considerable extent, the terms used in his description of therapy which is one of the foci of this dissertation. In the second place, they, together with Rogers' description of therapy, form the raw materials out of which my description of his anthropology will be fashioned in chapter four.

Turning now to my description of his view of personality, I feel justified in distinguishing three distinct descriptions, i.e. a structural, a developmental and a normative/ideal description. The structural description is taken from *Client-Centered Therapy* (p. 483), where Rogers outlines in nineteen propositions what, according to him, personality is and how if functions. It coincides with that phase of his development, when his thinking was still to a considerable extent "structurebound"[6] rather than "process oriented". In his second formulation [7] Rogers describes how personality develops into a rather rigid, incongruent structure as the result of certain kinds of child rearing practices. Here the suggestion that the development of personality into a structure rather than a fluid process is not inevitable, shows how Rogers' thinking is changing toward a more process oriented view. His third and final formulation [8] which deals with his view of the fully functioning person, represents his normative view of personality. It describes personality as being in perpetual process.

Lastly, there follows a description of Rogers' view of interpersonal relations. It comes in several versions, the last of which[9] only will be discussed in this chapter. This will complete my exposition of the development of Rogers' views on therapy, personality and interpersonal relations.

II. THE NATURE AND DEVELOPMENT OF ROGERS' VIEW OF THERAPY

A. Central Theme: Therapy as Autonomous Process Toward Personal Autonomy

Perhaps the most outstanding feature of Rogers' view of therapy[10] is that he sees it as an autonomous[11] process occurring entirely within the individual client. This therapeutic process is autonomous in the sense that the therapist can only facilitate its release but never cause its occurrence or direct its movement. In fact, quite the opposite is true. A therapist can quite readily obstruct the occurrence of this process by intervening into the life of his client or by directing its movement. This the more so since the therapeutic process is not only autonomous in terms of its character, but also in terms of its aim, direction and end product. The therapeutic process occurring in the client is basically a movement toward personal *autonomy.*[12]

Thus, intervention by one person into the life of another is therapeutically counterproductive because it contradicts the very nature, aim and direction of therapy. It belongs to the heart of therapy that it deals with the personal problems of the client which in the final analysis only the client can resolve. In some real sense, as we will see later, the basic problem of the client is that he must resolve *himself,* such that in successful therapy he *becomes* the therapeutic process, which, as a result of his contact with the therapist, was released *in* him.

B. Initial Application of Central Theme: Non-Directivity

1. therapeutic approach: non-interference

The autonomous character of this movement toward autonomy comes to an especially clear expression in Rogers' *Counseling and Psychotherapy.*[13] In this book he repeatedly warns the therapist against interfering with the life of his client. Thus he rejects the use of threat, exhortation, suggestion, advice, persuasion or intellectualized interpretation as proper methods for effecting personality change in persons (b, pp.20-25,138), and he warns the therapist against making moral judgments about the client (b, p.91), against assuming responsibility for personality change in the client (b, pp.96,115), against pretherapy diagnostics regarding the internal dynamics of the client (b, pp.

80,115) and against premature interpretation of material, not yet expressed by the client (b, pp.196,205). All of these are therapeutically counterproductive because in one form or another, they obstruct, or even prohibit, the spontaneous achievement of insight by the client into himself (b, p.195) which insight he must achieve if the major aim of counseling, i.e. the greater independence and integration of the client, is to be realized.

Instead, Rogers suggests that therapy should provide the occasion for the client to change (b, p.34), that it should *free* him (b, pp.89,90) toward self-directed integration and personal growth. This can only occur when the counseling relationship is characterized by warmth and rapport, and when it is maximally permissive of the expression of feeling (b, pp.87,88).

1.1 primary aim: catharsis

The client's expression of feeling, and its accompanying emotional release, or catharsis (b, p.131), is the primary aim of counseling and has priority over everything. Its occurrence can be facilitated by the therapist when he focusses on the client's feelings (b, p.133) rather than on the problems he presents. The problems which the client is unable to resolve by himself and for which he seeks therapeutic help are the result of emotional blocking. The client is stuck with conflicting feelings about himself and his situation, and these must be released first of all.

The activity of the counselor in facilitating this release is restricted to recognizing, accepting and clarifying these feelings (b, p.37). In his recognition of the client's feelings, the therapist should be guided by the pattern of feelings which the client himself presents (b, p.132). Thus the counselor should only recognize those feelings which have already been overtly expressed by the client, since the recognition of unexpressed feelings only retards the further expression of feelings (b, p.152). Second, the feelings expressed by the client are often conflicted in character. Therefore, it is important that, as the client goes into both sides of his conflicted feelings, the therapist shows equal acceptance of both sides, since this will free the client to express more of his contradictory feelings (b, pp.141,148). Third and finally, the counselor must clarify the feelings that are expressed by the client, to the client, by bringing their relationships to his attention (b, pp.38ff.).

Thus, the whole aim of therapy, in Rogers' view, is to bring the way the client feels about his situation, and especially about himself, to expression as fully and openly as possible in the counseling relationship (b, p.173). This kind of catharsis process gives the client the emotional release and physical relaxation he needs to become more comfortable with, and objective about, himself and thus enables him to further explore his understanding of himself and his situation as he goes along. In the course of this process the client also comes to accept more and more of himself as he learns that every feeling about himself that he expresses is met with equal acceptance by the counselor in therapy (b, pp.171,172).

2. therapeutic process: spontaneous achievement of insight

The achievement of insight by the client into himself is the second most important event in therapy (b, p.194). It is the inevitable result of the client's expression of his emotionalized attitudes, and its concommittant catharsis (b, p.174). It occurs spontaneously in the client when the counselor exercises the utmost of self-restraint when it comes to directive activity. It is obstructed, retarded or even made impossible when he tries to speed up the process of insight development by directive means or premature interpretations (b, pp. 195,196). Instead, the counselor does better to rely on the growth impulses, inherent in the client himself, to set the pace of the occurrence of insight (b, pp.200,201). These impulses guarantee that when the client spontaneously obtains insight in one area he will equally spontaneously see its application in other, new areas as well (b, p.205).

2.1 perceptual insight, emotional insight, personal choice

It becomes clearer to us that insight must be earned and achieved by the client and that it cannot be given to him through educative or directive means, when we look more closely at what it all involves. Basicaly, it involves the reorganization of the client's perceptual field (b, p.206). It is a new way of perceiving, a discovery of new relationships between percepts, that the client must achieve. While therapy facilitates the performance of this task by freeing the client from his defensiveness through catharsis, it nevertheless remains a task that only he can accomplish.

For one thing, such new perceptual insight cannot be transfered directly from the counselor to the client by an intellectual process, because it involves emotional components as well. Even if such new perceptions were directly transferable, they would not resolve anything for the client, since the key to their effectiveness is that the client accepts them as his own (b, p.207). Insight as a change in self-perception, implies that the client *feels* differently about himself now, as compared with before.

But even more than that, this reorganization of the client's perceptual field is a matter of choice as well. Insight includes more than a reorganization of self-perception and an emotional acceptance of this new self-perception. It further includes the making of positive choices (b, p.208). As the client achieves a more differentiated perceptual field, the range of possible choices available to his awareness also becomes enlarged. This places a demand on him to select those choices which yield him the greatest satisfaction. These positive choices more often than not involve the acceptance of delayed satisfactions over immediate satisfaction. Such personal choices no other person can make for the client, if for no other reason than that he is not likely to act upon those choices which others would make for him (b, p.210). Thus the fact that insight includes the making of personal choices further demonstrates that it cannot be induced but must be spontaneously achieved. If the client spontaneously achieves insight he will invariably act upon it. This is why positive action is often test of the genuineness of the client's insights (b, p.211).

3. non-directivity as facilitation of personal insight

It will be evident that *Counseling and Psychotherapy* very much stresses the point that therapy is an autonomous process, occurring entirely within the client. The relation between the therapist and client is important only insofar as it makes this autonomous process possible. The only therapeutic stance which the therapist can possibly adopt that would suit this notion, is a non-directive (b, p.126), permissive, nonauthoritarian stance. The therapist must zealously guard the autonomy, the psychological independence and the integrity of the client (b, p.127) by deliberately refraining from interfering with the activity occurring in the client. Only then is he truly therapeutic. The rationale governing this stance is clear: therapeutic insight cannot be given to the client. It can only be obstructed or allowed to grow. The client himself must achieve it spontaneously. That is, not only must he come to a new understanding of himself but he must also come to accept this new understanding of himself and choose to act positively on its basis.

C. Further Specification of Central Theme: Client-Centeredness

In his *Client-Centered Therapy*, Rogers continues to stress this basic notion of the autonomy of the therapeutic process, but at the same time there is a shift in emphasis from non-directivity to client-centeredness. This shift in emphasis allows for a richer description of the implications of this basic notion as it applies to the therapeutic stance of the therapist, the therapeutic process which the client experiences and the outcomes which result from such a process.

1. client-centeredness and therapeutic stance

1.1 basic trust in the client's capacity

Perhaps the best way to introduce this shift in emphasis is to ask the following question: Given the fact that the therapist takes a non-directive stance in his relationship with the client, on the conviction that the client must himself achieve therapeutic insight, how can he be sure that the client has in fact the capacity to do so? He cannot derive this certainty from the performance of the client in the relationship since the latter seems anything but capable of insight, especially in the initial stages of therapy. It is precisely because he is incapable of such self-insight by himself, that he has come to therapy. This trust in the client's capacity for self-insight cannot therefore be a hypothesis, a technique, which becomes stronger or weaker depending on the extent to which the client demonstrates this capacity in the therapeutic process. It is not conditional on the client's performance. For Rogers this trust is unconditional, a matter of principle, of first things (c, p.14). It is itself the central condition (c, p.35) *for* therapy. It precedes the therapeutic process and cannot therefore be its result. Rather it is that which makes therapy therapeutic. Only if, when, and insofar as the therapist starts from a basic trust in the client's capacity for self-insight, will the client demonstrate that he is in fact capable of this in therapy (c, pp.20-22).

Rogers concedes the possibility of adopting this trust in the client as a working hypothesis in therapy. He even sees some value in this approach in that its adoption will yield therapeutic results that might convince the sceptics about the rightness of trusting the client (c, pp.22-24). But he doubts that this trust can be maintained consistently when it remains only a matter of hypothesis or technique for the therapist. He shows, for example, how the best intentions notwithstanding, a lack of trust in the client can betray itself in such subtle matters as the inflections of the words which the therapist speaks (c, p.28).

1.2 attitude and technique

Thus, ultimately this trust must be a pervasive attitude on the part of the therapist rather than a technique. It must become a genuine part of his personality makeup if it is going to be pervasively present in the relationship and therapeutically effective for the client (c, p.21).

However, to have such an attitude of trust in the client by itself is not enough to be therapeutic. This trust attitude must be concretely implemented and communicated in the therapeutic relationship if it is to be therapeutically effective in the client's experience. It is in this context that Rogers sees a need for therapeutic techniques. For him, they are implementations of the therapist's attitude of trust toward the client. As such they provide the necessary and sufficient conditions for the therapeutic process to occur (c, pp.24-26).
But, as Rogers argues elsewhere, this function also exhausts their value for therapy, not just in client-centered therapy, but in all therapeutic approaches irrespective of their peculiar character. In and by themselves, therapeutic techniques are of no value to the therapeutic process. They are important only as implementations of the therapist's attitude of trust in his client. They can only serve as the tools by means of which he attemps to make the therapeutic relation totally client-centered.[14]

1.3 active expression of basic trust and anthropological presuppositions

It is Roger's preoccupation in *Client-Centered Therapy* with the active implementation of the therapist's trustful attitude toward his client that represents a shift in emphasis from his earlier nondirective conception of therapy (c. p.31). Earlier the main emphasis was on freeing the client from external interference, with the language being that of negative statements about what the therapist ought to refrain from doing. Now the language is positive, referring to what the therapist ought to be doing in the relationship. The attitude and actions of the therapist now make a positive difference in the therapeutic process which the client experiences. The therapist is now enjoined to actively facilitate this process. That is to say, he is now encouraged to actively attend to the client's internal frame of reference, to empathetically live into his subjective world (c, p.29), to duplicate his perceptual field, to become his alter ego and to do so acceptingly, without any kind of external evaluation. He is asked to demonstrate his trust in his client by actively following him into any direction and toward any outcome that he may determine. This basic attitude of total unconditional trust in the worth and capacity of the client as an individual, implemented by means of the "techniques" of empathic understanding and respectful acceptance of anything that the client may present in therapy, forms the central condition for the therapeutic process to occur in the client (c, p.35).

Earlier I mentioned that trust in the client is Rogers' principle of therapy. Behind this principle no *therapeutic* questions are possible because it forms for Rogers the basis on which therapy can occur. However, this is by no means the end of the matter. This therapeutic principle finds its base in Rogers' anthropological assertion that all individuals, without exception, have the capacity, the potential within themselves, for self-directed, constructive change (c, p.Xll).[15] A fuller discussion of this anthropological issue must wait until the next chapter, but it is mentioned here in passing because of its relevance to our present discussion on therapy.

2. client-centeredness and therapeutic process

A trust in the client's capacity for insight presupposes that the client is aware of, and can optimally utilize this potential in himself (c, pp.490,491). Or to put it another way, it presupposes that his self-awareness matches this inner potential. This can hardly be assumed to be the case as the client enters therapy. He is largely unaware of his potential. His self-awareness and his potential are mismatched, and he understands, accepts and trusts himself less than he could. In fact it can be said that this constitutes the very problem with which he comes to therapy. Yet it is precisely this matching of awareness and potential which the client obtains in a client-centered kind of therapeutic relationship. The therapeutic process which the therapist releases in the client via his implemented attitude is one in which the client gradually becomes aware of his potential and is freed to utilize it more fully.

2.1 short form description

I will first describe this therapeutic process in short form (c, pp.190-196) and touch upon its basic ingredients. Then, in order to deepen our understanding of the process, I will describe it in its various aspects, first as a learning experience and then as a change in the client's manner of perceiving. Following that, I will describe it as a change in the way in which the client experiences the relationship. Finally, we will look at its outcomes as they are observable in the changes of his bahavior. Much of Rogers' theorizing about the therapeutic process in *Client-Centered Therapy* centers around the self, the self-concept or self-structure of the client and its relation to the client's (self)-experience (c, p.15).

2.1.1 the problem: incongruence, self and experience

If we begin with a person who feels no need for therapy, then this is a person whose concept of himself is internally consistent and harmonious with what he daily experiences and perceives. His self-concept, which is an organized system of hypotheses about how to deal with life, based on an awareness of being, may contain some grossly unrealistic elements. But as long as the individual's experience does not contradict his self-concept, he will continue to find himself acceptable and to regard himself positively (c, p.191).

But suppose now that a conflict does arise between his self-concept and his social experience, between his self-concept and his perceived behaviour, or between two needs that he experiences. Suppose in short, that his experience becomes inconsistent with his self-concept. Then the perception of this "incongruency", as Rogers calls it, will threaten the self of the individual, such that he will move to defend it against these experiences by denying them to, or distorting them in, his awareness. As such he is still unaware of the exact nature of these experiences, but he is anxiously aware that "something" is the matter. When such incongruent experiences become so powerful or numerous, however, that he can no longer keep them from his awareness, then he may have come to a point where he is "ripe" for therapy (c, p.192).

If such a person now enters into a relationship with a client-centered therapist, he will experience this therapist as a person with warmth, interest and understanding, but also as a person who considers him responsible for the direction, movement and outcome of the therapeutic process (c, p.71).

2.1.2 the process: disorganization of self-concept

This therapeutic process when launched successfully is basically a disorganization and reorganization of the self of the client (c, p.193). As the client begins to explore himself in therapy he soon discovers more and more disturbing inconsistencies in himself. He discovers attitudes, feelings and experiences in himself of which he was previously unaware (c, p.76), and which appear to be highly incongruent with his current self-concept. These discoveries are so disturbing to his self-concept that its organization crumbles to the point where the client no longer has an organized self with which to meet life (c, p.79). He enters into an amorphous state (c, p.80), in which the major question after each new discovery is, "What does this do to the basis of my life?" (c, p.79).

Moreover, this disorganization process tends to be accompanied by intense emotional pain and racking torment, especially when a great deal of personality change is necessary (c, p.77). Thus violent fluctuations in the client's mood are the rule rather than the exception in therapy (c, p.83).

What makes the client continue his explorations, his intense discomfort notwithstanding, is his experience of the therapist's supportive attitude first of all. He finds that the therapist accepts every experience which he expresses, whether good or bad, as being of equal value. He further finds that the newly discovered experiences, which he himself finds so disorganizing of his self are not so experienced by the therapist (c, p.194). The latter seems to actually value them as signs of progress toward the growth of a new, enlarged self, which will include all the inconsistent and previously denied experiences that now appear so threatening. As a result, the client eventually obtains this sense of progress in himself as well, so that it becomes the backdrop for the intense feelings of despair that come over the client as a result of his self-explorations (c, p.85). It is this experience of progress which, in turn, makes the continued process of exploration possible until such time when therapy is completed (c, p.84).

2.1.3 the outcome: reorganization of self-concept

Towards the end of therapy the client experiences that, now that the worst is known and accepted (c, p.87), a new reorganized self is beginning to emerge within him, a self which is much more comfortable and realistic (c, pp. 194,195). Thus the process which started with a conflicted, highly defended self and moved through an experience of having no organized self at all, culminates in the emergence of a new enlarged self-concept which is organized to include all those experiences that were previously experienced as inconsistent with the self. When that occurs the client makes what could be his most significant discovery in therapy. He discovers that he is not a mere product of external forces shaping him into the person that he is, but that he is himself at least to some degree, the architect of himself. He discovers that he is the product of his own making, fashioned out of his own experiences.[16]

He begins to feel himself in action, frequently without quite knowing where he is going (c, p.88). He experiences that he is moving with his experience rather than against it. He experiences that the self, by relinquishing control, has gained control (c, p.96). In short, his concept of himself, and of himself in relation to others, has now become congruent with the sensory and visceral experiences of his organism (c, p.97). At this time he also finds that the experiences which were painfully inconsistent with his old self, have surprisingly lost their threatening character, now that they have become assimilated into his new self (c, p.195).

The motive force driving and directing this entire therapeutic process to its completion was not the structuring effort of the therapist in the relationship. It merely released and facilitated the process. Rather, it is the forward moving forces of life itself inherent in the client, but initially dormant, that direct therapy to its culmination. These are the forces that make the client move on toward the reorganization of the self rather than lose himself in its disorganization. As such, change in therapy is simply an instance of the growth and maturation which a person normally experiences throughout his entire life (c, pp.195,196).

Having described the basic ingredients of the process that occurs in client-centered therapy we can now look at its movement from a variety of viewpoints. In doing so we will not only deepen our understanding of the therapeutic process but also clarify more fully those of its events, that were left unexplained in the above shortform description.

2.2 therapy as learning process

For example, we can look at the therapeutic process as a learning process. What is learned in therapy comes to expression in the movement of the material which the client presents during therapy (c, p.132). Thus he characteristically moves from a preoccupation with the symptoms of his problem to a preoccupation with the problem itself, from a preoccupation with the manner and extent to which his environment and others in his environment have contributed to his problem to a preoccupation with himself (c, p.135). This is made possible by the fact that the therapist focuses consistently on his feelings, his perceptions and his evaluations, that is to say, on himself. Once the client becomes preoccupied with exploring himself in therapy he shows a movement from being preoccupied with material that was already available to his awareness, to a preoccupation with previously denied material, which only now has entered his awareness (c, p.135). From talking about past experiences he moves to talking about what he is now experiencing. In short, he gradually begins to deal with himself here and now as he moves through therapy (c, p.136).

As he does so, there is a noticeable change in his attitude toward himself from negative to positive (c, p.137), and it becomes possible for him to accept himself as worthy of respect (c, p.138). He becomes more able to view himself with objectivity and as a result, his ability to cope with life improves. He becomes more spontaneous and genuine and he learns that values are not inherent in the objects of perception, but rather that he himself is their evaluator (c, p.139).

In the main then, the client learns to perceive himself as more adequate and consequently he becomes more able to cope, for he has learned to allow all of his experiential data to enter his awareness, which tends to make his judgment more realistic. He has come to realize that it is he himself who places values on the objects of his experience so that his self and his values become less disparate. Thus, in every way he becomes more congruent, whole and integrated (c, pp.139-142).

2.3 therapy as a reorganization of perception

Another way of looking at the therapeutic process is to view it as a change in the perception of the client. During therapy an increased differentiation takes place in the client's perceptual field (c, p.142). Due to his defended state, the client perceives his experience at the beginning of therapy largely in terms of abstractions, in terms of high level generalizations which are superimposed upon his experience (c, p.143). In the course of therapy he gradually begins to perceive in terms of more limited generalizations that derive from and are rooted in his experience. In effect the client discovers that he has been living by a perceptual map which does not correspond to his experiential territory (c, p.144). What occurs in therapy is a loosening of the client's phenomenal field and as a result of it, he suddenly and spontaneously begins to see relations between percepts that earlier escaped his attention (c, p.146). That is to say, both differentiation and reorganization occur in therapy, with the latter following spontaneously upon the former.

On this point, Rogers cites Snyggs and Combs[17], who describe therapy as the "differentiation of the phenomenal self" and who argue that when this occurs, the client's "need to maintain and enhance the phenomenal self" will do the rest (c, p.146). Rogers suggests that we can understand the client's becoming aware of experiences that were previously denied in the same manner as a greater differentiation and a more accurate symbolization of his experience (c, p.147). The sequence in which these events occur is such that the client's self-concept must first change before his feelings and his behaviour can become more adequately symbolized (c, p.148).

2.4 therapy as a change in value system

The therapeutic process can also be viewed as a change in the client's value system. At the beginning of therapy the client lives by a set of values which he introjected early in his life from significant others in his environment, usually his parents. These values tend to wane in importance as therapy continues because the increased differentiation in his perception tends to expose their rigidity (c, p. 149). However, as the client lets go of these values, he begins to experience considerable confusion and insecurity, because he feels he no longer has any standards by which to judge his experience. But as he moves through therapy, it gradually dawns on him that he has no need of these values since he has within himself the capacity to weigh his experience. At first he experienced the locus of his valuation process as being outside of himself, (in his parents for instance, who therefore also determined the value judgments he made). But as a result of therapy he now begins to experience the locus of valuation as residing in himself (c, p.150). In client-centered therapy the client's evaluation of himself and his situation is accepted without question and as a result he no longer experiences values as fixed and threatening. Rather, he learns to think of them as based on his own experience (c, p.157).

2.5 therapy as a change in the experience of the relationship

There are those who believe that words, attitudes and perceptions are not nearly as important in therapy as they are made out to be. Instead, they see all of these as mere byproducts of the emotional experience that the client has in the therapeutic relationship (c, p.158). As proof for their belief, they cite the success that is booked with children in play therapy and instances of improvement in therapy with non-verbal adult clients. Both of these are examples that healing is possible in therapy where verbal expression and exploration is at a minimum. Thus, finally it would also seem possible to look at the therapeutic process strictly in terms of the client's changing experience of the therapeutic relationship. Viewed from out of that aspect of therapy, the client characteristically moves from experiencing himself as unworthy, unacceptable and unloved to an experience of being loved, (that is deeply understood and accepted) in the relationship (c, p.159). As a result, he himself will eventually come to respect, like or even love himself as well, and as a consequence of this he will also come to love others. Thus, viewed from this vantage point, the therapeutic process is simply a function of the relationship between the client and his therapist. (c, p.172).

2.6 summary

This completes my review of the therapeutic process as it is described in *Client-Centered Therapy.* Its essential characteristic appears to be the fact that during its course the client gradually becomes more aware of his (previously denied) experience (as being his own). One could also describe it as a process in which the client's self-concept is altered in the direction of a greater congruence with his experience. Yet another way of describing it is that the client has incorporated his experience into his (altered) self, or that he has reorganized his experience such that previously denied experiences are now available to his awareness. In short, as a result of therapy he has "owned" his experience and, therefore, it no longer threatens him. He has become genuine, congruent, integrated and whole.

3. client-centeredness and therapeutic outcomes

What, now, are the outcomes of this process according to Rogers? To raise this matter as a separate question may appear to be somewhat artificial, since many of the changes described thus far as part of the process could with equal reason be considered outcomes of this process. But Rogers has a specific purpose in mind when he distinguishes process from outcome. For him outcomes refer specifically to the changes which occur in the client's behavior as the result of the therapeutic process. These are overt, noticeable changes in the client. Thus toward the end of therapy we characteristically see the client once again making plans for himself. His judgment has clearly become more mature (c, p.180). There is a noticeable decrease in tension (c, p.181) and defensiveness (c, p.182), about him. He shows more frustration tolerance (c, p.183), and in general exhibits an improved, more independent functioning in his life tasks (c, pp.184,185).

3.1 process or outcome? a problem

This distinction between process and outcome is somewhat problematic in Rogers. On the one hand it seems to be a distinction between two ways of looking at the same event. Thus, for example, he describes the therapeutic *process* in "phenomenological" terms. That is to say, the changes that occur in therapy are described from the client's point of view (c, p.532). They are changes in his experience and in his perception. They are described as occurring in his "internal frame of reference". They are changes in the way the client experiences himself, feels about himself, perceives himself and values himself.[18] In contrast to this, Rogers describes *outcomes* in "behavioral" terms. Here the changes occurring in the client are described as perceived by outsiders. From this vantage point outcomes and process changes that can be observed by others, by society or by science.

In this first sense then, the distinction between process and outcome means to indicate that an identical series of events can be viewed from two different angles, internal or external, subjective or objective, individual or social. That is to say, it refers to the difference between individual perception and socially observable behavior.[19]

On the other hand, however, Rogers also refers to outcomes as the *result* of the therapeutic process and even goes so far as to say that changes in the client's perception of himself always precede and cause changes in his behavior. In this sense of the distinction, therefore, process and outcome clearly refer to two different classes of events (c, p.222).

This is not the place to deal extensively with this terminological ambiguity, nor is it all that important for our present discussion. Rogers himself largely ignores the distinction between process and outcome in his later writings, or where he continues to use it, he makes clear that it is only an analytical device that he uses to enhance the clarity of his exposition.[20]

3.2 perceptual change precedes behavior change

However this be, his intention with making this distinction in the context of our present discussion is far from ambiguous. He wants to make it crystal clear that no lasting modification of any kind can be initiated in an individual behavior by anyone, unless that individual himself is involved in these changes in a central and decisive manner. This is why he insists that behavior is caused by a way of perceiving. The client's experience of a change in his perception is the prerequisite for the occurrence of a change in his behavior (c, p.222).

3.3 therapy as internal diagnosis

In that sense therapy is experiencing that one's old ways of perceiving are inadequate and that they should be replaced by new, more accurate ways of perceiving (c, p.222). The experience of therapy is the perception of new relations between old percepts. Another way of saying it is that therapy is essentially diagnosis that goes on in the experience of the client (c, p.223). This diagnosis of his dynamics must be both experienced and accepted by the client before behavioral changes can take place. Specifically, he must come to a greater awareness of his defenses as self-protecting distortions of reality (c, p.223).

The constructive forces which bring about these altered perceptions reside in the client himself (c, p.222). Nevertheless, the therapist must provide the conditions for their occurrence. Chief among these conditions must be that the therapist does not evaluate or perceive the client's self for him (c, pp. 203,208,209). To do this would be especially devastating for the client, who, as a result of his constant self-exploration already experiences considerable threat to the organization of his self. The experience of *being* perceived and *being* evaluated creates dependence in the client and makes him lose confidence in himself. Instead, the therapist should do his utmost to facilitate the experience of increased independence and self-confidence in the client since this is the desired outcome of therapy (c, pp.214-218). The awareness by the client of the self as its own perceiver and evaluator appears to be central to the process of self-reorganization (c, p.218), which process the client must experience before alterations in his behavior can occur. Briefly put, therefore, therapy must provide the client with those conditions which make him feel maximally capable of changing himself (c, pp.224,225).

4. client-centeredness and therapeutic conditions

In a later article[21], Rogers has compiled a list of those therapeutic conditions which he considers necessary and sufficient for personality change to take place (d, p.96). The first condition is that the therapist and the client must be in psychological contact with each other. That is to say, each must make a difference in the other's experience (d, pp.96,97). Rogers calls this the minimum condition for two people to be in relation to each other.

The second condition holds that the client must be in a state of incongruence (d, p.96), whereas the therapist must be congruent in the relationship (d, pp.97,98). Particularly the latter part of this condition, that of the therapist's congruence, or genuineness, comes to be viewed more and more by Rogers in his later writings as the basic condition of therapy.[22] By making it the primary condition for therapy he means to indicate that all the other conditions, insofar as they depend on the therapist for their implementation are of no value to therapy, unless they are genuinely present in the experience of the therapist. To put it another way, if the end product of therapy is the achievement of congruence between self and experience in the client, then the basic condition for this to occur is that the therapist should psychologically be in this state at the beginning of therapy and throughout its course.

The third condition is a combination of two earlier conditions which were then mentioned separately. These were that the therapist should fully trust and accept the client as a separate person. Taken together they are now called "unconditional positive regard" (d, p.98). A fourth condition is that of empathic understanding. This means that the therapist must be able to live into the subjective world of the client and see the situation from out of his internal frame of reference at least to some degree, if he wants to have a therapeutic effect on the client (d, p.99).

A fifth and final condition states that the client must be able to perceive in his experience those conditions of therapy which depend for their actualization on the therapist. This simply means that it is not enough that the therapist experiences these attitudes within himself. He must also be able to communicate them to his client for them to be therapeutically effective (d, p.99). If these conditions are optimally present in therapy, then, Rogers predicts, all of the changes which were described as characteristic of the therapeutic process will inevitably occur (d, p.100).

D. Summary

Before I continue my discussion on Rogers' views I will first summarize the main features of his thinking about therapy as it had developed itself up to this point. Initially Rogers advocated a nondirective approach to therapy. This approach was based on the conviction that the therapeutic process cannot be induced into the client but must be spontaneously achieved by the client. The therapist can only obstruct this process by his interference, or facilitate its occurrence non-directively by allowing the client maximum freedom.

In his next and most comprehensive formulation of therapy, Rogers places the emphasis on the therapist's trust in the client's capacity for self-help and sees it as the chief therapeutic agent. This trust must be a genuine attitude on the part of the therapist however, and not the mere application of certain non-directive techniques, for otherwise it will be therapeutically ineffective. Therapeutic methods or techniques are now considered valuable for therapy only insofar as they implement this trust attitude in the therapeutic relationship. The therapeutic approach which Rogers advocates at this stage is no longer non-directive but client-centered.

As a result of this total client-centeredness a therapeutic process occurs in the client, in which he gradually becomes more aware of and congruent with his experience. He also begins to accept himself more fully as he is, and learns to appreciate himself as an individual who is capable of independent judgment and action. None of this can occur, however, unless the self-concept of the client has first been altered, and sufficiently enlarged to allow for the proper symbolization of all those experiences which he previously denied or distorted.

In that sense, the alteration of the client's self is the most significant event of therapy. In that sense also, all of the events of therapy can be said to contribute to but one all important movement, i.e. the disorganization and reorganization of the client's self-concept.

E. Final Expression of Central Theme: Becoming a Process

1. outcome as process

One further aspect of Rogers' thinking about therapy must be added to make it complete. Briefly stated it is this, that the client becomes the therapeutic process which as a result of his participation in client-centered therapy was released in him. Up until now, Rogers had consistently viewed the therapeutic process as a means toward the end, the outcome of increased psychological coping ability. However, in his later publications, particularly in his *On Becoming a Person,* he makes the occurrence of the therapeutic process itself the outcome of therapy (f, pp.64,66,125-159).

2. becoming your changing experience

The tenor of Rogers' argument about therapy in *On Becoming a Person* is in its essence accurately expressed by the title of the book. The outcome of therapy is that the client *becomes* a person, *becomes* his experiential organism (f, p.103), *becomes* living experience (f, pp.107-124). This formulation re-presents the result of Rogers' most mature reflection on the therapeutic process and its outcome, and implies a major extension of the view expressed in *Client-Centered Therapy.*

The end result of therapy is now no longer seen as congruency with experience. It is not the increased awareness of, or openness to experience. It does not mean the enlargement of the self so as to include all of one's experience. It is not a matter of basing your self-concept on experience. Nor is it a matter of owning that experience as yours. It does not even mean accepting that experience for what it is. Rather, the end result is that you *become* the experience that you *are* (f, pp.76,77,103,113).

This movement involves, first of all, that you relinquish all control over your experience. The language used in describing this process is one of surrendering your self to the wisdom of the experiential organism, which, one learns, is often wiser than the conscious self (f, pp.23,151). Thus it involves first of all a trust in your organism (f, pp.102-105,115,118,122,189). Or to use some interpersonal terms to describe this intrapersonal event, it involves more than being non-directive, or even empathic toward your experience. Basically it means that you become experience-centered. The self, as the thinker about, or tinkerer with experience, must in effect die, or at least drastically diminish in importance for the growth forces of the experiential organism to bear their fruit.

It is a matter of living in your experience to such an extent that you lose all awareness of yourself as experiencing and simply become the subject pole of that experiencing (f, pp.147,153,157,158). The self is now no longer the watchman over experience but rather an inhabitant in experience. Experience has its own meaning and the self must let it tell it its own meaning.[23] All the self was ever meant to do was to discover that meaning in the sense of uncovering it rather than inventing it, and having discovered it, to govern itself accordingly. Elsewhere, Rogers uses the image of a car on a slippery, icy road. If you steer it with the slide, you survive; if you go against it, you perish.[24] When things are as they should be then the self is no more than a tiny dot, floating on the stream of experience (f, pp.123,188,189).

Thus, the movement of becoming a person involves the movement of becoming your real self, which is now much less in control, much less separate from the experiential organism. It is the latter which now sets the tone for the direction in which the individual moves. In summary then, as a result of therapy the self has in effect become incorporated in, and identified with, the experiential organism (f, pp.187-192).

3. from fixity to constructive changingness

This leads to the description of one final aspect of becoming a person which receives the predominant emphasis in Rogers' later publications. It is this, that as a result of therapy the client *becomes a process*. That is to say, according to Rogers' most mature formulation the experience of therapy does not involve a change from an old, inadequate personality structure, through a process of dis- and reorganization, to a new more adequate personality structure. Rather, it involves a change from fixity to changingness, from rigid structure to flow, from stasis to process, as the major characteristic of the client's existence (f, pp.131,122,171).

This changingness is the direct result of the client's becoming his experiential organism. The nature of experience is such that it flows continually. The organism is in a perpetual process of change, of actualization. Consequently, as one becomes one's experiential organism, one also becomes process-, rather than structure bound in one's perceiving. One's self becomes a fluid gestalt, with figure and ground fluctuating freely depending on the change in one's experience. One begins to live existentially, quite literally changing from moment to moment, continuously transcending oneself (f, p.172), depending on the changes in one's experience.[25] One no longer *has* any values, but becomes a valuing process, changing one's values when one's experience seems to dictate such a change. In short, one becomes process rather than product (f, p.122).

The movement of this process is by no means at random, however. It is not a changingness of vacillation or confusion. It moves in a direction that is positive. The change that occurs is constructive. It is necessarily realistic. It is change for the better because it implies that one is open to all one's experiences, to those originating within, as well as to those without the organism. It implies that one is open to all one's impulses, open to the need for aggression, but also to the need for companionship. It means that one is aware of psychological needs, but also aware of physiological needs. It means, in other words, that one has the maximum possible information available on how to live meaningfully and adaptively.

4. the fully functioning person as experiential organismic process

Because one is fully aware of all one's experiential data, one makes choices which are inevitably much more realistic than was previously possible when one distorted or denied some of these experiences. The course of action one adopts has to be more satisfying because it strikes the best possible balance between *all* one's feelings, impulses and experiences.[26] Of course, this does not mean that one always makes infallible choices. Errors of judgment are bound to keep on occurring because the data available at any moment may not be sufficient to make the proper choices. But this is not nearly so serious when one is open to one's experience, since errors in judgment can be speedily corrected by noting the consequences they engender in subsequent experience. In summary then, the change for the better, which one experiences as a result of therapy, is that one becomes an experiential organismic process, and thus a more fully functioning person.[27]

F. Two Compact Formulations of Personality Change

This completes my description of the development of Rogers' thinking about therapy. Rogers has also written several summary formulations of personality change. These were recorded by him at different stages of his development. In terms of time, they come after his detailed description of therapy in *Client-Centered Therapy*.

The first of these is the most succinct, comprehensive and rigorous description of therapy ever formulated by Rogers. Rogers refers to it as his "theory of therapy". It basically states that if certain therapeutic conditions exist, then a therapeutic process will occur that has certain characteristics; and that, if this process occurs, then certain personality and behavioral changes will result. This systematic description of his therapy is quite detailed, but its content is identical to the material that I have already discussed in the previous pages. For that reason I will make no further reference to it, except to point the reader to its source.[28]

His two other formulations are less elaborate and also less rigorous than the first. They are worth quoting in full, because they very compactly, and in simple language, express the basic ingredients of Rogers' view of therapy.

1. personal formulation

In the following formulations Rogers speaks personally, as a therapist, or more specifically, as a helper when he states:

If I can create a relationship characterized on my part:

by a genuineness and transparency, in which I am my real feelings;

by a warm acceptance of and prizing of the other person as a separate individual;

by a sensitive ability to see his world and himself as he sees them;

then the other individual in the relationship:

will experience and understand aspects of himself which previously he has repressed;

will find himself becoming better integrated, more able to function effectively;

will become more similar to the person he would like to be;

will be more self-directing and self-confident;

will become more of a person, more unique and more self-expressive;

will be more understanding, more acceptant of others;

will be able to cope with the problems of life more adequately and more comfortably.[29]

2. an equation of personality change

Rogers' third formulation[30] relates more specifically to therapy proper. It is intended by him as a crude equation of what, based on the accumulated research, can be said to occur in successful therapy. As compared with the formulation above, this one places more emphasis on the fluidity of human functioning when it states that,

the more the client perceives the therapist as real or genuine, as empathic, as having an unconditional regard for him, the more the client will move away from a static, fixed, unfeeling, impersonal type of functioning, and the more he will move toward a way of functioning marked by a fluid, changing, acceptant experiencing of differentiated personal feelings. The consequence of movement is an alteration in personality and behavior in the direction of psychic health and maturity and more realistic relationships to self, others, and the environment.

III. ROGERS' VIEW OF PERSONALITY

If the therapeutic phenomena related thus far are what they were described to be, then what kind of individual would account for them? What sort of person is implied in these descriptions? To answer this question Rogers presents his view of personality.

A. Introduction: Three Formulations Differing in Time and Emphasis

There are three distinct formulations of his view of personality. Each of these originated at different stages of his development. In addition, they also differ from each other in the aspects of personality which they emphasize. Thus his first formulation seems more aimed at describing the structure of personality. That is, it deals more with what human personality is, and how it functions. His second formulation seems to concern itself more with how personality develops, more often than not in a distorted fashion, as a person grows up. Finally, his third formulation attemps to describe what personality could become under optimally facilitative environmental conditions.

Rogers' writings on personality are by and large characterized by an admirable conciseness of formulation. Unfortunately they are also rather detailed in their description. To quote him exhaustively would, therefore, seriously disrupt the flow of my exposition of his views. For this reason I will restrict myself to making summary comments about his views on personality in the text, and refer the reader to the sources for Rogers' own detailed description of the same.

B. Rogers' Structural View of Personality

Rogers' earliest theory of personality in print was presented by him in the form of nineteen propositions.[31]

1. nineteen propositions

The first seven propositions deal with the human organism and how it functions in its environment. According to Rogers it functions as an organized whole and as such it reacts to an experienced or perceived environment. It has only one motivating tendency, namely to actualize and enhance itself by fulfilling its experienced needs in a perceived world. This actualizing activity Rogers calls behavior.

The next five propositions deal with the development and function of the self. In accordance with the actualizing tendency the self differentiates out of the organism's total perceptual field. It becomes elaborated through the organism's interaction with its social environment and it carries within itself values that are derived from both the organism and the social environment. The latter values are frequently perceived distortedly as coming from the organism rather than from the social environment. Once it has become established, the self becomes that entity in relation to which all the experiences of a person become symbolized and perceived. Furthermore, the organism also tends to adopt only those ways of behaving that are consistent with this self-structure.

Propositions 13-16 deal with psychological (mal-) adjustment. Maladjustment occurs when certain organic experiences generate behaviors that are inconsistent with the self-structure. In themselves these may be significant experiences, and thus need to be related to the self. But because of their inconsistency with the self they are not taken up into the self-structure. The result of this is psychological tension. Experiences that are inconsistent with the self come to be perceived as a threat to the self and in defense against this, the self-concept tends to become more and more rigid, thereby shutting out an increasing number of significant experiences.

Finally, propositions 17-19 describe how this trend can be reversed. Under certain conditions when there is no external threat to the self-structure these inconsistent experiences may be allowed into awareness to be assimilated into a revised self-structure. When this occurs a person becomes more integrated within himself and thus also more acceptant of others. Finally, he will replace his present value *system* with a more fluid organismic valuing *process*, as the guide for his life.

C. Rogers' Developmental and Dynamic View of Personality

In what he himself calls his ''theory of the development of personality, and of the dynamics of behavior'', Rogers uses much the same sequence of description as in his earlier, structural formulation presented above. His developmental description differs from his structural description, however, in that it emphasizes how the human infant develops into a full-fledged personality and also how disintegrations and reintegrations can occur during this development. The text will again contain only a summary description of Rogers' developmental theory and the reader is referred to the sources for a fuller description.[32]

1. characteristics of the human infant

Rogers begins by postulating certain characteristics of the human infant, thus of a person at the beginning of his developmental process. These are essentially the characteristics of the human organism described above. For the infant his experience is reality. He reacts to his experience in an organized, total fashion and in accordance with his tendency to actualize himself. He values his experiences in terms of whether or not they enhance his organism and he behaves with adience toward those that do, and with avoidance toward those that don't.

2. development of the self and the need for positive regard

As the infant matures certain experiences related to himself differentiate out of his total experiential world and become perceptually organized into a self-concept. Together with this newly developed awareness of his self the growing infant also develops a need to be regarded positively by significant others in his surroundings. This need for positive regard by others and its satisfaction is a rather potent force in his life. Because of it the growing child is no longer exclusively oriented toward his own organismic valuing process but also becomes at least partially oriented to the values of others.

3. development of self-regard

These positive regard satisfactions and frustrations can also come to be experienced by the child *independent* from the positive regard transactions he may have with others around him. When this happens the child has, as it were, become his own significant social other. He has come to regard himself positively or negatively, independent of what others say about him. This Rogers calls self-regard.

4. development of conditions of worth

Whenever significant others selectively value some aspects of the child as more worthy of positive regard than others, the child himself tends to become similarly selective in his self-regard. He then begins to avoid or seek out certain self-experiences solely in terms of whether or not they are worthy of self-regard. Whenever that occurs the child is said to have acquired conditions of worth. If, however, such a growing child were to experience only *uncon*ditional positive regard from others, then no conditions of worth would develop in him. His self-regard would thus also be unconditional and his need for

54

positive regard and self-regard would never be at variance with his organismic evaluation. For Rogers, this would represent a fully functioning, psychologically well-adjusted individual.

5. development of incongruence

However, this is not what actually happens in child development. More often than not it produces individuals that have conditions of worth. Because of their need for self-regard such individuals tend to perceive their experiences selectively, symbolizing those experiences that are congruent with their current self-concept, and barring from their awareness those experiences that are not. An incongruence thus arises between their selves and their experience. This furthur tends to produce discrepancies in their behavior as well. Behaviors that enhance their self-concept will be at odds with behaviors that, while they enhance their total organism, are inconsistent with their self-concept.

This process is a bit of a vicious circle. Experiences which are incongruent with the self-structure tend to be perceived as a threat to its existence. Against this threat the individual defends his self by rigidly distorting the perception of his experience. This in turn tends to increase the incongruency between self and experience making it more of a threat to the self, which then becomes more defensive and rigid, etc.

6. disintegration

If an individual has accumulated such a large degree of incongruence between his self and his experience that he can hardly keep it from coming to his awareness, he becomes anxious. When his incongruence has increased to such proportions that he can no longer defend his self against it at all, his self disintegrates and his organism becomes disorganized. In such a state the organism may at one time behave in ways that are consistent with the self and at other times in ways that are not.

7. reintegration

This "confused regnancy" as Rogers calls it, in the individual's organism is the end result of the process of defense that started when the individual obtained his first conditions of worth. This process can be reversed in the individual by decreasing his conditions of worth and by increasing his unconditional self-regard. Earlier we saw that it was the conditional positive regard of others that gave the individual his conditions of worth, and caused him to be conditional in his self-regard. By the same reasoning others can also remove these in the individual by making their positive regard toward him unconditional. This would effectively eliminate the threat against which the individual defends his self-concept. With the threat removed, the process of defense could begin to reverse itself. The individual would symbolize more and more of his experiences into his awareness. He would revise and broaden his self-concept to include these new experiences, and as a result he would become more and more integrated. Thus, he would experience increased psychological adjustment and, like the infant, he would once again use his own organismic valuing process to regulate his behavior. The final result of this therapeutic process would thus be that the individual becomes more and more of a fully functioning person. This brings us to Rogers' normative or ideal view of personality.

D. Rogers' Normative or Ideal View of Personality

1. introduction: the fully functioning person

Rogers characterizes the fully functioning person as "the ultimate in actualization of the human organism", as "the goal of social evolution",[33] and as "the end point of optimal psychotherapy". He also states, however, that such a person does not exist and hence that we will never encounter him. What we see instead, says Rogers, are persons moving *in the direction of* fully functioning, without ever quite reaching it.[34] Thus the description of the fully functioning person, given below, is a "pure form",[35] an "ideal" or normative description of personality functioning. It is in this sense that I can call Rogers' view of the fully functioning person, his normative or ideal view of personality.

Over the years, Rogers has made a number of attempts in print to formulate his view of this ideal person. None of these formulations differ materially among each other in their basic elements. However, there are some important stylistic differences evident among these descriptions. His first formulation, obtained from the Koch article (e, pp.234,235), is analytic-definitional in character. It utilizes exact terms whose meaning content are described in the glossary of definitions appended to this chapter. His last formulation, however, is much less compact and concise. Its style is more intuitive-descriptional. In what follows I will restrict myself to summarizing his latest view only.

2. Rogers' latest formulation of his view of the fully functioning person

2.1 characteristics of the optimal person

What is the optimal person? What sort of person would presumably emerge from a highly successful therapy, or growthful education process? This is the question which Rogers tries to answer as he formulates his latest view of the fully functioning person in his book *Freedom To Learn*.[36]

To be sure, others had answered this question long before Rogers attempted to do so. The optimal person, some said, will be well adjusted to society. Others said, he will move from the diagnostic category called "pathological" to one which designates him as "normal". Still others held that he is a person who has achieved positive mental health. But for Rogers none of these answers are satisfactory, and it is against this background that he formulates his own view of the optimal person (h, p.280). In particular, he wants to describe the person who has experienced successful therapy of the client-centered type. What personality characteristics would develop in the client as a result of this kind of experience?

2.1.1 openness to experience and existential living

In the first place, such a person would be open to his experience. Every stimulus originating in the organism or the environment would be freely relayed through the nervous system without distortion. Whether the stimulus was the impact of a configuration of form, colour or sound in the environment on the sensory nerves, or a memory trace from the past, or a visceral sensation of fear of pleasure or disgust, the person would be 'living'' it, would have it completely available to awareness (h, p.282). He might experience love, pain or fear, living in this attitude subjectively, or abstract himself from his subjectivity and realize in awareness *that* he is in pain, *that* he is afraid or *that* he does love. But in either case the crucial point is that there would be no barriers to fully experiencing whatever was organismically present (h, p.284).

In the second place, such a person would live in an existential fashion. Each moment would be new to him. No one could predict what he would do the next moment, since what he would do would grow out of that moment. In such existential living the self and personality would emerge *from* experience, rather than that experience would be twisted to fit a pre-conceived self-structure. It means that one becomes a participant in, and an observer of the ongoing process of organismic experience, rather than being in control over it (h, p.285).

Elsewhere[37] Rogers has described this type of living from his own personal experience as follows:

This whole train of experiencing, and the meaning that I have thus far discovered in it, seems to have launched me on a process which is both fascinating and at times a little frightening. It seems to mean letting my experience carry me on, in a direction which appears to be forward, toward goals that I can but dimly define, as I try to understand at least the current meaning of that experience. The sensation is that of floating with a complex stream of experience, with the fascinating possibility of trying to comprehend its ever changing complexity.

Such living in the moment then, means an absence of rigidity, of tight organization, of the imposition of structure on experience. It means instead a maximum of adaptability, a discovery of structure *in* experience, a flowing, changing organization of self and personality, of which the most stable traits would be openness to experience, and the flexible resolution of one's existing needs in the existing environment (h, p.285).

2.1.2 organismic computator of experience: a trustworthy guide for living

Finally such a person would find his organism a trustworthy means of arriving at the most satisfying behavior in each existential situation. He would do what ''felt right'' in this immediate moment and would generally find this to be a competent and trustworthy guide for his behavior (h, p.286).

Rogers compares the organism of such a person to a giant computer into which all of the relevant data are fed and which computes the most economical course of action as a result. Because such a person is open to his experience, he would have access to all the available data in the situation: social demands, his own complex and possibly conflicting needs, his memories of similar situations, his perception of the uniqueness of this situation, etc. Out of all these the organism would come up with the most economical avenue of need satisfaction in this existential situation. That is, it would come up with a way of behaving that "felt right".

The process would become untrustworthy if we were to include non-existential material, or exclude material that would be relevant to the existential situation. If memories of previous learnings were to be included *as being this* reality and not memories, then erroneous answers would result. If certain threatening experiences were to be withheld from computation, or allowed to be included only in a distorted form, then this too would produce error. But such would not be the case in our fully functioning person, for he would be open to the whole of his experience and all of the relevant data would be accurately symbolized by him.

His organism would weigh, balance, compute all the incoming experience of the moment and select the best possible course of action for him to follow. But even at that, it would not be infallible. Even the organism of a fully functioning person would make mistakes, since, through no fault of his own, at times some data would be missing. This would not be serious however, since being open to his experience, the fully functioning person would quickly spot that error and could thus also quickly correct it. In fact, the computations would always be in process of being corrected, because they would be continually checked against resulting behavior (h, p.287).

The trust of the fully functioning person in his organism would be much like the behavior of the creative person who finds himself moving in a certain direction, trusting his hunches long before he is able to articulate the precise character of what was taking shape inside of him (h, p.287).

3. summary

Finally, Rogers pulls the three characteristics described above together into one unified descriptive strand. It seems that the person who emerges from a theoretically optimal experience of personal growth is able to live fully in, and with, each and all of his feelings and reactions. He makes use of his organic equipment to sense as accurately as possible the existential situation within and without. He uses all of these data in awareness, but recognizes that his total organism may be, and often is, wiser than his awareness. He allows his total organism in all its complexity to select from the multitude of possibilities, that behavior which in this moment of time will be most generally and genuinely satisfying. He trusts his organism in its functioning, not because it is infallible, but because he can be fully open to the consequences of each of his actions and can correct those that prove to be less than satisfying.

He can experience all of his feelings, and is afraid of none. He is his own sifter of evidence, but open to evidence of all sources. He is completely engaged in the process of being and becoming himself and thus discovers that he is soundly and realistically social. He lives completely in this moment, but learns that this is the soundest living for all time. He is a fully functioning organism, and because of the awareness of himself which flows freely in and through his experiences he is a fully functioning person. (h, p.288).

E. Postscript to Rogers' View of Personality: From Structure-bound to Process-Oriented Thinking

It should not surprise us that what we identified as Rogers' structural, developmental and ideal view of personality appear in his writings as successive stages of his development. They are indicative of a development in his thinking that we already encountered in his views on therapy. This development goes from a preoccupation with structure to a preoccupation with process.

Thus in *Client-Centered Therapy,* when his thinking was still very much structure bound, therapy is no more than the transition of an old, inadequate personality structure to a new more adequate personality structure. And similarly his description there of personality deals with its structure, old or new, and with how it, *qua* structure, functions. The emphasis on becoming rather than being, is more pronounced in the Koch article, both in his formulation of the therapeutic process as in the formulation of his developmental view of personality. In *On Becoming a Person,* Rogers' thinking had become fully process-oriented. Changingness, rather than a new personality structure, is now the result of therapy. Accordingly, his description there of the fully functioning person stresses the flowing, changing moment by moment existential becoming of the ideal person.

But other changes occur in Roger's writings as well. Up until now the significant events of both therapy and personality development have been described intra-personally. There is, however, another interpersonal dimension to Rogers' thought which receives an increasingly greater emphasis in his later writings. It is this dimension which will be discussed in more detail in the following section.

IV. ROGERS' VIEW OF INTERPERSONAL RELATIONSHIPS

A. Introduction

As is the case with therapy and personality, there are a number of places in Rogers' writings where he deals explicitly with the topic of interpersonal relations. The first formulation of his view on this matter is found in the Koch article referred to earlier. It is also his most concise statement on the matter. It includes his description of a deteriorating relationship, together with its outcome. It also describes the process of an improving relationship, together with its outcome. Finally, it includes his description of a tentative law of interpersonal relationships. Each of these are described in the most concise manner possible (e, pp.235-240).

However, because of the highly technical language employed by him in the first formulation, I have chosen to include only his second, more concrete description of interpersonal relationships. This second formulation was taken from chapters 17 and 18 of Rogers' *On Becoming a Person.*

B. Rogers' View of Interpersonal Relationships

The two chapters on interpersonal relations in *On Becoming a Person* deal with communication, its breakdown and facilitation. They form a whole in that they deal with communication as starting with, and ending in, the personal growth of individuals.

1. facilitation and breakdown of communication

As usual, Rogers first of all attempts to establish a link between therapy and interpersonal relationships by finding a common ground between them. This common ground is communication. He introduces the first chapter[38] by defining the task of therapy as that of dealing with a failure in communication. The emotionally maladjusted person is in difficulty and needs therapeutic help because communication has broken down within himself and as a result of this his communication with others has also been damaged. Through his relationship with the therapist in therapy, the client is able to restore this communication with himself. Therapy can, therefore, be defined as good communication within and between men. The converse is also true: good communication, free communication anywhere within and between men is always therapeutic. Communication is, therefore, the focal point of all good, (i.e. therapeutic), interpersonal relationships (f, p.330).

1.1 evaluation, a major barrier to free communication

A major barrier to free communication is our natural tendency to evaluate, to judge, to approve or disapprove of statements made by other persons. It is our primary reaction to evaluate what others may say from our own point of view or our own frame of reference (f, p.331). But, this is also the biggest stumbling block to adequate interpersonal communication. Happily, real communication can occur and our natural evaluative tendency can be avoided if we learn to listen with understanding to what the other has to say, i.e. if we learn to see the ideas and attitudes which he expresses from *his* point of view, rather than ours (f, p.332).

But this is not easy. The over-riding reason why we generally do not listen with such understanding is that it involves a risk and takes considerable courage to do so. If we really understand another person in a way that enters into his private world to see how life appears to him, without any attempt to make evaluative judgments (f, p.333), then we run the risk of being changed ourselves.

Especially when the point of view expressed by him is emotionally distant from our own, most of us find it impossible to listen with understanding. In such situations we often find ourselves compelled to evaluate. It would be too dangerous for us to do otherwise. Thus, whenever our emotions are strong on a given issue and our point of view is emotionally distant from that of the other we find it most difficult to achieve the frame of reference of the other person or group.

1.2 third neutral party as facilitator of blocked communication.

Yet this is also the time when an empathic attitude is most needed, if communications are to be established. What is needed to get communication going in such situations is a neutral third party who has the capacity to understand *both* points of view. When this occurs both parties will feel themselves understood by him in their own viewpoint. This experience has an emotionally liberating effect on them which is frequently sufficient to get them to listen with understanding to their opponent's viewpoint (f, p.334).

This approach to interpersonal communications, if properly executed and maintained for a sufficient length of time, can effectively do away with the insincerities, the defensive exaggerations, the lies and the "false fronts" which characterize almost every failure in communication. As a consequence, the process leads steadily and rapidly to the discovery of truth and gradually allows the parties to achieve mutual communication on things that really matter (f, p.335).

Summarizing then, the major barrier to meaningful interpersonal communication is our natural tendency to evaluate from our own point of view. The solution to this problem is for each party to understand the other from the other's point of view. However, to do this is risky because it may change us over to the other's point of view. Especially when emotions are high we find it impossible to do so, and thus a third party is needed who can empathize with both points of view and thereby act as a catalyst to precipitate better understanding and, therefore, communication between opponents (f, p.336).

2. (in)congruence and communication

In the second chapter[39] Rogers attempts to formulate in one hypothesis the elements which makes any relationship either growth-facilitating or its opposite. Specifically, the chapter deals with the effects of (in)congruence on communication in the relationship and the effects of communication, or lack of it, on the (in)congruence of the participants.

2.1 defense and deceit: incongruence in the relationship

Rogers first of all extends the concept of congruence to also include the interpersonal, so that it now covers the accurate matching of experience, awareness *and* communication (f, p.339). From this it follows that incongruence can exist in the relationship in two forms. First, it can exist when a person experiences a feeling and communicates it, without being aware of the feeling or that he is communicating it. In such a case the individual is not a sound judge of his own degree of congruence. He cannot evaluate it the moment he experiences it (f, p.340). A second form of incongruence exists when one is aware of one's experience but chooses not to communicate it, or chooses to communicate something other than whatever is experienced. In such a case the incongruence exists between awareness and communication. We generally speak of incongruence between experience and awareness as defensiveness or denial. But when incongruence exists between awareness and communication, we call it falseness or deceit. In either case however, it impedes clear communication.

2.2 personal expression: congruence in the relationship

If it is true that *incongruence* in the relationship hampers communication, it is also true that *congruence* improves communication. This becomes clearer when we look at an important implication of the construct of congruence. This implication is that if an individual is entirely congruent at a given moment in the relationship, thus congruent in both senses of the word described above, then his communications could never contain an expression of an external fact. Accurate awareness of *experience* would always be expressed as feelings, perceptions, meanings from an internal frame of reference. One never *knows* whether another person is stupid or bad. One can only perceive that he seems to be that way to oneself. Thus if a person is thoroughly congruent, then all his communication would necessarily be put in a context of personal perceptions.[40]

One cannot turn this last statement around, however, and say that whoever states his communications in terms of personal perceptions is, therefore, necessarily congruent, because this mode of expression may be used as a type of defensiveness as well (f, p.341). But given the fact that one is congruent in both senses of the word, then one's communication would indeed be in terms of personal perceptions only and this would necessarily lead to improved communication. It would have this as a result because it would demonstrate in the relationship one's willingness to refrain from judging or evaluating the other. By doing this one would effectively eliminate oneself as a threat from the experiential field of the other. To communicate oneself in terms of personal perceptions means that one is willing to be corrected in one's perception of the other, by one's experience of the other. It means that one is willing to be so open to one's experience of the other, that one could be changed by it (f, p.342-344).

2.3 being congruent in the relationship: a valuable risk

This last statement leads us to the existential choice anyone faces when involved in interpersonal communication with another. That choice revolves around the question: "Do I dare to communicate the full degree of congruence that I feel? Do I dare match my experience, and my awareness of that experience with my communication? Do I dare to communicate myself or must my communication be somewhat less than, or different from this?" (f, p.345).

To communicate one's full awareness of relevant experience is a risk in interpersonal relationships. But it seems to Rogers that it is the taking of this risk which determines whether a relationship becomes mutually therapeutic or disintegrative. Put another way, one cannot choose whether one's awareness will be congruent with one's experience. This is answered by one's need for defense, of which one is not aware. But one does have the existential choice whether or not one's communication will be congruent with the awareness of one's experience one *does* have. And this moment-by-moment decision in a relationship determines its direction (f, p.346).

C. Postscript to Rogers' View of Interpersonal Relations

This completes my exposition of Rogers' view of therapy, personality and interpersonal relations. Over the years a number of developments have occurred in Rogers' thinking in each of these areas. These developments were, however, never more than differential emphases around a common theme. In its basics Rogers' thinking has remained consistent throughout his life.

One such development was already identified earlier as a change from structure bound, to process-oriented thinking. There are two other developments that need to concern us in this section. The first has to do with the connection between therapy and interpersonal relationships in general. The second deals with a change in Rogers' thinking from an emphasis on the intra-personal to an emphasis on the interpersonal. In discussing this second development, Rogers' views on encounter groups will come into focus as well.

1. development of views regarding the relations: therapy and interpersonal relations

Looking at the first development, we notice that, starting roughly with the publication of his *Counseling and Psychotherapy*, Rogers initially stressed that the counselling relationship is unique as a social bond.[41] Unlike other relationships, e.g. those of a teacher to his pupil or a parent to his child, the therapeutic relationship is uniquely defined by warmth, by a permissiveness regarding the expression of feeling and by a complete freedom from pressure. These other relations, while differing from the counseling relationship, are nonetheless on equal footing with the counseling relationship. Counseling is just one of many ways in which people relate to each other. None of them is more important than the other. They are just different from each other. Such is Rogers' earliest view.

Then follows a period in which Rogers concentrates on the counseling relation as such. In the course of this pursuit, it dawns on him that what occurs in the counseling relationship is perhaps not at all unique to counseling, and that what occurs in it is to be found in every optimal interpersonal relationship. At this stage then, the counseling relationship becomes the paradigm for all other relationships. In the meantime, the list of characteristics describing the counseling relationship itself had been expanded as well, to include such elements as the empathy, and especially the congruence of the therapist. This relationship is now seen as the norm for the others.[42]

During the following stage of his development, Rogers begins to concentrate more and more on the interpersonal relationship as such, with its characteristics being those which were described above as being characteristics for the therapeutic relationship.[43] The concept of interpersonal relations is moved to center stage and is now no longer synonymous with any of the relationships people may enter into. It has taken on an ideal, normative quality. An interpersonal relation can be achieved *in* the everyday relationships in which people engage themselves, but is by no means the inevitable result of such activity.[44] If fact, these common relationships tend to place *limitations* on the extent to which interpersonal relations can be realized.[45] That is to say, the improvement in communication that occurs, when good interpersonal relations are established, is restricted to the roles which are connected with a particular kind of relationship. Thus the communication that can occur in a lawyer-client, or teacher-pupil relationship is restricted to the area of discourse that pertains to these roles. It does nothing for the achievement of communication in other role relationships.[46]

Rogers has arrived at the final stage of his development when he recognizes the therapeutic relationship as a mere particularization of interpersonal relations in general. Like the others, it *presumably* also places its limitations on the development of a full-bodied relationship between persons. But presumably only, because, as far as I can determine from Rogers' writings, he himself has never explicitly taken that step.

Summarizing now, it would seem that Rogers has come full circle to his position in *Counseling and Psychotherapy,* in that the counseling relationship has once again become merely one social bond among many. But there is a difference. Earlier such social bonds had intrinsic value as particularizations of human interpersonal relations. Now they are valued only by Rogers as limitations on the extent to which interpersonal relations can be achieved within their confines. They can become good interpersonal relations but even at that only to a limited extent because of their role boundedness. Finally there is the implicit, but never explicitly expressed suggestion, that even the therapeutic relation could contain such limitations.

2. change in emphasis from intra-personal to inter-personal

The second development that seems evident in Rogers' thinking is the gradual shift from an emphasis on the intra-personal to an emphasis on the interpersonal. This shift is followed by a movement in the direction of an emphasis on the communal. However, this latter movement was never completed by Rogers even in his preoccupation with encounter groups, as we will see later.

2.1 intra-personal: client and therapist

The development seems to go as follows. In the early part of his career Rogers seems to be entirely preoccupied with the state of, and the process occurring, in the client. The counselling *relationship* is of secondary value, and important only insofar as it facilitates the intra-personal process in the client. It is the task of the therapist to facilitate this process, non-directively in *Counseling and Psychotherapy,* or in a client-centered manner in *Client-Centered Therapy.* In both cases the *person* of the therapist must remain inconspicuous in the relationship.[47] The client is on center stage and the interview is essentially an intra-view.

Subsequently, Rogers' attention switches briefly to the therapist. It is as if he realizes that the therapist is also a person with feelings. Thus he elevates therapist congruence to a condition for therapy in the relationship.[48] But here too the focus remains on the intra-personal and not on the interpersonal. However, this shift may have provided the link necessary for the transition which subsequently occurs to the interpersonal.

2.2 congruence in the relationship

In his book *On Becoming a Person,* Rogers is still very much pre-occupied with the "becoming" *person.* However, in this book there is already a move noticeable toward an emphasis on the interpersonal. This is evident from his suggestion that the congruence of the helping person now be extended to include his communication to the other as well. Therapist congruence now means not only that the therapist should think what he feels, but also that he should say what he thinks. The emphasis is on the therapist genuinely, congruently being himself *in the relationship.* The term Rogers uses elsewhere for this is transparency.[39]

In *Freedom to Learn,* particularly in the chapter entitled "Being in Relationship" (h, pp.221-237), the interpersonal nearly comes to its own, when its enriching character for the persons involved in the relationship is stressed. What makes an interpersonal relationship enriching is its active and receptive empathy, Rogers states. In such a relationship one understands the other and is understood by the other. What's good about a relationship between persons is its character of mutual understanding (h, pp.222-226). Yet such a relationship can only exist when the parties are transparent in the relationship. Congruence remains the basic condition for interpersonal relations. A relation between two defensive, incongruent people is not an *interpersonal* relationship. It is not a relationship between poeple who have become persons, at least to some extent (h, pp.227-231). However, given an interpersonal relationship, in which mutual transparency prevails, then the enriching character of such a relationship lies in the mutual empathy by the persons in the relationship.

2.3 interpersonal but not communal

In his publication, *Carl Rogers on Encounter Groups,* the emphasis is fully on the interpersonal, as we would expect. The interpersonal is now appreciated for its own sake, and not only as a means for the intra-personal growth of the group members. In this book there is an emphasis on sharing (i, pp.120,123,173), on getting close to each other, on the intimacy of the interpersonal (i, pp.36,118), and there is an emphasis on the common bond that evolves over time, together with the beneficial effects which the group experience can have on the individual group members (i. pp.23-26,123,127).

Does this now mean that Rogers has returned to a position which he held when he wrote *The Clinical Treatment of the Problem Child?* In this book he described the child as a participant in his family, and argued that family membership can have a positive or negative effect on the child, depending on the quality of his family.[50]

Or to generalize this particular instance, does it mean that Rogers now recognizes that the group *as such,* whatever its type, has an effect on the individual, simply because he participates in it? Does Rogers mean to say that the "we", the communal, the interpersonal, the social bond has its own irreducible, positive or negative effect on the development of the "I", the unique, the self, the person, the individual, *independent from* the way in which the individual experiences, and/or perceives his participation in such a larger whole?

On the contrary! For Rogers it means rather that no grouping, no sharing, no closeness or anything common could ever come into being between people that do not respect themselves or each other as individual persons (i, pp.53,117,127). The group, or group process, is inter-*personal*, in the sense that its material, its content is necessarily the expression, the interplay and the facilitation of the internal frames of reference of the participants (i, pp.17-23,134-136). Being and becoming yourself necessarily precedes being together, sharing, and communal closeness in the group (i, pp.44,45). Transparency necessarily precedes empathy.[51] Encounter necessarily precedes relating (i, p.181). The interpersonal necessarily forms the basis for the common (i, pp.163-171).

Even though the experience of mutual understanding, of sharing, and of being together in a relationship is satisfying in its own right when it is experienced, in the final analysis it is of value only insofar as it helps the individual members to grow, to become congruent, genuine, insofar as it helps them to become persons (i, pp.93-115).

The closest Rogers ever comes to appreciating the communal *per se*, is in his emphasis on interpersonal relationships. Such relationships may mean that persons are permeable, that what takes place outside the envelope of the organism effectively changes the organization of the organism.[52] It may mean that through such relationships one discovers that what one considers to be most personal, has its counterpart in the universal.[53] But at no time does it imply that one becomes an indistinguishable part of that larger whole.

It does not mean that all men are basically the same. Rather, I believe Rogers to be saying that paradoxically, we have our difference from every man in common with every man. All men are without exception, universally unique. It is because of this fact, that one man's expression of his personal uniqueness can strike a universally familiar note of recognition in the heart of every man.

The autonomy of the organismic process that one is, and the primacy of the person that one becomes by living this process, are and remain the hallmark of Rogers' thinking also in its development.

CHAPTER FOUR:

ROGERS' VIEW OF MAN AND ITS IMPLICATIONS FOR THERAPY

I. INTRODUCTION

My aim in the preceding chapters has been to describe the development of Rogers' thinking from out of his own viewpoint. Thus far we have seen how historically he developed a notion which was destined to become the central theme of his life's work. We further saw how this theme came to expression in his description of therapy, personality and inter-personal relations.

In this chapter I will attempt to describe his view of man with reference to this same theme. In addition, I will relate the contextual implications of his anthropology for his approach to therapy. Thus the relation between therapy and anthropology will also receive considerable attention in this chapter.

A. An Anthropological Assumption

This chapter makes a significant assumption regarding the place of a view of man in human thought and action which needs to be discussed first of all.

1. the integrative character

1.1 integrator, basic understanding, commitment

It is assumed that in all approaches to human functioning some sort of integrator is discernable in terms of which these approaches make sense. Some kind of basic and comprehensive understanding regarding the nature, origin and destiny of man is assumed to be evident in every description that has to do with human functioning. This basic and comprehensive understanding I call one's anthropology.[1]

It represents an explicit, or implied commitment on the part of the writer regarding the meaning of human life and as such it functions as the integration point of all his views.

Specifically, I hypothesize that such an anthropology is evident in the writings of Carl Rogers, and the demonstration of this hypothesis will make up the bulk of the material of this chapter.

There is nothing mysterious about my assertion in this regard. In some mundane sense, it means to say nothing more than that, since all these views deal with the functions and aspects of *man*, some view of man *as a whole*, is implied in them. My thesis suggests that all descriptions of man's aspects by a given author or practitioner *cohere* in the view of man to which he subscribes, in much the same way as parts, or aspects cohere in the whole of which they are parts or aspects.[2]

1.2 implied character

The term "anthropo-*logy*" and the phrase "*view* of man" may create the erroneous impression as if I would wish to suggest that one's conscious, explicit *theory* of man serves as the integrator for one's approach to human part-functionings. This is not what I mean however. Writers or practitioners rarely explicate their view of man, or where they do make explicit reference to it, as Rogers does on several occasions,[3] their writings are never fully descriptive of the detailed view of man to which they subscribe. More often than not it takes the effort of others to explicate the view of man which functions without awareness in one's thinking. This is not strange. A view of man aids a person when he tries to make sense out of specific human behaviors. Thus it is supportively most successful, when it functions "subsidiarily" rather than "focally", to use Polanyi's terms.[4] In short, a view of man is seldom explicit and in view of its supportive character tends to function best when it is largely tacit.[5] For that reason also one often realizes only with hindsight that a particular view of man has been operative in one's thinking.

1.3 dynamic integrator

Finally, a view of man is likely to contain some themes that are more basic than others. Such themes tend to originate early in the development of the author's thinking and because of this, tend to persist over time without major alteration. This cannot be said for the whole of the author's anthropology, however. Through its contact with his changing experience, the anthropology of the author is likely to show change and development in its constituent parts. Thus there can be a considerable difference between the author's view of man earlier and later in the development of his thinking.[6] However, this does nothing away from the fact that the author's total view of man is at any given moment the integrator for all of his descriptions of man's aspects.

B. Anthropology as an Interpretive Category

1. description and interpretation

That anthropology functions as an integrator in human thought and action is an assertion on my part, with which Rogers may or may not agree. I know of no place where he himself refers to it as the integrator of his views in therapy, personality or inter-personal relations. Neither has he ever written a detailed description of his view of man. The task of describing his anthropology, therefore, takes me beyond the mere exposition of his views that was my aim in the previous chapter. In addition, it involves me in taking a position which Rogers himself has never explicitly taken. That is to say, the mere fact that I ascribe an anthropology to Rogers already indicates that my description of his view of man is interpretive rather than expository. To be sure, the sole intent of my interpretation is to understand Rogers' thought from out of his own frame of reference as deeply and comprehensively as I can. But insofar as this involves me in having to compose his view of man from the various hints scattered throughout his work in its development, I am open to the very real danger of misinterpretation.

2. interpretive validity: method and criterion

Such an interpretation requires a patient, deliberately receptive reading of the text to sense out patterns that are often more implied than explicitly stated. It further requires an equally painstaking re-reading of the texts to check whether the discovered patterns are real or imaginary. Thus interpretation is likely to increase in accuracy when one listens empathically to the texts. However, even after such a painstaking process, one is never entirely convinced of the accuracy of one's interpretation. Thus it seems that the definitive criterion as to whether I have understood Rogers in his basic intentions would be the extent to which he recognizes himself in my interpretation of his view of man.

C. The Heuristic Function of Anthropology as an Interpretive Category

My description of Rogers' anthropology must do more than merely be correct. Because it explicates Rogers' views to a deeper integration point than Rogers himself has done it must have heuristic value as well, or else it is redundant. In the first place it must be able to illuminate for Rogers, those aspects of his frame of reference of which he was previously unaware. My interpretation must therefore serve a "leading"[8] function with respect to Rogers' thought. To use Gendlin's terms, it must be my way of "focussing" so that the meaning "implicit" in Rogers' interpretation is being "brought forward".[9]

Secondly, because of its integrative, contextual character, my interpretation of Rogers' anthropology must help to resolve the alleged inconsistencies, contradictions and ambiguities which are often unjustly attributed to Rogers' thinking in the literature, and distinguish these from those that are genuinely part of his thinking.

Finally, the contents of this chapter, together with that of the previous chapters should provide me with sufficient material to be able to responsibly distinguish viewpoint from insight in Rogers' description of therapy, personality and interpersonal relations. This last task however, will be the subject matter of the next chapter.

II. ROGERS' VIEW OF MAN

A. Problems of Description

To undertake a description of Rogers' anthropology is an exceedingly intricate affair. This is so, first of all, because his view of man is highly complex, but also because he utilizes terms in his writings which, because of their overuse in psychology, have become nighwell totally devoid of any unequivocal meaning. Rogers uses such common terms as organism, behavior, motive, experience, feeling, perception and consciousness. If now one employs these terms in their popular, psychological text book meaning, one runs into considerable difficulty when trying to explain Rogers' view of man.

If for example, we take the term organism in the sense of "empty organism" or even in the sense of "physiological organism" we couldn't be more beside the point when it concerns Rogers' anthropology. For Rogers the organism is anything but empty and the mere fact that he also speaks of the "actualizing" organism ought to convince us that much more than physiological processes are intended by the term. Similarly, to understand the term behavior as a response to a stimulus, as is frequently done, is equally erroneous in Rogers' case, since for him behavior is first of all active and secondly free.[10] These two characteristics are utterly at variance with the S-R meaning of the term behavior.

Thus we do well not to take any of his terms at face value and to carefully circumscribe the meaning that *he* gives to the terms every step of the way. This will not always be easy since Rogers' own general definitions of the terms are often inadequate to describe their operative meaning in specific contexts. For that reason one must frequently infer their meaning from the context in which they function. In short, a description of Rogers' anthropology requires more than straight quotation from his writings.[11] Thus it will be clear that such an excercise is highly susceptible to the dangers of misinterpretation. At the same time I believe the enterprise to be rewarding in terms of the insight it will afford us into the basic intentions of Rogers' approach.

B. Man as Organismic Actualizing Process

I begin reviewing Rogers' anthoropology by describing the only motive that he postulates in his system, namely the actualization tendency. Man is an actualization process.[12] For Rogers this would be about the most general statement one could make about man, though it is not that which defines him uniquely as man. What it does is define man as an instance of ongoing life.[13] All forms of life can be said to exhibit this basic actualization tendency, and man is one form, one species of life. This is Rogers' starting point and even though he by no means ends there, it is important to note at the outset that he *begins* there. Man "is" *originally*[14] not the product of the push and pull of physical forces, but an active entity, an X "that is up to something", however that "X" may be further defined.

In the second place, it is important to describe man first of all as a tendency, a process, an activity or a functioning rather than an entity which then *does* this actualizing, etc. If man were defined as an entity that acts, this would imply that he could be described as (also) being something *other than* this activity, as a substance that is itself to itself, regardless of how it functions. Such thinking would be utterly foreign to Rogers' mind. Rogers thinks principally in terms of process, dynamics, movement and change.[15]

But there is more to be said "at the outset". This actualization process, this actualizing that man "is", however we further define it, is an organized activity. It functions as a whole, with all of its part-functionings contributing inescapably to this total activity. Man, as an actualizing process, has this total quality *originally* and every step of his development. Originally man is an organism, and remains this however he might change and however complex his activity may become.[16] Summing up then, for Rogers, man is always and everywhere an organismic actualizing process,[17] always and everywhere a total, active actualizing gestalt.[18]

C. The Meaning of Actualization

1. totality and change: man as dynamic unity

What now does actualization mean? Can we further define it as understood by Rogers? Clues for the answer to this question are to be found in the terms "total" and "change" used above. Ther term "total" implies parts or aspects, since there is no sense to the term "organization" unless it means the organization of parts or aspects into a totality. The term "change", in turn, implies that this organized totality does not stay the same in the organization of its parts, in its constitution.

If we speak of man as a totality that changes in its aspects, then we can only speak of him as such without contradiction when we see him as a dynamic whole. This means that man remains a totality by means of the continuous alteration of its parts, and only insofar as he never stays the same in his constitution. Man can only be and remain who or what he is as a *fluid* gestalt. His original unity is a dynamic unity, itself in motion, itself already changing.[19]

2. differentiation, assimilation, bifurcation

The terms "parts" and "aspects" must furthermore be taken in a genetic sense. That is to say, they are potentially present in the original organismic unity and come to be realized or actualized via differentiation. They differentiate over time *out of* the original unity. They are not entities *added to* the original unity, but rather differentiation *within* that unity. That potentials are realized in the organismic actualization process that man is, means that an originally undifferentiated organism becomes differentiated. That is to say, the fact that man develops, grows, actualizes, or actively realizes his potential, means, first of all, that he becomes increasingly more differentiated.[20]

This differentiation is one of the two movements, by means of which man remains the organized dynamic totality that he is. The other is assimilation

71

which follows differentiation spontaneously in a normal growth process. In this movement the organism integrates *earlier* differentiations at the newly differentiated level of complexity. Together they make up the growth or actualizing process that man is.[21] Throughout the course of his life man becomes an increasingly more complex system of contrasts, an organization functioning in terms of an increasingy diverse richness of shades and colours. Such is the process of growth that characterizes human life.[22]

This *differentiation* is not, however, a *bifurcation*. That is, it is not a splitting of an original unity into two or more, autonomous entities. Once they are actualized the contrasts do not become contradictions in, or opposites to, the original unity out of which they differentiated. At least this is not what occurs in a normal actualization process when the conditions are favorable.

However, under adverse conditions differentiations can indeed become bifurcations. This occurs when the actualization process is for one reason or another *arrested,* when it is blocked from further differentiation. Instead of being a way station in the actualization process toward further ends, the latest differentiation then becomes an end in itself, which seeks to actualize itself *against* the dynamic actualization of further potentialities in the original organic unity.

Under such conditions (to be discussed later) the latest differentiation fails to assimilate the earlier differentiations of the organism and thus fails to promote the maintenance of the harmonious organization of the original unity, inclusive its dynamic open ended character. Instead it becomes a bifurcation that splits asunder the dynamic totality that man is, into two or more actualization principles, each seeking to maintain and enhance themselves antagonistically at the expense of the other.[23]

3. integral connection, wholeness and actualization

Here then is another reason why the whole intent of man is normally aimed at the perpetual actualization of all his potentials (i.e. no static or-) ganization would ever do for Rogers) and why man as an actualization process is normally geared toward the maintenance and enhancement of his organismic wholeness. Organic, dynamic wholeness and differentiating, assimilating actualization are inseparably connected in Rogers' view of man.

D. The Meaning of Organism

1. criterion for actualization: organic wholeness, forward direction

Now that I have focussed extensively on the actualization process and its dynamics, I can concentrate more fully on what Rogers means by the organic wholeness of man. In some sense we can say that its maintenance and enhancement is the central aim for human life. In that sense it functions as the criterion for the actualization process. That is to say, man does not actualize every potential that he could possibly bring to realization. Speaking most generally, he certainly avoids the actualization of his potential for self-destruction. For Rogers the actualization process is directional[24] and its direction is always forward, constructive and self enhancing. It is this at least, whenever the environmental conditions are facilitative. Man's basic, innermost striving tends toward the "good".[25] Given the opportunity, man naturally works toward the "best" he can become. We meet here with a central article of Rogers' faith, and one of long-standing at that. There is no beast in man. Human nature is inherently "good" and moves in a forward, constructive direction.[25] "The human organism", says Rogers, "is active actualizing and directional. This is the basis for all my thinking."[26]

2. organism as gestalt relation

There is another sense in which the maintenance and enhancement of man's organic wholeness is the central aim of human life for Rogers. Earlier we had occasion to refer to the human organism as a (dynamic, fluid) *gestalt*. This gestalt notion must be taken in a relational[27] sense. That man functions at all times as an organized totality does not mean that he operates in a vacuum. On the contrary, Rogers has long held for the human species what Angyal held to be true for all forms of life, namely that:

Life is an autonomous, dynamic, event which takes place between the organism and the environment. Life processes do not merely tend to preserve life but transcend the momentary status quo of the organism, expanding itself continually and imposing its autonomous determination upon an ever inceasing realm of events.[28]

Qua organism then, man functions in relation to an environment, but his relation to it is that of a gestalt.

This gestalt nature of man's relations is characteristic for Rogers' view of man on more than one level of complexity. We shall take the level of organic need fulfillment as paradigmatic, since this is the level of least complexity at which it implies, and later illustrate how this same gestalt relation functions at other levels of complexity.

3. physiological organism, figure: physical environment, ground

The human organism is not merely one physical body among many in time and space, subject for its existence to the push and pull of physical forces. Rather it maintains its organization with respect to its physical environment in much the same way as the figure maintains itself with respect to the ground of a gestalt. In order to maintain and enhance itself as an organized whole, the organism must satisfy a certain number of organic needs, and in doing so, it *selectively* utilizes those physio-chemical processes that lend themselves for this purpose. That is to say, it determines which physical processes are to comprise its environment. It determines which of them are to be the ground of the gestalt relation of which it is the figure. This applies not only to such life-sustaining physical processes as food stuffs and air, but also to physical stimuli. All of these are taken up, or assimilated by the organism. Thus the organism has a physical *environment* at its disposal, and uses it for its own enhancement purposes. If, for any reason the organism is no longer capable of using its physical environment in this manner, it ceases to exist and becomes mere anorganic matter, in much the same way as a gestalt is no longer a gestalt when figure and ground are no longer distinguishable.

It should be noted that Rogers *starts* at level of need fulfillment. This implies that he knows of no physical "reality in itself" and thus does not pay any attention to it as an independent set of events. Physical reality is only the setting for the active organism, against which the organized, directional actualizing events of the organism stand out as figure. For Rogers, the activity of the organism that is "up to something" always occupies center stage. This becomes all the more clear, when we see what Rogers means by the term "behavior".[29]

E. The Meaning of Behavior

I will begin by giving a series of quotes by Rogers regarding the meaning of behavior:

"Behavior is basically the goal-directed attempt of the organism to satisfy its needs as experienced, in the field as perceived." Behavior is . . . "this goal seeking effort". Behavior is "the reaction (of the organism) not to reality, but to the perception of reality", . . . "it is the perception, not the reality, which is crucial in determining behavior". "The best vantage point for understanding behavior is from the internal frame of reference of the individual himself." "If we could empathically experience all the sensory and visceral sensations of the individual, could experience his whole phenomenal field, including both the conscious elements and also those experiences not brought to the conscious level, we should have the perfect basis for understanding the meaningfulness of his behavior and for predicting his future behavior." . . . "behavior follows definitely and clearly upon his perception."[30]

1. behavior as "what the organism is up to"

The first thing that stands out from these quotations is that behavior is not a mere function of physical stimuli. Behavior is not a reaction to (physical, or "objective") reality (and therefore not determined by it), but to the (subjective) perception of reality, and thus follows definitely and clearly upon perception, more accurately, upon experience, upon sensory and visceral sensations.

Secondly, behavior is a *goal-directed* attempt by the organism to satisfy its (experienced) needs. It is a *goal seeking* effort. We might thus say that the antecedants of behavior lie in experience (and subsequently in perception) which is the goal of behavior as organic need fulfillment. Experience is the goal of organic need fulfilling behavior *only* in that it represents the next differentiation to be made. It means to say that experience (naturally) emerges out of organic need fulfillment. It is experience, and not the physical environment, that determines the direction of this emergence. In other words, the physical environment does not direct the organism to further differentiate itself into experience. Rather, experience as the organism's own potential for further actualization beckons organic need fulfilling behavior, as it were by its ab-

74

sence, toward further differentiation. Behavior as organic need fulfillment is caused by what it aims for, by what it is not, by what it is up to, by what it is about to become, namely experience.[31]

Right from the start then, and certainly throughout the course of the organism's life, behavior is more than the satisfaction of organic needs, more than the reduction of physiologically induced tensions in the organism toward homeostasis. Instead, organic needs are fulfilled *in order that* the organism may realize its further potential, which potential, once it has been actualized, begins to determine *the way* in which organic needs are being fulfilled. We see thus a repeat at the experience level of differentiation of a pattern which we found at the level of organic need fulfillment with respect to physico-chemical processes, namely, that experiential events relate to physiological events in a gestalt fashion, such that the latter become the ground of a gestalt of which the former make up the figure.

2. behavior as activity and interactivity

There is however an important difference that may not go unnoticed. At the experience level the organism for the first time assimilates *its own activity.* What concerns Rogers in his writings is the *internal* functioning of organisms, not the way they behave, differentiate and integrate *as a function of their environment.* The organism, for Rogers, has its organization principle inherent in itself. It shapes itself. It is not shaped by the demands of its physical environment. With respect to its physical environment the organism is always *active.* However, with respect to its own internal differentiation levels, its activity is normally interactive. Its actualizing activity is always simultaneously differentiating and assimilating. The internal gestalts that are formed by the organism are always fluid and perpetually changing.

This I believe is why in Rogers' writings the human organism is consistently described as already differentiated at least at the level of experience, and why we find Rogers more frequently referring to man as the psychological organism. Only an organism that has already made at least one differentiation can be said to exhibit this interactive activity of simultaneous differentiation and assimilation, and to exhibit this fluid gestalt character in its internal relations.

3. general definition of actualization

If I were to put the preceding matter most generally, I could say the following: If actualization is the process of differentiation and assimilation, and if these movements are organismic, thus characteristic of the organism as a whole, then the activity of the organism at any given level of differentiation complexity is always aimed at the realization of the next *higher* level of complexity, thus "teleologically" responsive to and determined by it, while at the same time and with the same movement, it assimilates and determines the next *lower* level of organismic differentiation. This movement, which tends in the direction of greater differentiation complexity, has its lower limit at the level of organic need fulfillment, but, as I hope to show later, its upper limit is open ended, such that the process can continue indefinitely as long as there is life.

4. two meanings of behavior

Summing up now, we may say that in his writings Rogers utilizes the term "behavior" in two ways. Both these meanings of the term are essentially foreign to the S-R meaning which the Behaviorists give to the term "behavior". In the first, more restricted sense, it refers to the activity of the organism at the level of organic need fulfillment, per se. At this level, the organism *reacts to* and is determined by a *perceived* environment while fulfilling *experienced* (organic) needs. In its second, unrestricted sense it refers to the activity of the organism at any level of differentiation complexity. In its latter meaning, behavior is practically synonymous with the actualizing process that man is.

For the sake of highlighting the unity (one might almost say uniformity) of Rogers' conception of man, I would like to enumerate a number of terms utilized thus far, and connect them with an equal sign, where this sign carries the significance of "synonymous with" or even "identical to". Thus I assert that for Rogers, organism = actualizing = differentiation/assimilation process = behavior = becoming = growth.

The only difference that might be ascribed to behavior in the wider sense of the term, as distinguished from actualization, is to say that, whereas the latter is always forward-directional, the former is not. Thus in an "abnormal" state the organism might behave in ways that are *not* actualizing. But this is not a hard-and-fast distinction, since on occasion Rogers also uses the term "actualization" for this abnormal activity, as for example, when "the self" attempts to actualize itself *against* the growth activity of the total organism. [32]

5. the organism as an internally interactive process

All this leaves us with one central conclusion regarding the activity or the behavior of the organism and *ipso facto* of man. That is the fact that, this activity, this movement is always interactive in character. The concrete, dynamic behavior of the organism is always a combination of changing into what one is about to become and of assimilating or integrating what one was. It is simultaneously a process of continuous change and of changing continuity. Furthermore, this interaction process does not occur between the organism and the environment, understood as two separate, independent sets of events. Rather, it is a process "internal" to the organism, taking place between less and more complex levels of organismic functioning.

6. Rogers' anthropology as "interactive process", its interpretive value

This interactive process conception of Rogers' anthropology makes it possible, I believe, to avoid the pitfalls of a onesided interpretation of his views, as essentially "phenomenological", or as a "self-theory", or as a "holistic approach". Later I will have occasion to refer to these misinterpretations in more detail. For now I merely wish to point out that all of these interpretations forget that the levels of complexity to which they refer are only *way stations* of the actualization process that man is, according to Rogers. As such they define the specific *modus* of any concrete interaction, but for this very reason they cannot be definitive for the sum total of the organism's behavior.[33]

F. The Uniqueness of Man

Thus far I have said next to nothing about the uniqueness of man. What was said to this point could also be said of many forms of life other than man. This is so because I have as yet made little or no mention of the notions of "experience", of "perception", of the "self", or of "regard" in Rogers' system. This was done so as to first bring out those other aspects of Rogers' thought, without which the whole of his anthropology would be unintelligible.

1. the dual meaning of uniqueness

We should know that the notion of uniqueness functions in a double sense in Rogers' thinking. First, it refers to the uniqueness of man as distinct from other living beings. In that sense the distinguishing characteristic lies in the capacity of man for awareness, more particularly for self-awareness.[34] That sense of man's uniqueness will naturally come to the fore more and more when we come to the discussion of awareness and of the self. In the second place, the notion of uniqueness refers to one man's uniqueness as distinct from another.[35] In this sense, Rogers means to say that no two *people* are alike, that each has his own frame of reference, his own private, subjective, personal experiential world. This for Rogers is not merely one characteristic of man among many. Rather it is (one of) the essential characteristic(s) of man. It is what defines man as man. One's uniqueness, one's individuality, one's being or becoming a person is what one has in common with every man. This notion of Rogers reflects his frequent experience that what is most personal is at the same time most universal among men.[36] This second sense of the term "uniqueness" functions most explicitly in his thinking about social relations. In that context he insists that we ought to respect our neighbour first and foremost as a unique individual, as a separate person.[37] Uniqueness in this sense will thus come to more explicit discussion when we describe the regard level of differentiation.

G. The Meaning of Experience

My next task then is to deal more extensively with the functional meaning of the terms "experience", "perception", "self" and "regard" in Rogers' views. In the course of this discussion I will be able to deal more fully with man's uniqueness and at the same time I will be able to give further illustrations of the interactive character of human functioning as well.

First of all, how does the term "experience" function in Rogers' view of man? I will begin by presenting some quotations which deal with the notions of "experience" and "perceptual awareness". Thereafter I will initially restrict my discussion to only those parts of the quotations which refer to the relation of experience to organic need fulfillment.

"As a noun, experience . . . includes all that is going on within the envelope of the organism at any given moment which is potentially available to awareness." It is a "psychological, not a physiological" matter. Synonyms for experience are "experiential field" and "phenomenal field". It "covers more than the phenomena in consciousness". Other descriptions are "sensory and visceral experiences" and "organic experiences". It "refers to the given moment, not to some accumulation of past experience". Experience as a verb means "to receive in the organism the impact of the sensory or physiological events which are happening at the moment". Experience is a "process term" often used in the phrase "to experience in awareness". This means "to symbolize in some accurate form these sensory and visceral events at the conscious level".[38]

1. sensory, visceral, organic experience

The trouble with describing the functional meaning which Rogers gives to the term "experience", without reference to the terms "perception" or "awareness", is that Rogers himself almost never does so. But where he does, he speaks of experience as "sensory and visceral", and also as "organic". Experience as such is thus a matter that is "internal" to the organism. That is to say, it does not refer *directly* to "external" (physical) stimuli but to the sensory or visceral events occurring in the organism when it is stimulated. Moreover, it is not something that occurs in some part of the organism but is "all that is going on within the envelope of the organism". Experience is thus a total organismic event. It is the physiological organism differentiated into an experiential or psychological organism.

2. experience as "felt" functioning

However, experience as actualized activity is not the sensory or visceral events themselves. Rather, to experience means "*to receive the impact of* these sensory or physiological events" in the organism. Herein lies the defining characteristic of experience as the next level of differentiation complexity. At the level of experience man is affected, touched, moved by his own functioning. At the level of experience, man's potential for feeling or for sensing has been actualized. At this level his functioning is *felt* functioning.[39]

3. experience as actualized potential of physiological events for being felt

What is felt in experience is the organism's functioning on the level of organic need fulfillment, inclusive of its gestalt relation to its physical "reality". *Qua* actualization process, man functions at the experiential level of differentiation complexity when sensory and visceral events, occurring in the organism, have become actualized in their potential for being felt, for being experienced. When these organismic events have realized their capacity to affect, when they have become affects, then we can speak of the psychological organism, of the experiential organism, and of the experienced organism, rather than the physiological organism.[40] Physiological events have become differentiated and assimilated into experiential events when they function as ground to their realized affective capacity in the newly formed experiential gestalt.

4. interactivity between the psychological and physiological organism: a dynamic process

Thus at the experience level of differentiation complexity, the actualization process that man is shows the same tendency to maintain and enhance itself that we saw it exhibiting at the level of organic need fulfillment. In its downward direction it seeks to assimilate and integrate sensory and visceral events into an organized configuration in which experience clearly stands out as figure.[41]

This activity has a number of implications. It clearly assigns a functional place to these physiological events in the experiential gestalt. They function to actualize experience. Thus experience "teleologically" determines the function of need fulfillment. At the same time these physiological events determine the *kinds* of experiences that are possible. Only sensory and visceral events can become experience. The actualizing activity is therefore interactivity between two differentiation levels, which as boundaries determine the kind of interactivity that occurs. Behavior between these two is the interaction between the psychological and the physiological organism.

If now experience should lose its figure quality with respect to visceral and sensory events, this would reduce the activity of the organism to that of unfeeling need fulfillment. On the other hand, should experience seek to enhance and maintain itself without regard for these events, it would thereby lose its reality base. At the same time it would block the further flow of the actualization process. Experience needs to become figure of its own *gestalt,* before it can become the ground of a more complex gestalt. Once this is accomplished however, this further actualization movement inevitably occurs. Thus we see again that the process maintains and enhances itself dynamically. Experiences are meant to become "available to awareness".

5. experience: in touch with "reality", available to awareness

Experience thus puts man in touch with his own original reality and opens up the possibility of having this reality exist for him in awareness. As soon as the sensory and visceral events are experienced, they become potentially available to awareness. They become phenomena, that is to say, they become capable of being "symbolized in some accurate form at the conscious level". In that capacity experience functions as an experiential field, as a phenomenal field or as a perceptual field.

H. The Meaning of Awareness (Consciousness)

It is rather difficult to determine the functional meaning of the next level of differentiation complexity. Rogers uses several terms to describe the organism's activity at this level: awareness, consciousness, symbolization and perception. While he considers the meaning of these terms as virtually synonymous, they are nevertheless different terms.[42] As to the meaning of consciousness and awareness, these are practically identical for Rogers. Thus he uses them interchangeably.

1. symbolic representation of experience: the activity of awareness

It is somewhat different with the term symbolization. It is defined as the activity of awareness which occurs, when we become aware of certain events. In awareness we selectively symbolize some of all the events which we experience as available to awareness and in doing so we become conscious of them. Symbolization represents these events as words or images.[43]

Thus in awareness we discriminate, identify, label, picture, or refer to experienced events as *symbols that mean.* In awareness we grasp experiential events in their referential character. We say what these experiences *mean,* we interpret them. We ascribe meaning to them, or when we symbolize accurately, we ascribe them their meaning.[44]

The phrase, "symbolic objectification" is not out of place here, provided that we understand clearly that the events which we objectify are experiences, and that the objects which result from this activity are symbols or combinations of symbols rather than the events themselves. Rogers uses the term "symbolic representation"[45] to describe this objectifying activity. Thus in awareness we objectify or represent events that we subjectively experience in order to have them as symbolic objects of our awareness, to be manipulated in our awareness for our enhancement. In awareness our experiences stand before us in terms of what they mean. Their meaning determines whether or not we become aware of them, as also the extent to which they become defined in our awareness.

Summing up then, at the level of awareness the potential of experience for awareness, that is, its availability to awareness, its functioning as a phenomenal field, becomes actualized when symbolization ascribes meaning to it. To be conscious is to know what experiences mean, or refer to.

2. distortion and denial: failure to assimilate experience into awareness

Assimilation at the level of awareness can be illustrated by describing what occurs when experiences are not assimilated into awareness. The mere fact that some, or even many experiences are never made conscious is not itself an indication of a lack of assimilation at the conscious level. The fact that consciousness selectively symbolizes only some of the experiences that are potentially available to it is merely a normal case of the organism actualizing only those potentials that are presently enhancing for it (see note 29). Rather, only when the meaning of experiences is *distorted* or *denied* can it be said that the organism has differentiated without assimilation. Only such instances are harmful to the organism's actualization process.[46] This will become clear in what follows.

3. the symbolic, referential gestalt relation of awareness to experience

Our description of symbolization could lead one to believe that awareness is no more than the registration of the experience of the moment and that present experiences are symbolized quite without regard for past symbolizations.

Actually, there is no one to one relation between a symbol and an experience. While past symbolizations do not fully determine the meaning we ascribe to present experiences, they nonetheless modify them. There is a selective, regulatory principle involved in the symbolization of experience which codetermines whether and how a given experience is symbolized. There is an already existing gestalt, an already existing frame of reference, into which, or in terms of which, experiences are symbolized in consciousness. Awareness therefore is configurational in relation to experience. Symbolization has gestalt characteristics. Its gestalt relation to experience is symbolic, referential, representative in character.[47]

3.1 "meaning for us"

This is the key to how experiences are assimilated into awareness. When it functions properly, all those (and only those) experiences which have significance, meaning for us, are symbolized, and they are symbolized in the meaning that they have for us. Not to assimilate them (i.e. to deny or to distort them), means to deny that they have significance for us when they do, or to assign them a different significance than they in fact have for us. It means not referring to them when we should, or referring to them in this way, when we should refer to them in that way. A lack of assimilation results into incongruence between experiences and awareness.

I. The Meaning of Perception

1. the hypothetical, predictive character of perception

The nature of this gestalt relation becomes even clearer when we look at the function of perception in awareness. Perceptions are symbolizations that are interpretations. The designation of meaning that perception gives to experience is hypothetical, predictive and prognostic. In a perceptual act several elements are always operative: memories (i.e. past experiences insofar as they are symbolically present *now*), present experience of visceral events now going on *in* the organism, and the sensory experience related to the stimulus to be perceived (i.e. related to events sensorily experienced as occurring outside the organism).

Perception integrates these three into a predictive hypothesis regarding the stimulus. When it states that "this stimulus now experienced is an x", it makes the hypothesis that the present stimulus has the characteristics one remembers it having from past experience, while at the same time it makes a prediction that it will show itself to have these characteristics in future experience. Perception is thus *transactional* (interactive). Based on past experience it predicts that the present experience will have the same meaning in the future, that it is now perceived to have (differentiation), *provided* that no future experiences to the contrary will occur (assimilation).[48]

2. fluid interaction: future experience, present perception, past experience

The fluid, temporal, ongoing nature of the interaction process comes especially to the fore in the gestalt relation of perception to experience. This is best illustrated by what happens when this process is disrupted. Suppose that certain events were experienced in the past with such an intensity that they determined their past perception and symbolization completely. In that event the present memory status of these past perceptions or symbolizations could affect *present* perception to such an extent that the latter would become *conception*. That is to say, present perception could become so firmly lodged in memory, in past symbolized experience that it would take on the characteristics of conception, (and conception can be negatively defined as an event in awareness which is less affected by present experience that perception). When this occurs, then past experience, and subsequently present perception, would have acquired the power to bar future, contrary experiences from coming into awareness which is less affected by present experience than perception). When assimilating interplay between perception and experience that is normally characteristic of man as described in our model, would have become disrupted, making further actualization virtually impossible.

3. (in)congruence: relation between perceptual, symbolizing awareness and affective, felt experience

A summary statement regarding the relation between perceptive symbolizing awareness and affective, felt experience is in order. As was the case in relation between earlier levels of differentiation, so it is regarding human functioning between these two levels: its organismic activity is interactive.

Experience functions teleologically in response to awareness by actualizing its potential for becoming symbolized. Visceral and sensory (physiological) events, lived in their affective (psychological) character are meant to be grasped in their referential, phenomenal character. Experienced events are destined to become conscious. However, once actualized, perceptive awareness determines the kind of experiences that are to become focal in awareness, as also the extent and the shape of their symbolization. At the same time, present experiences can correct past perceptions to make them more accurate, more true to experienced reality.

In extreme cases, actualized perception has the capacity to deny large blocks of experiences to awareness, or to severely distort their referential character. But this would then represent a lack of assimilation, and a disruption of the actualizing process. Concrete human behavior is normally always the resultant of this interactive process. To emphasize one of its poles at the expense of the other, in either our description or in the actuality of behavior, is a violation of what occurs in man between these levels, or what would occur in man under the right conditions.

Rogers has much to say in his writings regarding the interactivity of the organism between these two levels. The (in)congruence between them are focal in his discussions on therapy.[49] It should be noted, however, that from the point of view of anthropology, incongruence in this sense is merely *one* of the disruptions that can occur in the total organismic process that man is.

J. The Meaning of Self-Conception

What now determines the kind of perceptions that the organism makes? Why are experiences symbolized thus and not so? Unto what end, for what purpose do certain experiences become focal in awareness, whereas others do not? What makes some experiences more significant, more clearly defined than others? Why are some experiences barred from consciousness? In short, what regulates the meaning that is ascribed to experience?

1. the regulative function of the self-concept in the organization of the perceptual field

The answer to these questions is found in the inherent tendency of all perception to organize its percepts at the conceptual level around its most important, most significant, most stable (group of) percept(s), in the case of man, around the perception of himself, or his self-concept. Perception, as Rogers views it, is always organized. For example, Rogers speaks of it as the "map" of one's "experiential territory" (*Client-Centered Therapy*, pp.144, 485), as a "perceptual field" (Ibid, p.486).

Furthermore, his chapter in A.E. Kuenzli, (ed.) *The Phenomenological Problem*, pp.49-73, (Chapter 3: "Some Observations on the Organization of Personality"), deals extensively with the relation between the self-concept and perception. In it he refers repeatedly to "perceptual reorganization" (p.60), to the fact that "the self can reorganize that perceptual field" (p.61), and to the organization of these perceptions into one "consistent system" (p.64).

Finally he explains in an oblique way why it is that the perceptual field tends to (re)organize itself around the self, when he states:

The individual is continually endeavoring to meet his needs by reacting to the field of experience as he perceives it, and to do that more efficiently by differentiating elements of the field and reintegrating them into new patterns. Reorganization of the field may involve the reorganization of the self as well as other parts of the field. The self, however, resists reorganization and change. In everyday life individual adjustment by means of reorganization of the field exclusive of the self is more common and is less threatening to the individual. Consequently, the individual's first mode of adjustment is the reorganization of that part of the field which does not include the self (pp.68-69).

Thus, once the self-concept, which is itself a perceptual gestalt has been actualized, it relates to perception and therefore to experience as a whole, in a gestalt-like fashion. That is to say, in relation to one's total awareness, or symbolization, in relation to one's total perceptual field, one's self-concept functions as a regulative, selecting figure, determining whether and how experiences are to be symbolized, determining what symbols are to be used in describing the meaning of these experiences. At the conceptual level of differentiation complexity, it can be said that the meaning which we ascribe to experiences is always the meaning that they have *for us*[50]

2. "for us" presupposes the content of the self as "awareness of being"

In describing man as a process which actualizes an increasingly greater number of potentials, it is, strictly speaking, illegitimate to refer to the levels of this process as "our" need fulfillment, "our" experience and "our" awareness. It is illegitimate to do so, when discussing the actualization of each of these differentiation levels step by step, as I have done. A being that in actuality functions only as yet at the level of need-fulfillment cannot refer to itself as functioning in this way, until such time as when he has become differentiated to the point where he is aware of himself. Prior to that he surely functions at the level of need fulillment, and others may describe him as functioning on that level. But he himself cannot have any knowledge that *he* is the one functioning on that level until he has acquired some notion of who he is.

A similar argument can be held for his functioning on the experience level. He may experience an event but would be unable to refer to it as *his* experience, because as yet he does not know the "he" to which the experience belongs. Finally, at the level of awareness he might be able to designate the meaning of whatever he experiences, but it would not *mean* anything *to him*, since he has as yet no notion of himself as that central entity to which all his other perceptions relate.

This may become clearer when I describe what Rogers means by the term "self-concept". I would first of all like to stress that it is a *self*-concept, that is to say, its content refers to those events of the organism which are internal to its own organization. Qua percept it contains self-experiences, that is the experiences by the organism of its own functioning and on the level of consciousness it entails an awareness of being, an awareness of its own characteristics past, present and future, actual and ideal. It is the perception of who one is as a separate gestalt and what one can do, or cannot do.[51]

3. from self-percept to self-concept

Yet on the level of awareness, a self-concept is but one percept among many, neither more nor less significant than another. It is merely the designation of one class of experiences, the class that refers to the self. On the perceptual level the self-percept is merely one perceptual object among many in the perceptual field. Like all others, it is an interpretation of, a hypothesis about the nature, the meaning of a given set of experiences, to be revised and corrected in the face of further experience.[52] For the self-percept to become the *most* significant percept in the perceptual field, symbolizing, perceptual awareness needs to differentiate into conception.

We should understand this clearly. It is of the essence of perception that it should organize its field into figure and ground. This holds for every percept individually and thus for the self-percept as well, but also for the sum of all percepts in relation to each other. A similar argument can be made for awareness and symbolization. Their activity is inherently configurational. As such all of these carry within themselves a tendency to organize themselves as "field" of a conceptual gestalt.

However, *which one* percept (or group of percepts) is to be figure and which others will be ground in the total perceptual gestalt depends on which percept obtains the status of concept. In man, according to Rogers, it is the self-percept which obtains this status (for reasons mentioned above). Furthermore, its gestalt relation to the other percepts is not itself a perceptual one. It does not *incorporate* all other percepts into its own gestalt. Rather, its relation to them is *con*ceptual. That is to say, the relation is regulative.[53] The function of the self-concept is not to make concepts out of percepts, but to regulate (i.e. to block or allow) the appearance and disappearance of percepts. Put another way, it regulates which *experience* will become conscious, that is, which will obtain figure status and which will not, in the phenomenal field, among all the experiences available to its awareness.

To the best of my knowledge, Rogers nowhere explicitly distiguishes a separate conceptual level of differentiation. By this I do not mean that Rogers fails to speak of concepts or of consistency, because he clearly does refer to the self as a concept and also speaks of self-consistency. However, like perception and symbolization, these seem, for him, to be matters related to awareness. Thus he does not distinguish the conceptual as sharply from awareness as he distinguishes experience from awareness. I feel, however, that the regulative, controlling function ascribed to the self-*concept* is sufficiently distinguishable from the symbolizing, referential function of awareness, so as to consider this a separate differentiation in the organismic actualizing process.

I suspect that the reason why Rogers does not distinguish the conceptual as a separate level, may be the fact that ultimately he considers the self-*concept* as an aberration in the total organismic gestalt. Earlier I defined conception negatively as "an event in awareness that is less affected by *present* experience than perception", and as I argue below, this characteristic gives it the control it has over human behavior.

If now, as Rogers argues more and more later in life, the key to integrated, whole, fully functioning for man lies in his increasing orientation to *present* experience, it becomes understandable that he also views the self-*concept* more and more as an obstacle on the road to fully functioning. All this suggests that for Rogers self *conception* is not a further actualization beyond awareness, but rather an *arrestation of* the growth process that man is (see also note 52).

I feel however, that such a distinction is necessary to make the regulative function of the self-concept, as described by Rogers in both its actualizing and its aberrant form intelligible in human life.

4. consistency: the defining characteristic of the self-concept

A concept is a (logical) entity which has consistency as its defining characteristic. An inconsistent concept is a contradiction in terms. It does not exist. Whenever something that is (meant to be) a concept becomes internally inconsistent, it ceases to exist. Put another way, a concept is a set of elements which stand in a relation of consistency to each other. Whenever that relationship is undone, the concept disappears and only the elements remain. At the conceptual level of differentiation complexity, therefore, the organism maintains and enhances itself by remaining consistent, by promoting self-consistency.

It is for that reason also that the self-concept is more resistant to change than the other percepts and tends to persist, notwithstanding changing experiences and perceptions. Within the dynamic actualization process that man is it tends to stand out somewhat like an immovable entity.

This characteristic would also seem to account for its significance, its figure status within the total organismic gestalt. By its sheer persistence it tends to make all other aspects of man's organismic functioning, whether these be behavior, experience or perception to gravitate around itself. From its position as a concept in the perceptual field it tends to regulate all other aspects of organismic functioning and assign them their place in the total dynamic gestalt, as elements which stand in a relation of consistency to each other.[54]

5. self-concept as enhancing or disrupting the organismic actualization process

Here again the situation is rife with possibilities for disrupting the process of organismic actualization. When the self-concept maintains its consistency *against* the occurrence of perceptions and experiences that might contradict its present gestalt, it thus defends its consistency against its own elements by refusing to assimilate them. Thereby it maintains its consistency for the sake of consistency, thus absolutely rather than as a relative function of the total organismic gestalt. The self then remains a consistent *concept*, but one which is by definition empty of any real self *content*. It is no longer the self it is, but at best the self it was, thus not (now) itself. It fails to assimilate the ongoing perception, experience, and need fulfillment process that man is. It becomes rigid.

Little wonder then, that Rogers places so much emphasis on the self as the determining factor, either disrupting or enhancing the psychological household of the individual. To be sure, self-consistency need not be rigidity. It is quite possible for the self to maintain its consistency by rearranging itself in the face of changing experience. But this implies that per definition the only lasting self-consistency is one of a self as a fluid gestalt. It is a fluid consistency that is always being disrupted and is always restoring itself. A healthy dynamic self-consistency is therefore possible and as desirable as it is necessary, even though it is not always actual.

6. self-consistency: man's capacity for "owning" his functioning

This self-consistency allows one to experience and perceive oneself as the center of one's own reality, as the anchor point for all the changing experiences and perceptions that one might have. It allows for the experience in awareness that *I* perceive, *I* experience, *I* function. Through self-consistency one acquires the capacity for "owning" one's functioning. It is the conscious awareness of being in control of one's functioning and therefore responsible for it.[55] It is particularly the question of responsibility (with its suggestion of some sort of answerability to the other, or to oneself) which ties human functioning at the conceptual level to one's functioning at the level of regard.

The question of responsibility points to a further need for ourselves, not just to value, but to *be evaluated*. This, it seems to me, is implied in being responsible *to* someone or something *for* oneself. Rogers recognizes this need as well. All this means is that we have a potential for regarding our *selves* positively or negatively that needs to be actualized for the flow to continue. *How* we regard ourselves will depend on the factors that are described in the following pages, but we cannot refrain from regarding ourselves without interrupting the actualization process.

K. The Meaning of Regard

1. organismic valuing, internal locus, self-worth

Up until this point, the discussion dealt exclusively with that intrapersonal process, where man comes to realize himself as a person. Throughout this actualization process the organism functioned selectively in this regard, evaluating its behavior and experiences in terms of whether or not they enhanced its own organization. Experiences and behaviors which did, were valued positively and sought after or repeated. Those which did not, were valued negatively and avoided. Thus a valuing process accompanied the actualization process every step of the way and had its locus of valuation in the organism itself.[56]

But the value of the organism as such was never questioned if for no other reason than that its enhancement was at all times the criterion for the valuing process. Whether or not it was *worth* enhancing, that question was never asked by the organism. Through its actualization process it had acquired an awareness of being functioning, but whether it had any right to be, to function, whether its functioning was acceptable, that never became a problem. In short, throughout its development the organism had always taken itself for granted as given.[57]

2. critical self-evaluation, and the ec-centric movement of regard

But now that it had realized itself as the center of all its perceptions, experiences and functions, the question concerning its own value becomes a possibility. A man can judge his self-worth only after he has become aware of himself. He can only evaluate the worth of *all* that he experiences and does, after he has conceived of himself as that entity in terms of which all his experiences and actions obtain their relative value. Only after he has come to know himself as the *criterion* for the value of his experiences and functions can he further actualize himself by critically inquiring into the value of the criterion itself.

However, such a critical question could never be asked, let alone answered, by an individual who knows himself exclusively in the position of a self in the center of his own world. Only from a place outside oneself can one regard oneself as having worth. One can only *be* regarded as having worth. Thus actualization at the regard level of differentiation requires that a man step outside of himself as the center of his world, and locate himself in a being, who like himself, is capable of valuing, that is to say, in a social other. For actualization at this level of complexity to take place he is necessarily dependent on another person, as the other person is likewise dependent on him. At this level therefore the interactions are relational, interpersonal rather than personal in character. At this level a man learns whether he is, or is not acceptable *to the other*.

3. social other or *alter ego*

It should be clearly understood that this formulation does not prejudge the question whether the value of an individual man is defined by the other or himself. That question is still wide open, as yet. Its answer could be that our worth is determined by how others see us, but it could also be that our own regard ultimately defines our self-worth. The latter answer would then affirm that we are in fact our own definers, based on our own perceptions and experiences, guided by our own valuation process, which has our own enhancement as its criterion. It would thus reaffirm ourselves as our own best judge.

The problem is, however, that we can only come to this realizaton with the help of others.[58] This growth movement entails that we put ourselves in the place of the other, that we regard ourselves as others regard us. This movement, in turn, implies that we recognize the existence of other valuators, who unlike ourselves, *could* value us negatively rather than positively, could value us conditionally rather than totally. It is for this reason that we must now speak interpersonally. We can only decide the question from the point of view of social regard. This merely means that differentiation at the regard level must take place before the question can be answered.

Which social other, the actual other or ourself as our own *alter ego*, defines our self worth, that question has to do with the interaction between the levels of regard and conceptualizaton. It means to deal with how we assimilate our personal functioning at the interpersonal level.

4. externalization of the locus of valuation

As a matter of fact, other people evaluate our actions and experiences in much the same way as we ourselves evaluate them, though not with reference to the same criterion. Normally others tend to evaluate them from out of their own frame of reference. They evaluate our actions and experiences by the same criterion that they would utilize to evaluate every other experience, namely, in terms of whether these would enhance *their* organismic functioning rather than ours.

At the level of regard these evaluations of us are not taken by us for what they are for us at the level of experience. We do not take them as *our* experience of the evaluations of others, concerning certain of our actions and experiences. Rather, we take them as direct indicators of our total self-worth, as viewed by others. In line with our need for self-consistency at the conceptual level, we generalize these part evaluations by others as whole evaluations concerning our total self-worth. In the face of these evaluations we experience ourselves as either *personally* "received" or *personally* rejected by others.[59]

Thus we could begin to regard ourselves as acceptable and lovable only on condition that we change or avoid that aspect of ourselves which is not to the other's liking. Perceiving that certain aspects of ourselves are not acceptable to others, we could come to make our positive self-regard conditional on the evaluations of others. In the extreme we could become exclusively oriented to the valuing process of the other rather than our own. As Rogers puts it, the *locus of our valuation* process would then reside in the other, rather than in ourselves.

In terms of our anthropological model this tendency in us to locate the locus of valuation outside of us is a matter of differentiation at the regard level, without the concommittant assimilation of the interactions of lower levels of differentiation.

5. personally inevitable, interpersonally reversible

Earlier in his career Rogers saw this tendency as a natural (albeit unfortunate) by-product of the way normal personality develops everywhere, as something with which every human being is afflicted to some degree. In later years he modified his judgment in this regard somewhat, and spoke of it as an unfortunate by-product of the way personality develops *in our culture*.[60]

But in either case he never meant to suggest that the process is inevitable or necessary. For him, it is quite possible to reverse this tendency or even to avoid it altogether. Given our culture, this tendency is indeed *personally* inevitable[61] to some degree. However, *interpersonally* this whole process can be changed. This occurs, for example, in therapy as well as in good inter-personal relationships everywhere. The main point in all this is, however, that in the nature of the case (it being a matter of regard) the undoing or avoidance of this tendency cannot be accomplished without the help of the other.

In our culture then, all of us tend to see ourselves to some degree as others see us, more accurately, *as we think that others see us*. This last phrase points to a further complication for man in his differentiation at the regard level. The process of developing some sort of self-regard is based to a considerable degree on what we infer from the frame of reference of the other. It requires that we step out of ourselves as the center of our world and perceive ourselves as we are experienced by the other. This is a difficult task frought with possibilities of misperception, if for no other reason than that the experiential field of another is never available to us to the extent that it is available to the other himself.[62]

6. social regard and self-concept

But whether accurately or not, we tend to experience ourselves at the regard level to some degree in terms of how others see us. These social experiences, together with those self-experiences which we found enhancing of our organism in other respects, form the material out of which the self-concept is (being) fashioned. Once a given self-concept is formed, those of its constituent parts which originated in other-evaluations tend to exert a modifying effect on the manner in which we perceive our experiential field. Experiences which we might otherwise have found enhancing of our organism are denied or distorted in our awareness if they are in some significant way perceived to be inconsistent with our socially acceptable self. This in turn results in the incongruence between the self and experience of which Rogers' therapeutic writings make such frequent mention.[63]

7. conditional regard and personal malfunctioning

Via our discussion of the regard level, we have located an important social cause for malfunctioning in the organism's development toward becoming a person. Conditional regard by one person for another, that is, regard for that person, or aspects of him, which evaluates him or what he does in terms other than his own frame of reference tends to have a stultifying effect on the intrapersonal actualizaton process of that person. This happens because in giving conditional regard we perceive him as a perceptual object in *our* experiential field, rather than as a subject of his own right. When we do this we say in effect that the other's functioning has worth only in terms of our evaluation of him, and not in terms of how he himself evaluates his functioning.

8. unconditional positive regard is growth facilitating

Only when one regards the other as a person, is the experience enhancing for that person. Thus the question regarding the value of the individual as a whole has to do with whether we allow him the freedom to be and become himself, irrespective of the differential value which we, from out of our own vantage point, might place upon his experience and behavior. It entails that we recognize, reckon with, respect, receive and accept him as an experiencing, perceiving and valuing subject *in his own right*, and not merely as an object in our own perceptual field.

The level of regard adds another dimension to man beyond the personal, without which it would be impossible to account for the destructive, as well as healing effects of human relationships on the growth of the individual person. It suggests that a person needs to be received by others, to be able to fully actualize his own potential. He depends upon the regard of others for his self definition. The unconditionality of the regard by others determines to a significant degree whether he will fully be and become the person his organism set out to become. To be fully received forms a precondition for one to be fully functioning. In this regard man is inescapably social. He must be affirmed in his worth by others to be able to work out his own destiny.

We touch here upon a very basic theme in Rogers' therapeutic philosophy, namely: *unconditional positive regard, first of all by the other but also by oneself, for oneself is growth facilitating.*[64] In summary then, we are only actualized by others and ourselves at the regard level, if/when the regard that others show us and which consequently we show ourselves, is unconditionally positive, that is, if/when it is such that personality development can be interpersonally assimilated.

Finally, while Rogers would hold that no one can personally grow without the unconditional positive regard of others at some time in his life, he is *not* saying that our growth is perpetually dependent upon it. If a person would consistently receive this unconditional positive regard by others up to the point where he has actualized himself at the level of regard, he would then have attained an unconditionally positive *self-regard*, without "conditions of worth" (see glossary construct 35). Such a person would be personally fully functioning *independent* of whether the positive regard of others toward him was unconditional or not. Anthropologically speaking he could thus actualize himself further at the communal level and begin to facilitate the personal growth of others towards an unconditionally positive self-regard by receiving them. Whenever two or more persons are mutually receptive of each other, then true communication will emerge.

L. The Meaning of Communication

Thus this type of regard not only facilitates personal growth, but interpersonal communication as well, and it further opens up the actualization process that man is toward the communal level of differentiation complexity. Only people who are regarded by others and themselves as having unconditional worth can properly communicate. Only people who regard themselves and each other as persons can truly share of themselves at the communal level.[65] Anything less than that results inevitably in miscommunication. In such situations each feels himself threatened and misunderstood by the other and as a result can neither be himself nor freely express himself in relation to the other. Rather than share one's inner self which may not be acceptable to the other, one is inevitably driven to be and to express something that one is not. One cannot be genuinely oneself in the relationship. Good communication, then, can only be inter-*personal,* and inter-personal communication is always mutually enhancing, and mutually growth facilitating.[66]

If we view the whole matter anthropologically, we can say that at the communal level the organism seeks to share, to have things in common with others. This drive to differentiate can become so absolute that one attempts to deny one's own uniqueness in the relationship. Thus one fails to share one's individuality and totally identifies with the other. On the other hand, since this differentiation is realized inter-personally, one can also attempt to achieve this goal by denying the uniqueness of the other. Through manipulation one then attempts to incorporate the other in one's own uniqueness. In either case the actualizaton process is disrupted because differentiation occurs without assimilation at the communal level.

2. transparent sharing one's uniqueness with the other

Both partners can actualize themselves and each other only, and share their individual uniqueness with each other only insofar as they are (allowed to be) trasparently, genuinely themselves in the relationship. When each partner is fully genuine, or congruent, or transparent in this manner,[67] then they think what they feel and they say what they think. Furthermore, transparent expression itself implies that each respects the other's uniqueness, for the evaluations by each partner of the other are not offered in terms of common fact but in terms of individual perceptions. One thus speaks hypothetically about the other and expects to be corrected by the other's response in subsequent experience.[68]

M. Summary of Rogers' Anthropology

My description of Rogers' anthropology insofar as it relates to personality development, therapy and interpersonal relations is hereby completed. It can be summarized in the following concluding paragraph:

The aim of human life is the growth of the organism into an ever richer, maximally differentiated and integrated, fully functioning person. The fluid, process-like character of this ongoing human event is, to some degree, interpersonally determined by the extent to which one is received by others. One can only be that actualizing growth process insofar as one is regarded as a person by others, i.e. insofar as one is granted the freedom to be oneself. Conversely, one can only grant this freedom to another and thus promote his growth to the extent that one has come to accept oneself unconditionally as an everchanging, organized growth process. Personal growth thus precedes interpersonal acceptance. Finally, true communication can only occur between two people insofar as they regard themselves and each other as persons. The reason for this is that what is shared in communication is one's unique world of experience. Such mutual expression of one's private world to another, is an event that is only fully realized between persons, and when it occurs it is mutually enhancing.[69]

N. Postscript: Openendedness as Actualization Beyond the Communal

My description of Rogers' anthropology as an autonomous actualizing process may be regarded as complete for our purposes. However, it would be inconsistent with Rogers' intent to regard the communal level as the culmination point of man's actualization. If it were, its growth arresting effects would immediately be felt downward, and result in an incongruence between the lower levels, of the kind which Rogers describes as occurring earlier in the process between the threatened self and one's total organism. Thus if the organism is to continue to enhance itself at the lower levels of differentiation, the process of growth must be allowed to go on beyond the communal level. For that principal reason my description of Rogers' anthroplogy must remain openended.

I do not know what further differentiating steps Rogers would possibly take. But, based on his increased interest in the Eastern religions in recent years, I would speculate that this would go in the direction of some form of universalism, where the individual would become one with the universal stream of the life of becoming.

Certainly, Rogers, who at seventy-eight considers himself very much alive, is too much of an optimist to regard death as the culmination point of the organismic actualization process that man is. Some sort of transpersonal, transcommunal actualization would thus seem to be the next differentiating step. However, this is pure speculation on my part and in any case falls outside the purview of this dissertation. My reason for mentioning it is only to show that a further differentiation is both possible and, as it seems to me, potentially required in the development of Rogers' view of man.

III. SCHEMATIC REPRESENTATION OF ROGERS' ANTHRO-POLOGY

The preceding description of Rogers' anthropology had to ignore a great many details of Rogers' thinking, which in themselves are highly important insights. This was unavoidable. To present a unified description one has to be selective. A schematic representation, in either verbal or visual form, such as the one that follows below, is an even greater impoverization of the rich, dynamic complexity of Rogers' thought. However, its merit lies in the fact that it allows us to focus our attention more directly on the salient structural features of Rogers' anthropological thinking.

Nevertheless, I wish to emphasize again that what follows is not a quote from Rogers' writings but rather *my model* of his basic anthropology. It thus represents an inference on my part, based on my scrutiny of his writings and as such it is subject to all the hazards of interpretation.

A. A Verbal Representation

1. human life: a continuous everchanging flow of forward movement

According to my model, Rogers would hold that human life is an ever-changing process of organismic actualization. More specifically, it is an ongoing, continuous process of differentiation and integration (assimilation), on increasingly complex levels. It is a unified, whole process of continuously diverging contrasts, which interact with each other in a forward direction, that is, in the direction of levels of increasing complexity. Interaction between lower or earlier, less complex levels, preceeds, calls forth, and has as an inevitable consequence, the divergence of a higher, later, more complex level. The higher, more complex level simultaneously assimilates, integrates the interactivity between the levels lower than itself. The interaction between the levels is distinct in kind from level to level, and receives its characterization wholly from the character of the two levels between which the interaction occurs.

This process is a harmonious, total process of growth if it is allowed to occur naturally, that is, when it proceeds from the one motive power of human life, nl. organismic actualization. If this condition obtains, then human life is a continuous everchanging flow of forward movement.

This flow is arrested when, and to the extent that, interaction of levels of greater complexity begin to dominate, to determine, to take precedence over the interactivity between levels of lesser complexity. As a result, human life becomes less fluid, the levels tend to rigidify, contrasts tend to become opposites, life loses its wholeness, tends to become fragmented, disharmony occurs, and differentiation and integration cease to occur in a forward direction. Each level of differentiation and integration begins to actualize itself auton-omously and in conflict with other levels, rather than organismically.

Only when this process is reversed, that is, only when the autonomous actualization of the levels is deliberately undone, will growth once again inevitably, naturally reoccur. This process of undoing occurs in good interpersonal relations and more specifically in psychotherapy. In the psychotherapeutic situation the undoing of interactivity between more complex levels occurs first. This frees the levels of lesser complexity to undo their interactivity. When this process is completed, the motive of organismic actualization inevitably propels human life, once again, in a forward direction.

2. monistic geneticism

Rogers could be called an anthropological monist. For him, there is but one unitary organismic process of growth, of actualization, both in terms of its origin, its process and its end. The differentiations, contrasts, interactions, integrations and levels of complexity are but characteristics *of* this growth. Secondly, Rogers is an anthropological geneticist. Human life is for him primarily a matter of process and only secondarily a matter of structures. It flows continually and structures are only temporary way stations in that process. The process itself is one of actualization, that is, it moves from the simple to the more complex. In that sense it is a genetic process.

3. anthropology in terms of individual development

Thus far, my description of Rogers' anthropology has been deliberately abstract. This was done to avoid confusing his anthropology with one of its manifestations in a particular life area, as could have occurred, had we filled our terms with more definite content. To make the connection of Rogers' anthropology to his psychotherapy more evident, I will now attempt to describe his anthropology in developmental terms. Thus I will describe the way in which, according to Rogers, an infant grows into an adult human being. When I do so, however, it is when the understanding that this growth process is *not* a once-in-a-life-time affair for Rogers, but that it repeats itself continuously and indefinitely throughout one's entire life.

At birth the actualization process occurs at the level of least complexity, the level of *physiological need fulfillment*. Action on that level immediately calls for activity on the *experience* level, as well as subsequent interaction between these two levels. Need fulfillment and experience are thus the first contrasts to diverge out of the organismic actualization process, or the organism, as Rogers refers to it. On the level of experience, the "physiological organism" has become a "psychological organism", and can be spoken of in phenomenological terms. This activity on the level of experience calls for activity on the level of *awareness, of perception, of symbolization,* with the resulting interactivity between awareness and experience now becoming a possibility. On the level of awareness, the organism can be spoken of as consciousness. The activity on the level of awareness in turn gives rise to the conceptual. Here the organism functions in terms of a self (concept), and this again, together with all of the foregoing activity, has to be assimilated on the level of *regard,* and the communal level where one can properly speak of society and social interaction. This entire process is, I believe, what Rogers would call the process of becoming a mature, independent person, inclusive of its activity at the regard level of complexity in the interpersonal process, and its activity at the communal level, where it shares its uniqueness with others in a process of communication. Finally, this actualization process does not culminate in this level but is principally ongoing and openended.

If we now see what happens when this process is arrested and actually reversed, we note that when the communicated activity at the regard level begins to dominate, the activity at the conceptual level begins to diminish, as is the activity at the level of awareness, of experience, which finally results in a loss of need fulfillment. The fact that this movement never fully completes itself, is a testimony to the fact that it is an artificial one, whereas the upward movement is a natural one. Rather, the levels begin to actualize themselves autonomously and disharmony between the levels is more likely to occur, since each share in the actualization force of the organism, which can never be stopped entirely, as long as there is human life.

In terms of an individual human being, what occurs is that as he begins to live exclusively by the dictates of others, he loses confidence in the directing channeling powers of his self. He becomes defensive and as a result of this, denial and distortion of the experience, rather than awareness and symbolization must occur. The solution to this problem is the deliberate undoing of this artificial process, via the communication of regard without condition, followed by a relinquishing of control by the self over awareness, and a total openness of awareness to experience, up to the point where "experience begins to tell you its own meaning". The meaning of experience is the realization by the individual that there are basic needs within him that require fulfillment. When this occurs one has gained a working insight, has become more of a fluid process, more of a fully functioning person in which growth processes inevitably reoccur.

Schematically, all of the foregoing can be represented in a diagram, as is done on the following page.

Rogers' Anthropology

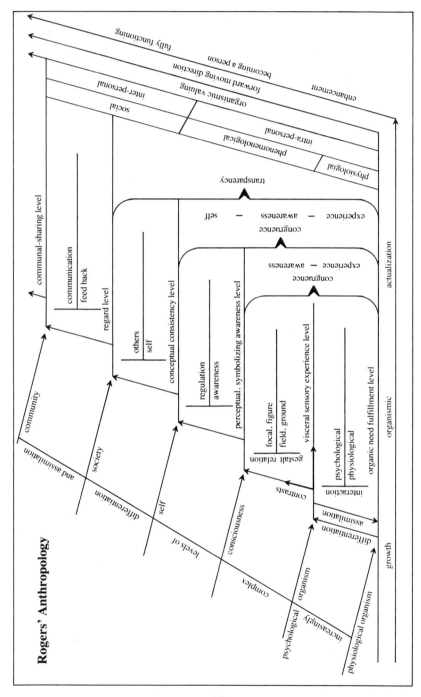

IV. THE INTERPRETIVE IMPLICATIONS OF ROGERS' ANTHROPOLOGY

A. Introduction

By describing Rogers' anthropology I have tried to present the whole of his thought in its interrelatedness. I have attempted to show how all of his past productions hang together in a coherent, anthropological whole. The intent of my description was at all times to understand Rogers as deeply and as broadly as I could from out of his own viewpoint.

What, now, was the interpretive value of this exercise, over and above our descriptions in the previous chapters? The fact is that a discussion of Rogers' views on therapy, personality development and interpersonal relations in isolation from his anthropology can be factually accurate in its description of his views, and nonetheless do injustice to his basic intentions. It is, after all, one thing to describe Rogers' approach to therapy accurately, but it is quite another to show why he chose this approach to therapy, rather than another. The latter can only be explained in terms of the anthropological significance which his therapeutic approach has for him. Thus the main value of an anthropological description is, as I see it, that it safeguards us against a distortion of Rogers' intentions in our description of his views on the various areas of human functioning.

To illustrate this point in greater detail I will first of all attempt to show the interpretive implications of Rogers' anthropology for the central theme of his work. That is to say, I will show how a knowledge of his anthropology has increased our understanding of the significance of the "idea" to which I referred at the end of the chapter two. Thereupon I will attempt to demonstrate some of the implications of his anthropology for the dominant themes in his view of therapy. Thus I will attempt to describe the anthropological meaning of his view on the therapeutic relationship, the therapeutic process and the therapeutic outcomes.

Finally, I will discuss some of the reviews of Rogers' thought in the literature, to show how each of these distorts the basic intention of Rogers' thought to a lesser or greater degree, depending on the extent of their insight into his anthropology.

B. The Implication of Rogers' Anthropology for his Central "Idea"

1. "society should free the individual"

I gave several descriptions of Rogers' "idea" at the end of chapter two, but one description of it was his *dictum* that "society should free the individual" (VII,A). Taken by itself this "idea" could be interpreted in various ways, each of them in violation of Rogers' basic intention. It could be taken to mean that Rogers advocates a situation where each individual would do whatever was "good in his own eyes" without regard for the concerns of others and where society would be abolished. It could be taken to mean that in the ideal state each individual would be an island unto himself, without the need for any bridges between them. It could be taken to mean that Rogers would consider any form of "togetherness" as *anathema* for the individual. In the extreme, it could be taken to mean that he would advocate social anarchy.

2. primacy in the order of priority

Obviously, none of these are in line with Rogers' basic intentions. Rogers' lifelong concern with communication and human relations are a testimony to the contrary. Thus, his central "idea" does not intend to promote the separation of individuals from each other, nor the separation of individuals from society. What his "idea" does insist on is the *primacy* of the individual over society. What it advocates is that *in the order of priority* the individual should come first and society second, this, note well, in the interest of society as much as in the interest of the individual.

That Rogers' "idea" is motivated by something deeper than his preference for the individual over society becomes crystal clear when we view it from out of his view of man.

Anthropologically speaking, social interaction is preceded by personal development. Anthropologically speaking, any form of "togetherness" necessarily implies a sharing of "uniqueness". Without the interpersonal respect for the "the unique" in man, "the common" is not possible. Personal growth precedes and moves in the direction of social growth, not *vice versa*. For society to control and direct personal growth is to reverse the direction of the actualization process that man is. Its result is to make both personal freedom and social harmony impossible. This, I believe, is the import of Rogers' plea, that society free the individual.

3. reverence for growth deeper than respect for the individual

Thus in an anthropological context we come to understand that Rogers' deep and pervasive respect for the individual is ultimately rooted in an even greater reverence for the forces of growth. The ultimate reason why Rogers advocates that "society free the individual" is, therefore, that he sees it as the only way in which both the individual and society can grow. For Rogers, growth is in the final analysis the origin, pathway and destiny of man, alone and together.[70]

C. The Implication of Rogers' Anthropology for the Relation Between his Non-Directive, Client-Centered, and Interpersonal Views of Therapy

1. later view: departure or continuation?

One important question in the Rogers-interpretation is whether his later development shows a departure from his earlier views on therapy, comparable to the one he made he initiated his non-directive approach to therapy. Specifically, the question is whether his later interpersonal, or "person to person"[71] view of therapy, with its emphasis on genuineness as the core therapeutic condition, represents a switch from, or is an enriched continuation of, his earlier non-directive, and client-centered descriptions. Throughout my dissertation I have consistently maintained that the latter is the case, and I believe that my anthropological model allows me to demonstrate this hypothesis more concretely, as I hope to do in what follows.

2. non-directivity, client-centeredness, interpersonality: from intra-view to inter-view

Already early in his career as a therapist Rogers saw the therapeutic value of not interfering with the client's own actualization process, the value of not directing the resolution of the personal problems of another. The client, he held, must himself achieve the insight, which inevitably occurs when feelings are expressed. In terms of his anthropology, we recognize this achievement of insight process as an interactive movement between awareness and experience, where experience is assimilated at the awareness level, which means at the same time ("inevitably"), that new perceptions will occur to the client (see chapter 3,II,B,2).

Rogers' client-centered description was a further (and better) specification of this approach to therapy. It basically stated that the client *has to be given* the freedom to be himself at the regard level, if the actualization from experience to awareness is to take place (see chapter 3,II,C,1.3). This was a richer description of Rogers' therapy than his earlier non-directive view, because it also included the interactivity between the conceptual and the awareness level into the process that occurs in the client during therapy.

But in both his non-directive and his client-centered descriptions Rogers had expressed the healing effects of therapy strictly in terms of the intra-personal process going on in the client. Therapy, according to these descriptions, is the facilitation of the therapeutic process by one person (the therapist) in the other (the client). That is to say, non-directive or client-centered therapy is essentially not an inter-view but an intra-view. It does nothing for the therapist himself in the relationship. From this vantage point the therapeutic relationship is clearly asymmetrical.

Rogers broke with the last vestiges of a view of therapy where an expert applies his skills in the service of another person (thus with the traditional view of "professional" therapy) when he defined any relationship that is interpersonal as therapeutic (see chapter 3,IV,B,1; IV,D,1; IV,D,2; IV,D,3). In this kind of relationship both parties were seen to change as a result of their contact, and this change was understood to be mutually actualizing and, therefore, therapeutic for both. By being interpersonal, the therapeutic relationship had thus become symmetrical. This change in view seems to have been accompanied by a change in practical therapeutic interest from individual to group therapy.

3. genuineness in the relationship: primary therapeutic condition

This mutual therapeutic effect of interpersonal relationships is predicated on the notion of genuineness in the relationship, or transparency. This transparency is congruence in the fullest possible measure and comprises both intra-, and inter-personal genuineness. To be transparent, to be oneself in the relationship, means to have achieved the greatest differentiated, integrated, dynamic wholeness that one can ever hope to attain. When one can think what one feels and can say what one thinks, one is most fully oneself, and that, according to Rogers is always therapeutic for the other in the relationship. This, I believe, is the primary reason why Rogers later in his career elevates genuineness to the primary condition of therapy.[72]

4. non-directivity, client-centeredness, transparency: enrichment rather than contradication

My anthropological model now shows that there is no contradiction, as is sometimes alleged, between this transparency and the earlier described non-directiveness or client-centeredness as the central therapeutic agent in the relationship. It shows that, on the contrary, the former flows directly out of the latter two, and is a richer, more accurate realization of their intent. If this can be shown, then the question as to whether Rogers' interpersonal formulation of therapy is a deviation from, or a continuation of his earlier two formulations will also receive an answer. Thus my next task is to see how transparency can anthropologically be understood to be an enrichment of client-centeredness and non-directiveness.[73]

For one to be transparently, fully oneself in the relationship means that one expresses oneself strictly in personal terms. One does not evaluate the other in absolute terms but expresses how one perceives the other to be (rightly or wrongly). In essence, this implies (see chapter 3,IV,B,2.2), that he thereby gives the other in the relationship the freedom to be himself. Thus transparency implies the respect for the separate personality of the other in the relationship which the non-directive or client-centered approach to therapy meant to convey to the client. Anthropologically speaking this transparency means, if it is mutual, that the partners actualize each other's personal growth at the regard level of differentiation. This would also seem to be the reason why mutual transparency is therapeutic.

But transparency does more than that. In addition, it means that each partner discloses himself to the other, or shares himself with the other. In short, it means that they actualize each other at the communal level as well. They communicate themselves to each other and in doing so they both change each other and are changed by each other (for the better).

Interpersonal communication thus yields the greatest possible therapeutic effect because it is maximally growth promoting, and that for both partners in the relationship. It entails mutual genuineness in the relationship, mutual unconditional positive regard, a mutual change of selves, a mutual reorganization of perception, a mutual openness to the experience of the other in awareness, and a mutual living in the experience of the moment, rather than in terms of some preconceived notions. It ties non-directiveness (which is a matter of technique), and client-centeredness (which is a matter of attitude) in with communication (which is a matter of relationships). The final description of interpersonal therapy, and *ipso facto* of good communication, would thus be that in it *one respects the other's personhood by transparently communicating one's own.*

5. summary: anthropological insight into the development of Rogers' therapeutic views

In summary we could say that the interpretive value of my anthropological model for our insight into Rogers' view on therapy is as follows. It shows how his non-directive, client-centered and interpersonal descriptions of therapy are not in conflict with each other. It shows that, instead, they are progressively richer formulations in therapy of Rogers' basic intent and his central theme for human relations. Thus we can also view the development of his thought in regard to these matters which was described in chapter 3,II as an increasingly more mature formulation of his views on therapy. It would further entail that his interpersonal view of therapy assimilates and thereby *relativizes* his earlier non-directive and client-centered formulations. For this reason also I would consider it incorrect to label the therapeutic approach of the *mature* Rogers as non-directive, or client-centered therapy. A better term in my view, would be interpersonal, or person-person therapy. Finally, the parallel between the development of Rogers' thought and the actualization process, described in my anthropological model, is striking. It represents another tribute to the fact that Rogers has always tried to live what he stood for, also in his thinking.

D. The Implications of Rogers' Anthropology for his View of the Therapeutic Process

Looking anthropologically at what occurs in the client during successful therapy (as distinct now from the therapeutic relationship or the therapeutic outcomes), we see that Rogers' descriptions deal nigh well exclusively with the interactivity that occurs between the conceptual, the awareness and the experience levels. As such the events or processes to which his descriptions refer are what they are described to be, but only their character as anthropological part processes makes their significance for man fully intelligible.

1. insight as seeing new relationships: a partial solution to a more basic problem

To take the term "insight" as a designation of this process by way of first example, its achievement basically means nothing more than that the client obtains clarity during therapy about matters which were previously unclear and confusing to him. It means no more than that he now begins to see relationships that were previously hidden from him. However, unless we take into account the anthropological function which the achievement of insight has for man in Rogers' view, we will fail to understand why Rogers rejects outside interpretation as a way of obtaining this insight.

In an anthropological context, the achievement of insight as such by the client is only a partial solution to a more basic problem that he has, one which the induction of insight through interpretation by the therapist does not resolve, but rather aggravates. We might put it this way: that the client is confused is merely one expression of what is basically the matter with him, and his confusion will only disappear to the extent that this basic problem is being resolved.

Basically the problem is that the forward direction of the growth movement that the client is, has been arrested, and that as a result the client is now actually trying to reverse this movement into a self-destructive direction. His confusion stems from the fact that he is telling his experience what he ought to feel, instead of letting his experience tell him what he is actually feeling. For another person to point this out to him, does nothing to get this process moving forward again. It merely compounds the problem, because it makes the client feel even less capable of actualizing himself.

2. insight requires a redirection of the total growth process

Before a client can reorganize his perception in this regard, he must first *let go* of his present perceptions (which he maintains largely *against* his experiences) so as to be able to live his feelings expressively (=catharsis) and thereby assimilate them on the level of awareness (=insight). As soon as this assimilation has taken place, insight, as a further differentiation, will occur spontaneously, as is always the case with differentiation whenever the proper assimilations are being made.

Not only that, but once this insight has been achieved, there occurs an additional spillover effect in other areas of the client's functioning. These effects, usually described as outcomes of therapy, show themselves in the client by a reduction of tension. He also gets along better with others than before and, unlike before, he now acts spontaneously upon his insights. In general, therefore, he appears to be able to cope much more adequately.

These improvements are not the result of the acquired insight as such, but rather the result of the work which the client had to do to obtain it. The achievement of insight required a redirection of his entire life, even as it focussed on only one differentiation level in his functioning. To achieve insight, the client had to start actualizing his *total* organism again, and the occurrence of *this* process is therapeutic at any level of differentiation. Thus it is not the fact that the client gains insight in therapy that is therapeutically most significant, but the fact that the insight that is obtained is a *working* insight. The fact that *he achieved* insight is therapeutically much more significant than the insight which he achieved, because its autonomous achievement is the event that puts him back in control of his own functioning again. Diagnosis and interpretation are thus only therapeutically significant if they occur in the client and not in the therapist. Herein lies the root of Rogers' rejection of the induction of insight as a therapeutic technique.

Finally, this anthropological description of Rogers' earliest version of the therapeutic process (see chapter 3,II,B) illustrates that we cannot call his approach to therapy "insight oriented" without distorting the basic intention of his views. It would be better to call it "relationship oriented", (C.R. Rogers, and G. Kinget, *Psychotherapie en menselyke verhoudingen.* [1974] p.59). But even this term will not do since it refers to the therapeutic conditions, rather than the therapeutic process. For this reason, I prefer the term "growth oriented".

3. alteration of the self-concept

3.1 from self-disorganization to self-reorganization

A later version by Rogers describes the therapeutic process as the alteration of the client's self-concept in a manner that allows him to become aware of hitherto denied or distorted experiences. In this sense, he views the process as a disorganization and reorganization of the self-concept which has to occur before the self can assimilate experience again (chapter 3,II,C,2.1).

Anthropologically speaking, self-disorganization means that the self-concept has become less consistent. This, in turn, is experienced by the client as a "loss of self" (understood here as a loss of "anchorage point", (chapter 3,II,C,2.1.2). This loss of self is made possible when the client knows himself to be received *in* his inconsistency on the next higher differentiation level, the level of regard. This procedure allows the self to open itself toward the "bottom", i.e. toward experience. Instead of a concept, the self becomes but one percept among many and as a result all manner of perception now becomes possible. The client begins to perceive his experience much more extensionally[74], and congruence between the self and experience once again becomes possible. The client knows himself to be much less in control of *where* he is going, yet he experiences himself as going in the right direction and feels himself much more totally in action than before. Without knowing it exactly and consciously, reorganizaton was occurring in the client contemporaneously with the disorganization which he experienced in awareness. In short, by relinquishing control he (re)gained control.

3.2 relativising the self-concept: gaining control by relinquishing it

What now to make of this last paradoxical statement? How can it be understood that by giving up one gains control? Anthropologically speaking, self-alteration is basically the relativization of the self-*concept*, whereby it once again becomes an *aspect* of the total dynamic actualizing *anthropological* gestalt that the client is.

The change of the self-concept is not one from one (unrealistic) system to another (realistic) system. It is the change from the self as a rigid construct to the self as a fluid gestalt process. Consistency, structure and identity may be the essential characteristics of the self-concept, but it is not the defining characteristic of the whole of the client.

This is not to say that to be self-consistent is wrong or that to be inconsistent is right. The self-*concept* has a definite anthropological function. But it is a limited function. It is when the self-concept becomes absolute and dominant, when consistency is organismically maintained at the expense of organismic becoming, that one needs to become less consistent.

Man is a process which has structure, consistency as *one* of its characteristics. But when man becomes a structure at the expense of process, then he violates his own becoming. The self-concept is a central, regulative, channeling anchorage point in man, but it should never become dominant and all-determining. The self-concept in man is no more than actualization process "having-become-consistently-aware". When if functions properly, it is registrative, coordinating rather than domineering in its functioning. This is how it can be anthropologically understood that one gains control by relinquishing it. Man is inherently a "being on the way", a "becoming", a process of continual change. This is the anthropological reason why the absolutization of the self-concept or structure goes contrary to man's basic intent. It is an arrestation of man's becoming.

3.3 from controlling system to open, changing gestalt

To summarize, during the therapeutic process, the self (again) becomes a relative aspect of the total organism. This involves the reorganization of the self as such, from a rigid, persistent, once-for-all, controlling *system* to an open, differentiated and differentiating, persistently permeable, fluid, and consistently changing gestalt. Until such time as when the client has accomplished this relativisation of the self-concept, he remains powerlessly stuck with himself.

4. reorientation of self-concept

4.1 pivotal character

The pivotal character of the self in the anthropological household carries with it the possibility of an openness to either the "top" or the "bottom". By "openness" I mean that, whereas the self-concept has consistency as its unique qualification, it has no content of its own, but derives its content from the other levels of differentiation. This derived content characteristic is not unique to the self, of course. The same could be said for man's functioning at other levels of differentiation. An experience, for example, derives its content from the visceral or sensory events of which it is the experience. But the fact that the self-concept has this characteristic seems to be more significant for the total functioning of man in Rogers' system than that any other entity should have it. While the self is not dominant, it is regulative and central in the organism actualization process, according to Rogers. Thus he also views the actualization of the self against the actualization of the organism as a uniquely disrupting factor in the overall actualization process. This state of affairs is what I refer to as the pivotal character of the self-concept in Rogers' views. It makes the question whether the self orients itself to the level of regard or to the level of experience for derivation of its content, centrally significant. As I see it, the self-concept is pivotal both in terms of its unique character as also its place in the actualization process. *Qua* concept, it has the inherent tendency to generalize its regulating control, while in terms of its place it is open to both the evaluations of others and its own organismic valuing process.

4.2 public self: orientation to regard

Thus, "at the top", the self-concept can orient itself socially toward the regard level and become overly sensitive to the regard of others. When it does so, it at the same time becomes defensive toward its own experience. When this occurs, the unique character of social regard tends to define the *content* of the self. The self that then emerges is one which "tries to keep up with the Joneses". It is a self that wonders continually: What will the neighbours think (of me)? It is a self that wants to *"seem"* good (in the eyes of others). It is a self that defends itself against its own "bad" impulses. Thus the self that then emerges is for the most part a *public* self, which becomes more and more rigid, more and more defensive, and more and more a system as it becomes more public.[75]

4.3 self-process, self-system

However, the self *is* not a system, but a process that can become a system, depending on its orientation. The very fact that the self-concept can become *more* rigid, etc., testifies to this process nature of the self. The term "system" is a "being" term, not a "becoming" term. The fact that the self can change in the direction of greater rigidity itself shows that it is a "becoming" term.

4.4 fluid self: orientation to the experience of the moment

Returning now to the therapeutic process, we see that during successful therapy the self changes toward greater openness to the "bottom". That is to say, it orients itself to its own experience. This movement also has definitive implications for the self which then emerges. That is, the fact that the self orients itself, not to the social regard of others, nor to their communications *per se*, but rather to experience, determines the content of the self which then emerges. It is because the self assimilates *experience*, and not some other qualitatively different aspect of the organism, that it becomes a fluid *changing* gestalt.

Experience as an aspect of organismic actualization is by Rogers' definition always experience of the moment. It must never be understood as referring to "past experience", as that fund of experiences which one has accumulated over one's lifetime. On the contrary, per definition experience is always new. Experiencing puts one in touch with what is going on *here and now*.[76] What experience is, therefore, changes from moment to moment and for the client to orient himself to his experience means that he commits his *self* fundamentally to consistent, persistent permanent change.

It means that the client is permanently changing the view that he has of himself, to conform it to the experience of the moment. It keeps his self-image permanently up-to-date and in touch with "felt" reality. The therapeutic process, therefore, as the opening up of the self to experience means at the same time an alteration of the self from structure to changingness[77] and thus also a relativization of its distinguishing characteristic within the total anthropological gestalt.

5. conclusion

Thus in conclusion I can say that the further interpretive value of my anthropological model lies in this, that it shows how anthropologically speaking "self-alteration", "openness to experience" and "living in one's experience" do not contradict each other as designations of the therapeutic process. Rather, they prove to be successively more penetrating formulations of the same therapeutic movement.

E. The Implication of Rogers' Anthropology for his View of the Outcome of Therapy

If therapy aims at the alteration of personality, the change it aims for is not one toward a more comfortable personality structure, but rather one that moves from structuredness to fluidity as the defining characteristic of concrete personality functioning. For Rogers, personality change is not merely the means toward therapeutic outcomes but the goal of therapy, itself the outcome. When personality structure becomes an aspect of personality change (albeit an indispensible aspect), then, for Rogers the goal of therapy has been reached. For him the process *is* the outcome.[78]

1. the dissolution of the conscious self: regression or healing?

There seems to be agreement among most approaches to therapy that its process involves a certain lost of self-control. The difference in this respect between Rogers' view and most other views lies in the differential value that is ascribed to this process. Many view this process negatively as a regression, an infantilization, as a semi-psychotic process, as a semi-submersion into the unconscious, which in itself is unpleasant and even dangerous, though necessary for healing to begin. For Rogers, this dissolution of the self, this loss of self-control is itself the healing that occurs. He, therefore, values this process positively.

2. differential localization of the principle of organization

The reason for the differential valuation of the same therapeutic movement lies, I believe, in the fact that Rogers localizes the principle of organization or integration elsewhere in man than do most other approaches. For most approaches the conscious self is the principle of organization in man. For Rogers it is an organism. For most approaches the expression of feeling, the (re)living of (past) experience is a necessary part process of therapy to get at the facts, the dynamics of the problem. But it is also clearly understood by them that some form of interpretation, insight or decisive action must follow if the client is to become reintegrated and whole. For Rogers this living in his experience *itself* is integrative and healing in character.

3. the goal of therapy: self-consistency or growth?

For those approaches which have the self as organization principle, the ultimate goal of therapy is self-consistency, or conscious, conceptual, "analyzed" control over ones' functioning. For Rogers this principle lies in the organism and thus for him the ultimate goal of therapy is growth, or dynamic integration, or the integrated change, or fully functioning.

4. integration as trusting one's total organismic actualization process

For him, man is most integrated, and most fully functioning when he realizes that he is *not* consciously in control of all that goes on within him. He becomes whole when he learns to trust that this largely unconscious process going on inside himself will move him in the right direction. He becomes whole when he learns to respect this organismic actualization *process* as wiser than his conscious, consistent self-*structure*. It is only when man becomes aware of himself as borne by an unconscious, *but benevolent*, organismic process, over which he has no exact control, which rather carries him like an ocean carries a ship, that he becomes personally and interpersonally integrated. It is when he has learned to respect *this* process, that he has become mature, autonomous and dynamically real.[79]

V. ANTHROPOLOGICAL EVALUATION OF SOME ROGERS- INTERPRETATIONS

The question to be investigated in this section is the extent to which a description of Rogers' anthropological intent aids us in judging the validity of the various interpretations of his views found in the literature. My aim will not be to determine whether these interpretations are valid external criticisms of Rogers' views, but rather whether they have adequately understood his basic intent. Furthermore, it is impossible to deal exhaustively with every inter- pretation of Rogers' views in existence. For that reason I have grouped these reviews under two broad categories, namely those relating to his view of personality and those dealing with his views on the interpersonal relationships. Within each category I will restrict my discussion to some representative reviews only.

A. Rogers' View of Personality as a "Phenomenological Self Theory"

One group of reviews focusses on Rogers' view of personality and labels it variously as a "phenomenological", or "perceptual", or a "self"- theory. Considering Rogers' anthropology as I have described it in this chapter, are these the correct labels for his view of the human person? I will attempt to answer this question by discussing each of the reviews in this group in some detail.

1. the "third force" interpretation of Dagenais

In his *Models of Man*[80], Dagenais calls Rogers a spokesman for the so-called "third force" in psychology (p.35). According to Dagenais, this movement is presently in a quandary because it has renounced the mechanistic, experimental model of the natural sciences as a paradigm for psychology but being a psychological movement, it also hesitates to turn to philosophy for an alternative model. Hence, instead of being a "third force", it is in danger of becoming "the odd man out" by the renunciation of their "scientific" char- acter, and their inability to remember their "philosophical phenomenological roots." Re-establishing their link with their philosophical past could save the third force movement, according to Dagenais. This is why he wants to demon- strate that the movement is a "branch of phenomenology" which finds its "origin" in Brentano (pp.32-33).

However, if Brentano is the grandfather of third force psychology its father is not the transcendental phenomenology of Husserl but the empirico-experimental phenomenology of Stumpf (p.34). The latter pursued his *"philosophical"* investigations in an *"empirical"* manner (p.28) and thereby became the father of Gestalt psychology, which in turn influenced such third force figures as Lewin, Snyggs, Combs, Rogers and Maslow. Holism, too, was made possible by the Gestalt tradition. In short, the connection between phenomenology and third force psychology goes first of all via the influence of Lewin's *field theory*, with its self in a perceptual field. Then there is also *holism*, which linked the perceptual field to real bodily existence. Next, the connection entails the notion of *Gestalt* which was developed philosophically by Merleau-Ponty and clinically by Rogers. Finally, it includes Maslow's transformation of clinical psychology from a medical model to a *growth model* (pp.34-35). As a result of all these theoretical contributions, third force psychology set out to rehabilitate the "self in its subjectivity and dignity" and to replace "a mechanomorphic model of the robot" by an "anthropomorphic model of the person". It turned its attention "from determinism to self-determinism, from causality to purpose, from behavior to experience and from manipulation to actualization" (p.33). In this manner Dagenais wants to make amenable to us that third force psychology was set into motion by the phenomenological concerns of its precursors (p.33).

If we add to this list of influences the notion of perception as the integrating concept, it adds up to a self theory which is based on perceptual principles, especially those pertaining to the perceptual field of the self as a gestalt. Furthermore, since this self is a human organism it must be understood in a holistic sense. According to Dagenais this is Rogers' theory of personality.

In this manner Rogers' theory of personality incorporates all the basic options of (phenomenological) third force psychology and subsumes them all under the single integrating nuclear concept of the self (p.36). On the one hand Rogers' self theory is the result of highly sophisticated experimentation with operationally defined scientific concepts. On the other, its content is precisely expressed in terms of possibility, potentiality, growth, person and selfhood, all of them notions derived from a phenomenologically inspired third force tradition (p.37). Reminiscent of Stumpf, Rogers has thus been able to bridge the gap between scientific psychology and the phenomenological bases of the third force options. Dagenais therefore hopes that the movement will recognize the paradigmatic character of Rogers' theory, for this will help them to become, if they wish, both scientifically respectable and philosophically relevant (p.38).

From this phenomenological position of self theorist, Rogers is also said by Dagenais to have "incorporated" the "biological tradition", or to have "harmonized" psychology and biology. Via this incorporation and harmonization Dagenais wants to bring the influence of Darwin's evolutionism on third force psychology to the fore (p.39). In a model based on evolutionistic biology a person can go in one of two directions, according to Dagenais. One can move towards a teleological or a mechanistic view of man (p.41). Rogers' holistic-biological-psychological theory does neither of these. Rather, it chooses for an innate tendency in the organism to grow, to enhance and maintain itself but which tendency is also *directional* rather than teleological. That is to say, it is not a tendency that moves *towards* growth but one that itself *manifests* growth. Rogers thus holds with Angyal that the direction defines the goal and not *vice versa*. In this manner both Gestalt theory (psychology) and evolutionism (biology) are harmonized in Rogers' self theory, according to Dagenais (pp.42-43).

By way of criticism we may ask Dagenais whether in Rogers' case it is indeed a question of the "phenomenological tradition" incorporating the "evolutionistic tradition". The development of Rogers' thought seems to suggest that a better case can be made for the reverse. Historically speaking, Rogers stands in the American tradition in which evolutionism has exerted a strong influence. This influence was certainly very pronounced when Rogers first conceived his "idea". Furthermore, it was not until later that he underwent a direct influence of phenomenology (particularly via Snyggs and Combs). Thus to accept Dagenais' view would seem to entail that we must ignore the development of Rogers' thought prior to his publication of *Client-Centered Therapy*, where for the first time he speaks in phenomenological, perceptual or self-theoretical terms about personality. On these historical grounds, I believe, we must rather view his self theory as a variant of his more evolutionistic, growth oriented conception of man which was not only conceived much earlier, but also prevailed throughout his life.[81]

I believe we could even take this one step further. Insofar as the influence of the phenomenological tradition on Rogers included the notion of "self-determinism", it caused more problems than that it aided him. The postulate of the self that determines is foreign to Rogers' growth oriented view of man, because it introduces a determining factor *other than growth itself*, into the actualization process. Instead, the notion of the self often seems to function as the "undigested lump" in Rogers' process-oriented view of man.

2. the "self-theory" interpretation of Combs, Hall and Lindzey, Patterson, Beck and Smit.

Systematically speaking, there are also difficulties in describing Rogers' view of personality as a (phenomenological or perceptual) self theory. Combs[82] has described the phenomenological frame of reference as follows: People respond to reality in terms of their perception of it, and differ from each other in terms of that perception. The latter is due to the differential way each regards himself. Each person has a self-view, a self-concept or a "phenomenal self" which they want to preserve at all cost. This characteristic has a consequence that the phenomenal self becomes the most stable element in their personality. For that reason it determines the way they perceive reality and thus also the way they behave (pp.198-202). The fact that Rogers' view of personality is phenomenological thus boils down to it being a "self-theory", as Hall and Lindzey refer to it.[83]

In his review of client-centered therapy, Patterson[84] also calls Rogers' view of personality a self-theory "because of the central importance of the self, or self-concept in it". He goes on to say that more broadly, however, both Rogers' theory of therapy and his theory of personality "constitute a perceptual theory, or more specifically, a phenomenological theory". Citing Combs and Snyggs,[85] he describes phenomenology as follows. It . . .

"assumes that although a real world may exist, its existence cannot be known or experienced directly. Its existence is inferred on the basis of perceptions of the world. These perceptions constitute the phenomenological field or the phenomenal world of the individual. Man can only know his phenomenal world, never any real world. Therefore he can only behave in terms of how he perceives things or how they appear to him."(p.432)

The process of client-centered therapy, according to Patterson, is the reorganization of the perceptions of the client about himself and the world. Its outcomes include self-direction and the perception of the locus of valuation and of choice in the self. The individual is conceived as a free agent, capable of and with the right to make his own choices and decisions. The individual is capable of changing (p.433).

At the same time, however, Patterson argues, phenomenology is deterministic. In this connection he quotes Combs and Snyggs again who state that . . . "All behavior without exception is completely determined by, and pertinent to, the perceptual field of the behaving organism."[86] If this is so, Patterson argues, following Beck,[87] then Rogers' phenomenology is in conflict with his client-centered view of therapy. Even the fact that the self influences the phenomenal field cannot resolve this conflict, on grounds that it provides man with his freedom of choice. For, since the self is a self-*percept* or a *phenomenal* self it is itself also determined and thus the conflict remains. As Kellerman[88] has noticed elsewhere, Rogers appears to be guilty of circular reasoning here when he holds simultaneously that the self-concept determines the nature of perception and that perception determines the nature of self-concept. Thus Patterson concludes that there exists an apparently unrecognized conflict in Rogers between his phenomenology and his system as regards individual freedom and choice (pp.433-434).

Smit,[89] another reviewer of Rogers' thought, has also called Rogers' personality a "self theory". For Smit this implies that Rogers has made the serious mistake of equating the concept "ego" with the concept of "self" in his personality theory. This further means that Rogers ends up with an "ego-less self", which in turn entails that he has no *person* as the necessary "sub-stratum" for his *personality*. Because there is no room for an "ego" or "person" in Rogers' man he remains caught in his own phenomenal world and can never "transcend" his phenomenal world to the real world, "outside". In short, because Rogers knows only of an "ego-less self" he has fallen prey to "phenomenological solipsism". This is also why there is a lack of inten-tionality and activity in Rogers' man. Instead of describing man as a person, Rogers describes him as a "biological organism which develops into a per-sonality". Since organisms only respond passively toward their environment, this makes man relate only reactively but never in an active, outgoing fashion towards his phenomenal field (pp.34-37).

3. summary evaluation of these interpretations

Via his alleged phenomenological, or perceptual or self-theoretical view of personality Rogers thus would appear to have gotten himself into a number of rather serious conceptual inconsistencies. These would seem to include first of all that he begins halfway down the development of his thought and then "incorporates" the earlier development of his thinking. They would further seem to include that he adopts a deterministic phenomenological viewpoint in order to be able to demonstrate that man is free. Next, they would include that he involves himself in circular reasoning by stating that the self both determines and is determined by perception. Finally, they would include that he gets himself caught in phenomenological solipsism in an effort to improve interpersonal communication and restricts his view of man to an inactive actualizing organism. All these inconsistencies allegedly plague Rogers' thinking because in an effort to demonstrate that behavior is self-determined he presumably adopted a "self-theory" of personality.

With regard to this notion of self-determinism a few more "inconsistencies" could be added directly from Rogers' writings. There Rogers argues that insofar as the self-concept dominates the perceptual field it is a rigid self-concept which is by and large made up of external introjections. Hence insofar as the self determines perception man's actions are governed by others and hence he is not free. Man is only free insofar as his self-concept becomes a self-percept, thus insofar as it loses its determining status over perception, and man is only free insofar as his self-concept is continually changed by perception. Thus also the less man is a determining ego the more active he becomes. But at the same time all this goes directly contrary to Beck and Patterson's assertion according to which man is not free when the self is determined by the phenomenal field. It also goes counter to Smit's assertion that unless the self becomes more of a determining ego over his perceptual field man does not become more active but passive.

In view of all these contradictions, I believe we do well to ask whether Rogers really adhered to a self theory of personality, or whether it exists only in the mind of the reviewers. To the best of my knowledge Rogers himself never refers to his view of personality as a "self theory", even though he does of course refer extensively to the self-concept, to perception and to the phenomenal field.

If we view all these matters from out of his basic anthropological intent, as described in this chapter, then a dramatically different picture emerges. For then it becomes clear that Rogers localizes neither man nor the human person in the self but in the organismic actualization *process*. This means first of all that structures of any kind, the self-structure included, must be taken as aspects of flow. Thus a theory of man that is self-directive in the sense described above does not at all appear to be Rogers' view of man or the human person. Rather, it would seem to be his view of "pathology", of *mal*-functioning, rather than *fully* functioning. A determining self-concept is a static self-concept, which as such represents an element in human functioning that is foreign to man's dynamic nature. Similarly, Rogers does not appear to espouse a phenomenological view for its own sake, but does so rather to safeguard the self from becoming a rigid concept through the introjection of outside values. His phenomenological view would thus seem to have the function of allowing perception to have access to *changing experience,* which in turn receives its dynamic character from the dynamic growth process that man is. Thus, as soon as we see that the central integrating concept of Rogers' view of personality is not perception but growth, we can begin to understand that the phenomenological is not the heart of personality *structure* but rather an aspect of personality *growth.*

Furthermore, if we look beyond Rogers' view of personality to his view of man we see that it is a process of actualization that has both assimilation and differentiation as its characteristics. In that context a self-concept that is derived from and reflective of perception, but also regulative for it, presents no problem. It is not contradictory to say that the self changes perception and is changed by it if both self and perception are aspects of the assimilating and differentiating process that man is. Neither is it contradictory to say that perception is both selective of, and informed by experience, if both of these are viewed as process aspects. Then, finally, it can also be understood how organic need fulfilling behavior can be both responsive to experience and perception, as well as capable of actualizing them.

The fully functioning *person* for Rogers is not the self but the organismic actualization process. This entails that not even the person "himself" can or ought to control this dynamic proces. All he can or ought to do is yield to this dynamic flow that he is. From this anthropological perspective, a description of Rogers' view of personality as a self, or phenomenological, or perceptual theory would thus appear to be an attempt to *anchor* this flow in terms of something other than itself.

B. The Relationship as the "Dialogical Context of Personal Growth"

There have been more attempts in the literature to anchor this flow in terms of something other than itself. In what follows I will discuss a group of Rogers-interpretations which have this in common that they all view personal change as a function of man's interpersonal relations. My anthropological model will again be the criterion for determining whether this group of reviews has correctly interpreted Rogers' view of therapy and interpersonal relations. The procedure to be followed will again be that I will attempt to answer this question via a detailed discussion of each review.

1. the "dialogical-monological" interpretation of Dijkhuis

In his dissertation[90] on Rogers' process theory Dijkhuis characterizes Rogers' description of the therapeutic interview as "monological". By this he means to say that for Rogers the therapeutic relation is a function of the therapeutic process that occurs in the client. He further attributes Rogers' monological view of therapy to his anthropological conviction that man is individually independent of others, or to his conviction that, given the right conditions, man has a single, unified tendency to constructively actualize himself (p.175).

Dijkhuis himself does not share Rogers' conviction in this regard and thus he comes to different conclusions about the nature of man. In the first place he states that even under optimal conditions man's tendency to actualize himself is not unified but continues to be characterized by ambivalence and uncertainty. This is why the individual will always need the concrete inter-actions of others to bring about a unification in his self-actualization. For that reason also man will never become fully independent (onafhankelijk) from others. At best he can only become "self-governing" (zelfstandig) in inter-action with others. Thus he defines self-governance as the capacity to "be yourself" in the everchanging relations with others (pp.175-176).[91]

It is because of these anthropological considerations that Dijkhuis advocates a "dialogical" rather than a "monological" view of the therapeutic interview (p.180,p.143). This in effect means that he views the therapeutic process that occurs in the client as a function of the therapeutic relationship. It further means that for him therapeutic change results from the "co-operation" (samenwerking) between client and therapist in the context of a "common experiential frame of reference" (gemeenschappelijk ervarings kader) (p.178).

This is why Dijkhuis wants to pay a great deal of attention to the concrete behavior of the therapist in the relationship (p.176). He does not consider it sufficient that the therapist holds a certain number of therapeutic attitudes. The important thing is that his concrete behavior also communicates these attitudes to the client (p.177-178). This concrete communication process, with its more specific "concrete interactions in the interview" (concrete gespreksinteracties) is central to Dijkhuis' view of therapy. In this regard he accuses Rogers of neglecting these concrete interview interactions in favor of an emphasis on the more global (holistic) attitude of the therapist and on the transactional therapeutic process of the client (pp.175,69-71). In that context Dijkhuis speaks of a need for knowing the "interactive techniques" (p.178) of the therapist. That is to say, he advocates a more differentiated understanding of the therapist's interactions with his client than a mere list of attitudinal conditions is able to give us. Elsewhere he states that "the therapeutic activity, however spontaneous it may occur, must regularly be checked to see whether it is in line with the intentions of the therapist" (p.174).

Dijkhuis' central objection to Rogers' view of therapy appears to be aimed at its alleged over-emphasis on the global attitude of the therapist at the expense of a focus on the concrete interacting behaviors that implement this attitude. He appears to link this holistic emphasis in Rogers' view of therapy to a conflict in his view of science (p.83) as this comes to expression in his *Person or Science?*[92] Dijkhuis describes how Rogers resolves this conflict in this article by arguing that science occurs in people (p.57), thus by making science "personal" (p.51,53). By resolving the conflict in this manner, according to Dijkhuis, Rogers chooses for a view of psychotherapy that must remain complex and transactional. That is, it can only view it in terms of the total interdependence of all of its variables. It never gets to analyzing the interaction of these variables in terms of their effect on each other. In short, Rogers' view of therapy does not make clear how the interactive events of the therapeutic relation bring about the change in the experience of the client that occurs during therapy. His approach is thus holistic rather than operationalistic (pp.67-71).

Dijkhuis' criticism notwithstanding, Rogers' research output in the area of psychotherapy has been prolific. He has further described many of the facets of psychotherapy in extensive detail. Moreover, using these research data and these descriptions he has constructed at least one rigorous theory of therapy that utilizes operationally defined constructs. Thus we do well to ask whether Dijkhuis has correctly interpreted Rogers' view of science and of therapy as well as their relation. Rogers has always advocated a unified approach to psychotherapy. This would indeed seem to be the background for his emphasis on the therapist's attitude. But this fact never kept him or his co-workers from doing detailed research about the factors involved in his approach. Thus Dijkhuis himself has a hard time convincing us that Rogers has a tendency to neglect experimentation (pp.84-87). Only if Rogers had advocated a unified approach *at the expense of* detailed experimentation could he be faulted with a holistic over-emphasis. But this, as far as I can see, Dijkhuis has been unable to prove thus far.

In order to correctly gauge Rogers' appreciation for science we must first of all understand its functional significance for the goal of human life as Rogers sees it. That goal, briefly put, is the enhancement of the individual's growth. Whatever contributes toward that goal is to be pursued. But, equally, whatever obstructs the growth of the individual should be avoided. A basic prerequisite for the perpetual achievement of this growth, in Rogers' view, is that the individual should be or become a person and for this he needs to have freedom, autonomy and independence. Thus the primary function of therapy and all interpersonal relations is for one individual to help another to become a person by giving him the freedom, the autonomy and the independence that he needs.

It is in this context, first of all, that we must understand Rogers' "conflict" between the person and science, and his solution to this conflict. Rogers does not object to science because it is operationalistic or interactive in its method, as if he would prefer a more holistic or transactional method. He does not object to science because it analyzes or discovers regularities. Rather, as I have attempted to show in chapter two, he objects to its becoming the guide for human life. For if all its accumulated findings would become the exclusive determinator of our lives, Rogers urgues, these could end up *restricting* the freedom of the individual and thus obstruct his growth. It is the restrictiveness of a "common" science on the free creative growth of the human person that worries Rogers.

Science is per definition a common, public activity that yields commonly accepted results. But in Rogers' growth-oriented anthropology the personal has priority over the common in the order of growth. Thus Rogers' "personalization" of science does not at all represent a devaluation of science as such, but merely an attempt to put it in its proper place. Science must serve the individual and not *vice versa*, is all that Rogers is saying here.

There is one more way in which Rogers places science and its results in the context of human life. This refers to his assertion that human experience rather than science is the source of knowledge in human life. The anthropological background to this assertion is that since science is a matter of conceptualization, it follows experience in the order of growth. For that reason science cannot determine human experience but must be reflective of it. Experience is the source of knowledge in which scientific conceptualization can only bring *order*. In summary therefore, I conclude, contrary to Dijkhuis, that the alleged conflict in Rogers' view of science has little to do with the issue of holism versus operationalism. Rather, it is more concerned with the issues of the common versus the individual, with the issue of the conceptual versus the experiential and ultimately with the issue of structure versus process.

2. the "relational dependence" interpretation of Wijngaarden

Wijngaarden[93] has described Rogers anthropology as a "consistently applied individualism" (verdoorgevoerd individualisme) that "strongly accents the autonomy and independence of the individual" (1961, p.423). Central to this view of man is a respect for "man's capacity for self-help" (1961, p.421). The latter, which Wijngaarden calls "Rogers' humanistic credo", is directly operative in Rogers' therapeutic practice. But in this scientific theory this capacity for self-help is represented by a series of "powers" which are then ascribed to an "organism" by Rogers. In doing this Rogers has fallen prey, according to Wijngaarden, to a common prejudice that would hold that a theoretical-scientific approach to the phenomenon of man may only operate with natural-scientific concepts, if it wants to call itself "scientific". Rogers believes that by using only such concepts he has avoided introducing "homunculi" into his theory of man. Wijngaarden argues however, that Rogers can only accomplish this feat by ascribing all manner of *human* creative activities to the organism. This means that the organism becomes a "substantial entity" and thus *it* becomes the homunculus or mannikin in Rogers' scientific theory of man (1961, p.423). In an earlier publication Wijngaarden had questioned Rogers' theory along much the same lines. There he had concluded that as a result of Rogers' "dogmatic positivism" his theoretical constructs end up being a "series of riddles" (1958, p.7).

Thus Wijngaarden has little appreciation for Rogers' personality *theory*. At the same time, however, he has great admiration for his *practical therapy*, particularly because it is such a completely genuine and consequential application of his humanistic credo. Wijngaarden signals three factors in which he appreciates Rogers' approach to therapy over that of others.

a) Apart from a trust in the individual's capacity for self-help, no theory or construct about man is operative in Rogers' therapy.

b) There is a de-emphasis on the use of techniques in Rogers' therapy. This entails that the activity and "self-governance" (zelfstandigheid) of the client is stimulated.

c) More than with other approaches, Rogers' approach places a greater emphasis on the "relational events" of therapy (1961, pp.425-426).

However, while Wijngaarden is highly appreciative of Rogers' approach to therapy, he does not share his view of man. This leads him to differ significantly from Rogers in his own approach to therapy. Briefly, with Dijkhuis, Wijngaarden holds that while man can indeed become "self-governing" (zelfstandig) he can never become "independent" from others. He can only achieve this self-governance in an inescapably dependent relation to others. He depends on his relation to others for his self-governance. From this vantage point therapy means helping others to become self-governing in their relation to others (1961, pp.425-426).

This difference from Rogers in his anthropology not only leads Wijngaarden to a different approach to therapy but also to a different kind of respect for his client. Rogers' tendency to reserve this ability to respect the client exclusively for the adherants of his anthropology is not to Wijngaarden's liking for it entails that all those who do not share Rogers' view of man are by implication guilty of a lack of respect for man (1961, p.423). Over against that, Wijngaarden argues that a different view of man leads to a different kind of respect for man. He illustrates his point from his own approach to therapy, in which as therapist he freely expresses his own feelings and "hunches" concerning the client's self-expressions to the client during therapy. Not to share his feelings and hunches with the client would for Wijngaarden constitute a lack of respect for his client. It would constitute withholding from the client something which he needs in order to become self-governing (1961, p.428).

Thus we see that both Wijngaarden's approach to therapy and his respect for his client are closely tied to his view of man, and further, that on all three counts he differs markedly from Rogers. But there is also considerable overlap. For one thing, Wijngaarden's approach does not entail that the therapist tries to bring his client around to his interpretation. His feelings and hunches are always offered as hypotheses that mean to stay entirely within the client's frame of reference. Moreover, it is always the client who determines whether the hunch or feeling of the therapist was a correct insight. Thus Wijngaarden insists that whenever the client rejects a given hypothesis, the therapist must immediately do likewise. For, if the "hunch" is not *felt* to be adequate by the client it is therapeutically worthless (1961, p.428). In summary then, Wijngaarden accepts Rogers' notion that the client must himself achieve an insight for it to be therapeutically valuable. But he rejects the idea as if the client should have to come to it *by* himself. For Wijngaarden only the fact that the client makes the discovery is important, not however the fact that he was the first to make it (1961, pp.430-431).

Wijngaarden believes that his approach to therapy is more likely to lead to an acceleration of insight than would be the case in the approach of Rogers. For him this does not entail however that an equal acceleration of the client's growth process would be noticeable and he leaves himself entirely open to the possibility that an accelerated insight might actually retard the growth process of the client. However, he feels that further research would have to determine that question (1963, p.162).

Finally, in a number of subsequent publications (1965, 1970) Wijngaarden has argued that Rogers' later emphasis on the congruence of the therapist as the core condition for therapy, together with his stress on transparency and his later preference for the label of Person to Person Therapy represents a major switch in his approach to therapy (1965, pp. 578, 588; 1975, p. 210). He sees this as a switch, moreover, with which Rogers' theoretical productions have not kept pace (1965, p.582). Basically he sees the switch as a change from non-directivity to non-imposition (1965, p.579). In this trend Wijngaarden further sees Rogers' earlier emphasis on the unconditionality of the respect one shows to the client becoming increasingly more problematic (1965, pp. 581, 582). In short, he sees Rogers' later views becoming much more relational and much less individualistic. Because of this he feels that there is little or no difference between his approach to therapy and that of the later Rogers (1963, p. 163).

As I mentioned above, Wijngaarden has considerable appreciation for Rogers' practical approach to therapy (as distinct from his personality theory) because, according to him, it contains no constructions regarding man other than the one referring to his respect for man's capacity for self-help. In saying this, Wijngaarden is technically correct since Rogers' anthropology shuns constructs or structures of any kind. However, I question whether his interpretation is in line with Rogers' intent for therapy. For in it the *notion* (if not the *construct*) *of growth* is equally present. It is present in the sense that it qualifies the respect for man's self-help capacity as a respect for man's capacity *to grow*. Thus it would seem that the notion of "organism", with its connotations of growth and actualization, are not only important for Rogers' personality theory, but also for his practical approach to therapy.

Furthermore, with reference to the second quality that Wijngaarden appreciates, it is because growth is the goal of Rogerian therapy that the use of techniques is de-emphasized in favor of attitudes. Rogers' argument in this regard goes roughly as follows: Techniques that are not connected with a client-centered attitude are by definition directive. Directivity shows a lack of respect for the client. A lack of respect for the client hampers his creative independence and when the latter is hampered the client cannot grow. Hence therapy is then ineffective in achieving its goal. It is this line of argument, I believe, that undergirds Rogers' de-emphasis of techniques. Rogers is not saying that every technique can be effective in therapy, but rather that only growth-promoting techniques are permissible, and further, that such techniques can only be those that implement the non-directive attitude. Thus Rogers maintains a narrow, rather than a broad, criterion for therapy; so narrow, in fact, that it would exclude Wijngaarden's approach as non-growth promoting.

Lastly, Wijngaarden shows appreciation for a Rogerian approach to therapy because it presumably lays more emphasis on the relational events of therapy than do the other therapies. It is true that particularly the later Rogers emphasizes the relationship rather than only the "analysis of the patient"

(1961, p. 425). But it is never so with Rogers that *personal* growth is function-ally dependent on the relationship. Rather, it is personal growth that makes any meaningful interhuman relationship possible. The latter is always a function of the former in Rogers' view. Schematically (and not quite correctly) I might put it as follows: A fully functioning *personal* development is conceivable to Rogers outside of a relationship to others. But it is inconceivable to him that a sharing, communicating relation should exist between people that are not persons. Thus I believe that we must always guard ourselves against turning Rogers' interpersonal relationship into a ''dialogical'' relationship.

Given his view of man, and considering the above factors, I wonder whether Wijngaarden's appreciation for Rogers' practical therapeutic approach is not misplaced to some extent. I further wonder whether Rogers' choice of the term ''organism'' for man is correctly interpreted as a positivistic influence on his theory which then plays no significant role in his therapeutic practice. I believe that the term ''organism'' is very much in line with Rogers' view of man as a growth principle, which as such dominates both his theory and his therapeutic practice. Thus, there appears to be a much closer connection between Rogers' therapeutic approach and his theory of personality than Wijngaarden seems to believe there is. Furthermore, as I have attempted to show in II.B. of this chapter, if we take the term ''organism'', not as the designation of an entity but rather as a characteristic of the actualization process, then the use of the term as applied to *human* functioning is not nearly as problematic in Rogers. Finally, in IV.C.4. of this chapter, I have attempted to show that Rogers' later interpersonal emphasis in therapy is not necessarily inconsistent with his earlier non-directive or client-centered emphasis. To speak of it as a switch in Rogers' approach seems to me to be an overstatement of the development that occurs. Thus I believe it is more correct to speak of an enrichment rather than a switch. Finally, I wonder just how problematic the notion of unconditional positive regard really is in the later Rogers. Far from being conditional, Rogers' later stress on the therapist's congruence, on gen-uineness and on transparency actually represents a better expression of the original intent of the unconditionality of positive regard.

3. the ''dialogical'' interpretation of Upshaw

Finallly, a brief analysis is in order of some themes in Upshaw's dissertation[94] regarding the relation between Rogers' views and those of Martin Buber. His dissertation attempts to investigate the relation between the ''re-ligious'' and the ''psychological'' as ''two dimensions of human experience''. Upshaw's underlying assumption is that ''the realm of relational experiencing lends itself equally to religious and psychological investigation'' (p.28). The basic question appears to be whether the ''religious'' determines the ''psycho-logical'' or vice versa (pp. 100-101).

Upshaw converts the discussions of this question into a comparison between the views of Buber and those of Rogers by substituting Buber's terms ''dialogical'' and ''relational'' for his term ''religious'' and by substituting Rogers' term ''interpersonal'' and ''experiential'' for his term ''psychological'' (p.118). He first shows that, their differences notwithstanding, Buber and Rogers are one in the way they describe ''meeting'' (or ''the highest point in human interchange''). He subsequently wants to consider how the ''dialogical'' (Buber) and the ''interpersonal'' (Rogers) interdepend in ''that process which leads to meaning in personal existence'' (p.118). He wishes to do this without reducing the views of the one to the views of the other.

Thus, he comes to the assertion that . . . ''Rogers' descriptions of therapeutic meeting reflect an implicit dependence upon certain assumptions which Buber has developed more fully in terms of ''relation'' and the ''between''. He further asserts that likewise . . . ''Buber's description of dialogical meeting reflects an implicit dependence upon certain assumptions which Rogers has developed more fully in terms of ''experiencing'' and ''subjective becoming'' (p.119). Thus Upshaw sees the relation between Buber and Rogers as ''potentially complementary''.

What interests me, in the context of our present discussion, is the part of the above quotation regarding Rogers' dependence on Buber's ''between'', his ''relation'', and his ''dialogical''. This concerns the question, which we already met in Dijkhuis and Wijngaarden whether for Rogers, *in the final analysis*, the relationship is presupposed in ''personal becoming''. It concerns the question whether the ''monological'' is a function of the ''dialogical'', and whether ''growth'' is a function of the ''relationship'' in Rogers. In this regard Upshaw does his utmost to argue that Rogers really accepted the ''between'' of Buber. In my opinion he makes a good case, but he does not succeed entirely.

In the final analysis there remains a crucial difference between Buber and Rogers which also clearly came to the fore in their debate.[95] Upshaw shows how for Buber it is not the self or the organism that is the bearer of meaning, but *the other as ''Thou''*. Hence Buber also argues that if you stress the importance of the inner flow of experiencing in the relationship, as Rogers does, then you run the risk of cutting yourself off from the power of the relationship itself (p.141).

As Upshaw shows at length, Rogers does indeed *speak* of the ''between'' in his writings. But such ''communal'' matters as mutual empathy, the co-personal, and the interpersonal are for Rogers only aspects or outgrowths of the personal and the organismic. The heart of man for Buber is located in the relation, in the ''between''. For him man is always ''man with man''.[96] For Rogers the heart of man is located in the organismic actualization process, and that, it seems to me, makes all the difference.

C. Conclusion

This concludes my anthropological evaluation of some of the Rogers-interpretations in the literature. What now has been the value of my anthropological model for the evaluation of these interpretations? In the main, it allowed me to illustrate how there is a persistent attempt in the literature to anchor the flow that is characteristic of Rogers' anthropology in terms of something other than itself. Thus we have seen how attempts were made to anchor this flow in terms of the "self" and also in terms of the "relationship". The misinterpretations of Rogers' basic intent that result from these attempts were also documented.

What conclusions can we draw from the above discussion in support of the central hypothesis of this dissertation? In the main it shows, I believe, that whenever we discuss the views of another person from out of our own anthropological commitment we inevitably end up distorting the basic intent of the other to a greater or lesser degree. The only exception to this general rule that I have thus far been able to locate in the literature is Vossen's description of Rogers' view.[97] Better than anyone I know, Vossen has been able to capture the dynamic flow that is so characteristic of Rogers in his description of his views. Thus I also believe he is entirely correct in characterizing Rogers' approach as a "developmental-psychological psychotherapy" (p.14).

However, Vossen was able to correctly interpret Rogers because there appears to be no essential difference between his view of man and that of Rogers. This, therefore, still leaves the question whether one is able to correctly represent the views of another if one does not share the other's views. I believe this can be done, provided one constantly strives to interpret the other's view from out of the other's own basic intent as I have attempted to do in the preceeding chapters. Once this is accomplished however, genuine conceptual difficulties will still remain in the view one has attempted to describe. Thus even in my "Rogers-centered" description of Rogers' view of man, of personality and of therapy a number of problems have come to the fore that need to be dealt with as well, in time. Therefore a critique of these problems will be part of the subject matter of my next chapter.

CHAPTER FIVE:

CRITICAL EVALUATION OF ROGERS' VIEW OF MAN IN RELATION TO PSYCHOTHERAPY, PERSONALITY AND INTERPERSONAL RELATIONS

I. INTRODUCTION

In the previous chapter I gave an extensive description of Rogers' basic anthropological intent. With the completion of this chapter the main objective of my dissertation was achieved. Via a process of empathic understanding I was able to, in Rogers' own words, "indwell" his work in such a way that he felt "clarified" (personal communication by Rogers).

Yet now that this deepened understanding of Rogers has been achieved, I am personally left with a considerable number of questions (and even some misgivings) regarding Rogers' view of man and the way it decisively influences his view of therapy, personality and interpersonal relations.

These questions tended to accumulate during my study of his writings, but they could not come to full expression as long as it was my aim to give a Rogers-centered description of Rogers. Now that this task has been completed it is possible to put some of these questions to Rogers in a concluding chapter. Accordingly, my aim in what follows will be to critically evaluate Rogers' view of man and its relation to his views on psychotherapy, personality and interpersonal relations.

It should be noted first of all that my approach in this chapter will differ from the one taken in the previous chapters. Then I attempted to speak *for* Rogers. Now I will attempt to speak *with* Rogers. I will speak personally, from out of my own basic intent and offer an evaluation that is essentially external to Rogers' frame of reference. Thus, I expect that my own view of man will now quite naturally become more visible in the issues that I will raise.

Not that my critique of Rogers will be based on my own personal viewpoint only. Other reviewers have expressed difficulties similar to mine with Rogers' views. Their views will be discussed as alternatives to Rogers' view. I will also refer to Rogers' own writings for instances where he himself appears to be inconsistent with his basic intent.

In my evaluation I intend to follow a pattern that moves from discussing more abstract, general considerations related to Rogers' anthropology as a whole, toward a discussion of more specific considerations related to his views on therapy, personality and interpersonal relations. First of all, since Rogers is principally a dynamic thinker his views have changed continually over the years. For that reason I would expect him to keep changing his views in the future as well. Thus I will begin my evaluation by once again describing the basic direction of his thought, this time with the intent of showing where, in my opinion, it is headed. In this connection, I will further attempt to briefly place Rogers' conception in its cultural-historical context, in order to also show where it originated.

Secondly, it is one of my main contentions that the works of all notable writers show a central theme, or basic intent. This is not to say, however, that all of their part productions are therefore necessarily consistent with their basic intent. But this then at the same time shows how strong the integrative power of their basic intent is. Thus, in this section I will attempt to evaluate to what extent Rogers' various theoretical productions have been consistent with his own basic intent. In addition, a number of important external critiques of Rogers' conception, found in the literature, will be reviewed. In this discussion I will find the occasion to briefly deal with the possibility, as well as value, of external criticism. That is, I will evaluate whether criticism that crosses anthropological viewpoints is conducive to further insight.

In the next section I will evaluate the possible consequences of Rogers' basic intent. Anthropological viewpoints are not just viewpoints. They tend to have concrete implications for the practice of living. Thus this section will investigate the effects of Rogers' viewpoint on therapy, personality and interpersonal relations. Finally, in a concluding section I will attempt to summarize succinctly both my debt to Rogers and my critique of Rogers.

II. ROGERS ADVOCATES A RECEPTIVE ATTITUDE TO "LIFE"

A. Active Receptivity versus Laissez-faire

If there is one word, next to 'growth' that describes the pervasive characteristic of Rogers' work, that word is 'receptivity'. Rogers' life-long preoccupation is with receiving. This receptive attitude is so much a genuine part of him that it pervades his writings, characterizes his approach to therapy and indeed colours his entire personal life style. As an attitude to life this receptivity is by no means passive however. It is not a form of laissez-faire, as if one had to wait to let things happen to him. It is not a form of resigning oneself to the inevitable influence of one's surroundings. On the contrary, this receptivity is active. It takes effort. It is hard to achieve and worthy of pursuit. It is essentially an intentional concentration of oneself on being open toward a life of growth. Receiving is the one thing that man can do, according to Rogers. It is the one way in which he can act. All other events only occur, they happen to him, inevitably. If Rogers were asked: What must I do to be fully functioning? (for Rogers *the* way to live), then he would undoubtedly answer: Be receptive, be open! If life is growth then receptivity is the condition of all conditions of human functioning.

B. Interpersonal Receptivity

Interpersonally this receptive attitude comes to expression as an intentionally empathic openness to (the internal frame of reference of) the other, and a pervasive respect for (the individual separateness of) the other. The aim of such interpersonal receptivity is to receive the other person unconditionally, "as is".

Initially this openness toward the other takes the form of "freeing" the other $(2,VII,A)$[1]. In therapy this is reflected in the non-directive, non-authoritarian, permissive attitude of the therapist, who deliberately refrains from interfering with the activity occurring in the client. It is an expression of the conviction that the therapist must follow, as the client takes the lead $(2,VI,C)$, of the conviction that the therapist must "rely upon the client for the direction of movement in the therapeutic process" $(2,IV,B)$.

Later, it comes to experession as a pervasive unconditional trust in the other. Again, in therapy this takes the form of client-centeredness, where the therapist communicates his trust in the client by focussing on his feelings $(3,II,B,1.1)$, by actively attending to his internal frame of reference, by empathically living into his subjective world $(3,II,C,1.3)$, or by listening to him with understanding $(3,IV,A,1.1)$.

Still later, when Rogers discusses the interpersonal communication process, this receptivity comes to expression in his suggestion that genuine communication can only occur if the persons in the relationship are in touch with their own experiencing and can communicate this experience transparently to each other. The communication enhancing value of such transparency appears to be that the parties thereby open themselves to being changed by each other. A further communication enhancing device that he suggests is that the parties refrain from evaluating, judging or (dis)approving of each other from their own point of view since this has the effect of closing oneself off from the other. Instead they are asked to express their experience as personal feelings, as perceptions, as meanings rather than judgments $(3,IV,B)$.

Finally, this interpersonal receptivity comes to its fullest expression in Rogers' discussion on encounter groups. In these groups mutual active and receptive empathy (thus mutual receiving and being received) is said to form the basis for interpersonal sharing. What is shared by this empathic process is each other's uniqueness. And this kind of sharing is of value for the personal growth of the parties participating in the group $(3,IV,C,2.2,2.3)$. Apparently Rogers believes that one needs to be open to, and be changed by, the other's differentness from oneself to be able to truly be and become oneself.

The discussion so far might lead us to a conclusion that many reviewers seem to have reached about Rogers, to the effect that his receptivity is mainly rooted in an ultimate, basic and primary concern for the subjectivity, the individuality, the uniqueness, the wholeness and the integrality of the other in the relationship. Thus, the conclusion that his receptivity is based on a respect for Buber's other as "Thou". Beyond a doubt, Rogers is certainly a respecter of persons, but I do not believe that this is the ultimate reason why he advocates a receptive attitude to the other. Rogers' openness to others is not an end in itself but a means toward a more deeply rooted goal. This will become clearer as we look at what is involved in intrapersonal receptivity.

C. Intrapersonal Receptivity

If we look at receptivity from the vantage point of intrapersonal functioning we see that it involves a process that closely dovetails with interpersonal receptivity. Sometimes the former precedes the latter as its condition and sometimes it flows from the latter as its result.

This process starts when a total openness to the self-that-one-is is substituted for a critical, and therefore controlling regard of self based on values that we introjected from others. It implies an acceptance by oneself of oneself "as is", where no one part of oneself is valued more than any other part (glossary, prop. 30). This first movement of an intrapersonally receptive process is thus one of receiving oneself free from any conditions of worth (glossary, prop. 35,3,III,C,4). Such total, unconditional self-reception can only occur after the condition of interpersonal receptivity has been met at least to some extent. That is the link between interpersonal and intrapersonal receptivity (4,II,L,8).

This activity of self-reception in turn gives the self the room it needs to change from a rigid self-structure into a fluid self-process. Thereby it becomes more receptive to, and aware of, meanings and perceptions that were previously inconsistent with itself. This in effect means that the self *concept* now becomes one of many *percepts*. In doing so it loses its status of first among equals (4,II,J,3), and thus it relinquishes some of its regulatively controlling power *over* awareness, symbolization and perception. As a result perception becomes more extentional. Figure-ground relations become more fluid rather than rigidly structured. There is more awareness and less denial, less distortion and more accurate symbolization. In short, what in essence happens in this self-receptive movement is that a person's self-awareness becomes more receptive to the experience(ing) of the moment. As a result a person listens more intently to his experience, which has its own meaning to impart (3,II,E,2). The meaning of which the person then becomes aware is that next to the regulative force of the self there are other, more basic, organismic, actualizing, forward moving life forces operating within him, to which he must become more and more receptive. Intrapersonal receptivity thus ultimately entails an active openness to one's everchanging experiential process, or actualizing tendency, or differentiating/assimilating, forward moving direction. Active interpersonal and intrapersonal receptivity are thus Rogers' ways of bringing us in contact with the forces of growth (4,IV,D,3,4).

What was said thus far could be misconstrued to mean that the self and awareness should periodically open themselves to experience in order to embrace and incorporate this moment by moment experiencing within themselves so as to keep both the self and awareness from losing touch with reality. This would mean that Rogers, along with many other theorists, is simply insisting that, as a condition for mental health, a person's actual experience must become part of his self-awareness.

But this is not the case. Actually Rogers advocates the reverse, and this subtle, but highly important difference distinguishes him from many other theorists, notably the self theorists. It is truer to Rogers' basic intent to say that, as a condition for mental health, one's self-awareness must become part of one's experiencing. This, I believe, is the meaning of his later formulation of active receptivity as *becoming* our experience, *becoming* our organism and *becoming* a person.   So receptive must the self become to experience that it completely relinquishes its control *over* experience and merely becomes a tiny dot on the sea of experience (3,II,E,2). Similarly, the functional importance of consciousness or awareness must likewise be reduced to that of a spotlight that only periodically lights up the actual goings on in the envelope of the organism.[2] The whole point of this active receptivity is to make a person's self-awareness a mere reflection of his experiencing of the moment. This would allow him to live subjectively out of his experience and to literally change his identity from moment to moment in accordance with the dictates of his experience (3,II,E,3).

To sum up, there is a process within ourselves, with which we can only come in contact via our experiencing. This process is wiser than our intellect, and therefore our self-awareness must either become identified with it, or if not that, then certainly it must become, as it were, symbiotically dependent on it. For Rogers this process must gain total regnancy in the internal household of a person if he is to become fully functioning. That process to which Rogers calls us to be totally and actively receptive is the organismic actualization process. Active receptivity as a way of life means a lifelong intentional surrendering to that process without ever quite being that process (3,III,D,1).

What this means for the way we live and move and have our being is illustrated by a quote from Rogers in an article that he wrote recently. In it he writes: "The things that seem to be seeking expression in me make me aware that it is my belief that . . . ."[3] It is an example of what he once wrote already much earlier in *On Becoming a Person*, p. 27. There he states: "I am at my best when I can let the flow of my experience carry me in a direction which appears to be forward, toward goals of which I am but dimly aware, . . . floating with the complex stream of my experiencing, . . . trying to understand its ever-changing complexity."

D. Characteristics of the Growth Process

1. the autonomy of the process

In view of the importance that Rogers ascribes to this process it seems advantageous to explicitly enumerate some of its characteristics. First, we do not generate his process and it is beyond our conscious, deliberate control. For while Rogers speaks many times of congruence between the self and the organism, between awareness and experience (which congruence could conceivably be achieved in either direction), it is clear that the organism never receives the self. Furthermore, Rogers never speaks of awareness changing experience, except in the negative sense of distortion and denial.

Thus it seems that the only deliberate, conscious, self-initiated activity that a person can have with respect to this process is either to resist it, to deny it, to avoid it, to his own detriment, or to receive it actively, to seek it out, to move with adience toward it, and that for his own wellbeing. For this too must be said, the process is only benevolent, and will only function in a positive, forward direction insofar as we actively receive it. Active receptivity is the sufficient, but at the same time also the necessary condition for this process to occur in a positive direction.

That leaves us with a process which we have not generated, which we cannot control and which will only work for our profit if we actively become part of it. Fortunately for us, this process thus received is a benevolent process, if at least we can believe Rogers. Others, not so trusting of the process, might consider these aspects of the process enough to characterize it as a threatening, foreign entity within our internal households. For Rogers this organismic process could never be foreign to the person however, since he believes and has actually stated a number of times that the organism *is* the person (3,III,D,3). Neither could it ever be threatening to the person since its main characteristics are described by him as enhancing, maintaining and actualizing. Thus it can never be foreign or threatening except in a pathological sense.

Nevertheless, as our own process that enhances our organization it still seems to operate in the concretely functioning person as a ready made entity, which needs no correction, and which cannot be improved upon by either ourselves or our awareness. With respect to it the only conscious decision to be made is to reject it or accept it. Other than that there is nothing to be done by us with respect to the process. It "happens" within us. It is a question of becoming the process, not one of acting with respect to it. Furthermore, this receptive/ becoming characteristic of our relation to the process is not a once-for-all happening in therapy. Rather, it is a continuous lifelong task.

E. Consequences of Receiving the Growth Process
What are now the consequences for us when we receive/become this process?

1. intrapersonal dynamism
Specifically, the self is constantly reformed by the process. The self literally changes from moment to moment. There is hardly any constancy to our being anymore. One cannot say for long: This is who I am. One can only say: This is who I am becoming. The self becomes dynamic. So do symbolization and awareness. There is no one way of looking at things any longer.[4] Perception is constantly being modified. It too becomes totally dynamic. Rogers says

somewhere that change is the only constant in his system. Indeed, the consequence is that *we* become changingness when we become fully functioning. We become dynamic. I would characterize this emphasis on change as ''intrapersonal dynamism''.

2. intrapersonal monism

Furthermore, the process is totalitarian. It cannot tolerate anything or any activity within us that is not generated by itself. It cannot tolerate an entity that functions independent of itself or an activity with which it has to reckon. A self that maintains, actualizes and enhances itself against the organismic process is problematic in Rogers' view. It creates incongruence. The self must become (dependent on) the organism for congruence to exist. In this connection it is interesting to note that the growth process itself generates the occasion for its own problems. Via its part process of differentiation it opens itself up to the possibility of self-actualization against its own direction.

Thus, intrapersonally at least, genuine structural differences are neither appreciated nor tolerated by the process because they set limits to its own activity. Diversities threaten the process and must therefore be eradicated wherever possible. This is not just shown in the fact that the process constantly seeks to change as it were the content of these diverse realities within us, such that diversities rather become diversifications, or ways of changing. But it also shows in the process' drive to *diminish* the activity of these diverse realities, wherever it can. It is not only a condition for fully functioning that the self and awareness should change constantly, but also that they should be reduced to a ''tiny dot'' and a ''flickering light'' with respect to experience, and thus become mere ''reflections'' of the process (see note 2).

I conclude therefore that intrapersonal differences are only appreciated and tolerated insofar as they are necessary to keep the process going, thus only as diversifications, i.e. as themselves part of the growth process. The aim of active receptivity seems to be to make the person a unity at the expense of his diversity. This emphasis on personal oneness is what I call intrapersonal monism.

F. Monistic Dynamism, a Threat to Personal Uniqueness?

I have thus far described Rogers' basic intent for human life as a dynamism, that is as an extreme emphasis on change (more correctly, on growth). I have said further that because of its totalitarian character this dynamism is monistic, that is to say, it neither appreciates nor tolerates longlasting, structurally diverse realities other than itself. Rather, it constantly seeks to turn them into diversifications, which as such cannot have influence *on* the process, because they are viewed as expressions *of* the process.

If one prefers, I can also formulate this descriptively rather than prescriptively as follows: If one adopts active receptivity to growth as a way of life, then one's life will continually be in the process of becoming monistically dynamistic. Rogers' writings exhibit an intense preoccupation with describing the characteristics of this process and the life conditions that must obtain for its realization.

In discussing the issues involved in Rogers' preoccupation with active receptivity and its consequences, I have by and large restricted myself to a discussion of intrapersonal functioning. It seemed to me that the diversity reducing characteristics of Rogers' basic intent are more clearly evident there than in interpersonal functioning. Nevertheless, we can also ask whether this same monistic tendency does not show itself interpersonally as well. And if it does, is it not possible that it will eventually lead to the eradication of the boundaries between persons? Is Rogers' basic intent not ultimately a threat to man's personal uniqueness? One would hardly expect this from the champion of persons, but let us look closer.

Looking at Rogers' fully functioning person we see that changingness is the major characteristic of his life. For such a person becoming a person seems more important than being one. For him changing (growth) seems to be more important than staying the same (identity). If such a person now enters into a relationship with another fully functioning person then the fact that they are relat*ing*, seems more important than that they have formed a relation*ship*. For them communicating seems more important than being part of a community.

The *ad hoc* character of encounter groups is a typical example of this. In them one can achieve almost instant intimacy and interpersonal contact seems to be as casually terminated as initiated. In them also it is the sharing of self-expressions that counts most. Whether the people involved are compatible, whether they *can* in fact relate to each other or not, because their lifestyles are so diverse, seems quite irrelevant to the group activity that occurs. Active and receptive empathy, changing the other and being changed by the other via mutual self-expressions appear to be the mainstays of such a group relationship (3,IV,C,2.3).

Formulated abstractly, an ideal relationship, that is, one that exemplifies Rogers' basic intent appears to be one where the relata are in total flux and where the one freely flows into and through the other. It is a relation where the relata are essentially interchangeable and where the flow meets with no obstruction whatsoever.

Formulated less abstractly, an interpersonal relation is one between fully functioning, internally congruent, mutually empathic persons who are transparent in the relationship and who thereby risk being changed by each other, which risk is worth taking because it promotes communication. In such a relation one person can say what the other thinks he feels (3,IV,B).

What strikes me again and again about Rogers' description of an interpersonal relation in comparison to his description of a fully functioning person is that, although he uses slightly different terminology, a description of the one could just as easily be given in terms of the *meaning content* of the other. Intrapersonal functioning can be described in interpersonal terms, and *vice versa*. This holds for transparency and congruence, for empathy and openness to experience, and it holds for unconditional positive regard and respect for one's organism which is wiser than oneself.

A true relation is characterized by perfect communication within and between persons (3,IV,B,1). In such a relation the question of identities, of subjects, of who or what is right, of who must be changed by whom are irrelevant obstructions. Openness toward, becoming and flowing into each other is all that counts. It is *The Process* that gives unity to the description of both persons and relations. In terms of the condition for its occurrence that Process is called active receptivity. In terms of its actual occurrence it is called growth.

So the question seems valid: Where is Rogers headed with his basic intent? Undoubtedly he always has been and still is a staunch defender of the irreducible uniqueness of individuals. Yet given his basic intent, will not persons also eventually become diversifications of that one dynamic principle called growth (4,II,N)?

There are already some hints in that direction in Rogers' latest writings. In a recent article[5] he speaks of a "formative tendency", evidenced by a universal "stream of evolution" into which at "a higher plane of consciousness" the individual self appears to "dissolve". Furthermore, Rogers' interest of longstanding in Eastern religions and his latest preoccupation with parapsychological and mystical phenomena[6] also seem to point in that direction. Thus it is possible that his latest thinking is headed toward a view in which the uniqueness of persons is exchanged for their participation in the evolutionary stream of 'Life'. If this should ever occur then the monistic tendency of his dynamism will indeed have triumphed fully. For it seems to me that when the condition of total, active receptivity to Life is fully met, the result is monistic dynamism.

G. Brief Cultural Historical Excursion

What has been written thus far appears to be characteristic of Rogers' basic intent but not necessarily of the whole of his work, which is of course much richer in scope and even at times at variance with his basic intent, as I hope to show in the next section. Yet being his *basic* intent it is clearly at the centre of his work. This leads me to ask what may have motivated Rogers to adopt this position, which might ultimately lead him to repudiate the very thing which initially led him to this position, specifically his respect for the autonomy of persons. Anthropologically speaking this question is little more than second guessing of course, since Rogers can hardly tell us the basis for his *basic* intent. Nevertheless we might get a little more insight into this question if once again we look briefly at the development of his thought from out of the cultural-historical context in which it occurred.

Tying into my discussion of chapter 2,V,B we note that as a post-Deweyan American, Rogers inherited the "individualism versus conformity" problematics. He also inherited Dewey's "solution" to it, which the latter accomplished by introducing the notion that all reality is naturally dynamic rather than static. Dewey held that everything is naturally in a process of interacting development. But on the human level, this development is clearly dependent for its occurrence on the reconstructing activity of the human subject. At that level the interaction is between the established, settled, common reality of existing society and culture and the (re)constructing, (re)forming activity of the individual, who is also designated as the agent of innovation and change.

Thus, Dewey held that man, more specifically his intellect, can improve the natural development of things by (re)forming this natural process via the scientific method, and in accordance with his needs. Furthermore, man does not have autonomy, as it were by birthright, but conquers his autonomy over existing society and culture by exercising control over them. No man, Dewey held, can be free unless he also reconstructively frees his society and his culture as well (2,VII,A). Therefore, this pursuit of individual autonomy is a culturally-formative pursuit and development at the human level is historical development.

It is specifically this element of culturally-formative control *over* nature in Dewey's thought that seems to have been rejected by Rogers (2,VI,B;VII,A). He did so, it seems, because he saw that this would once again tie the naturally innovative capacity of the individual for self-actualization to something other than itself.

The notion that each individual has the capacity to realize his inner potential, as we saw in chapter 2,V,B,1, has always been a particularly cherished notion in American culture.

It was also held that this capacity would function best if it were allowed to develop naturally, spontaneously and without any outside interference. Dewey's "solution" to the cultural dilemma of his time had the unfortunate side effect of stifling this creative tendency by linking it to the scientific method. This meant that henceforth there would be only one way of realizing human potential, rather than many. That way was the rational, scientific way.

In response to this problem Rogers seems to have renounced human cultural control over nature as a way to individual and social growth and freedom. Thus for him man does not intervene formatively in the natural stream of life. Rather life itself has a formative power to which (in particular man's intellect) must be receptive. If man opens himself to nature and participates in the stream of life, he will discover that he too has the capacity to actualize, to (re)form himself, naturally. In the final analysis therefore man does not form the natural development of things. Rather it is the natural development of things, if not obstructed by man, that forms man.

III INTERNAL CRITIQUE OF ROGERS' CONCEPTION

How successfully has Rogers worked out his basic intent into a consistent theory? This is a question about the inner coherence of his thought (4,I). In this section I will explore the unity of his conception of man as a process of actualization.

A. The Organismic Actualization Process Revisited

To do this, I shall first have to list the salient features of the organismic actualization process. For a more detailed discussion of this notion the reader is referred to my discussion of the process in 4,II,B,C, and D.[7]

According to Rogers all the diverse characteristics of the process are initially potentially present in its original unity and are actualized via a process of differentiation/assimilation. It is a unified, organized process but its unity is dynamic. That is to say, it is and remains unified only insofar as it continues to actualize its potentials. Originally it is already actualizing its potentials and there is principally no end to this process. It is, as it were, a midway process without any clearly discernible beginning or end other than itself.

It is a diversifying process, which actualizes its potenial by perpetually moving from relative homogeniety to relatively greater differentiated functioning. It is this genetic direction that allows the process to function at levels of increasingly greater differentiation complexity. To keep the process going indefinitely however and thus to keep it unified it must also continually assimilate its functioning at levels of lesser differentiation complexity. Thus assimilation must always follow differentiation if the process is to remain dynamic. When it does, it perpetually provides the process with new homogeneous material to be differentiated.

In a properly functioning process differentiation and assimilation are identical. They are merely two ways of looking at one and the same process. Differentiation means that homogeneous functioning pushes itself upward and thus actualizes itself to become differentiated functioning, while assimilation means that differentiated functioning draws up homogeneous functioning and thereby actualizes it to become differentiated functioning. But both are essentially the same actualizing movement. That is to say, when something is assimilated it is thereby also differentiated, and when the process differentiates itself it thereby naturally also assimilates new material for differentiation.

This identity does not obtain however when the process is disturbed, as occurs in bifurcation. The latter involves a splitting of the original unity into two or more autonomous self-actualizing processes, rather than a differentiation process *within* the original unity. Bifurcation takes place under certain adverse environmental conditions. It occurs when the organismic actualization process is arrested or blocked from further differentiation. In such situations the latest level of differentiation becomes an end in itself that seeks to actualize itself against the further actualization of potentials in the original organismic unity. When this occurs the latest level of differentiation thus fails to assimilate functioning at earlier levels of differentiation.

A further characteristic of the process is that it is directional. It is goal directed, but then without any predetermined goal toward which it is directed. Rogers wants to make clear that the process is not random movement, that it is going in a definite direction. But he does not want to involve the process in a movement that will eventually stop when the goal to which it is directed is reached. The movement is perpetually purposeful. It is always "up to something". But its purpose is its direction and not its end. Hence the process is directional. Furthermore, the direction of the process is described as constructive. It enhances, maintains, actualizes the process. The direction is also forward. It moves in one direction only, from less to greater differentiated complexity. It does not reverse itself unless it is blocked.

Finally, the process does not actualize those of its potentials that are harmful to its own preservation. To bring that across in a dynamic way we must think of the relation between the various levels of differentiation complexity as a fluid gestalt. That is to say, the levels relate to each other as figure and ground. Thus the figure emerges (differentiates) out of the ground. But also, the figure partially determines what its ground shall be by selectively assimilating *this* to become part of itself and *that* to remain ground.

This way Rogers can maintain that the process is configurational, that it maintains itself as a fluid *gestalt* by selectively assimilating only that which is relevant for its further differentiation. At the same time he can avoid saying that the more complex levels exclusively determine the less complex levels of functioning. For to say that would go against the tenor of his whole argument thus far. In essence he means to convey to us that the process is both unified, organized, configurational *and* perpetually changing in its component "parts." It is his way of describing the structure of the process without negating its central characteristic, namely its fluidity.

B. An Image of Rogers' Conception

Rogers' description of the process is not easy to understand. His basic intent is clear. He constantly seeks to guarantee the fluidity of the process. But in doing so his description of the process becomes a rather complicated affair.

By way of introduction to some internal criticism I will first deal with Rogers' conception in terms of the visual image of a river. The origin of this river is beyond our view. It flows in one direction only, downstream. It is clearly a unified body of water and yet it is never the same water that we see. New water passes by continually. Further downstream the river develops into a delta network of smaller streams which in turn branch out into an ever increasing number of still smaller rivulets. This developmental process repeats itself as far as we can see and even further. In fact, it never ends. The river is initially homogeneous but carries within itself the possibility of branching into ever smaller streams. It is the flow of the river pushing itself downstream that fills up the smaller streams, but it is also the flow of the smaller streams into the rivulets that makes room for the river.

It can further be said that the original river is larger than any of its smaller streams downstream, because it contains within itself all of the smaller streams potentially. But it can also be said that the river is fuller the more it divides itself into smaller streams. Finally, from its point of origin up through its delta formation it is the same river that flows. The difference is that in its delta formation the river is a more complex body of water than in its initial development. If now any stream of its delta network were to be dammed off, that stream would have an end in itself. It would fill to overflowing. It would no longer receive the water of the river and eventually it would attempt to form its own delta network. It would act as if it were the river itself rather than one of its offshoots.

C. Complications

Because of its fluidity the image of a river turning into a delta network of an increasing number of smaller streams seems to me to depict Rogers' process conception more accurately than his own often used image of a growing plant. But it also shows up more clearly the complications that are present in his conception of man as a process.

1. problems around the source and destiny of the process

In the first place, a river has a beginning. It is formed by something that is not itself a river, e.g. melting snow or rain. Rogers' conception of the process is that in its origin it is already "up to something" (4,II,E,2). Rogers neglects to tell us what started the process, except for one instance, where his reference is to the "formative tendency" of the "evolutionary stream of life." But this reference, as we saw, presents him with the difficulty of losing the uniqueness and autonomy of the process itself. So the question is: What is the *source* of the process? The problem of the source of the process is not just a once-for-all problem of where it started either. Because of the ongoing reoccurring character of the process it is a perpetual problem. Thus the question is essentially one of what keeps feeding the flow. A river that is not fed, runs dry and ceases to flow.

Secondly, a river eventually empties itself into a larger homogeneous body of water which does not form its own delta network. Thus it flows into a lake or an ocean which itself does not flow, is relatively stagnant, and is an end in itself, as well as the end of the river. This is also at variance with Rogers' conception, unless he is presently thinking of some "Universal All" into which ultimately all individual beings dissolve. But this notion would generate further complications for the perpetuity of both individuals and the process. Perhaps Rogers is thinking of something like the water-cycle, where the water in the ocean evaporates into clouds which then empty themselves as rain or snow on the earth and thus in turn feed the rivers? But this too cannot be, for Rogers' thinking about the process is not cyclical, but linear. It is forward directional.[8]

Thus, I have difficulties understanding Rogers' conception of man as an internally unified, self-directional, autonomous process. A process that flows in one direction but is principally without either beginning or end seems to me to be a contradictory concept. It is much rather a description of a pool without motion. Or if it has motion, it is the motion of a whirlpool.

2. problems around the dynamic unity of the process

A second question which I have about Rogers' conception is whether by itself the dynamic character of the process can indeed guarantee its unity. Using the image of the river again, no river runs uphill or over a mountain. Instead it runs through valleys. It is the lay of the land plus the law of gravity, more than the flow of the river itself, that determines what shape it will take, how big it will be, how fast it will run, and where and how it will form into a delta. Water is notoriously dependent of a container to keep its shape. Thus it is the riverbed more than the flow of the river itself that keeps the river unified, that keeps it from dispersion. Moreover, to remove every obstacle from the path of a river does *not* facilitate its development into a delta network of smaller streams. On the contrary, it is more likely to cause it to rush forward in an undifferentiated, destructive torrent.[9]

3. process and reality

What I miss in Rogers' view of man as a dynamic process is a recognition that this process is faced with a "reality" not of its own making, with which it has to reckon, also for its own internal functioning. By "reality" I mean a given structure in man himself or in his environment that exists independent of the process, that is not determined by the process, that itself determines the process to some extent, and which the process needs to maintain its unity.

The above formulation presupposes a tacit assumption on my part that the phenomenon of man cannot be exhaustively described in process terms alone. It implies that there is a diversity to man and his world that is not reducible to growth. This diversity is "reality" for growth, in the sense described above. In holding this view I differ sharply from Rogers. But in the next section I hope to show that by maintaining that these diversities in man and his world are or will eventually become aspects of growth. Rogers involves himself into quite a number of conceptual difficulties and ultimately ends up in a conceptual impasse.

My main objection is that Rogers does not seem to take this "reality" seriously enough. Insofar as this reality is an obstacle to the actualization process, the power of this obstacle is much greater than Rogers seems to realize. Concretely speaking, organismic actualization is much more a struggle with a solidly resisting reality than Rogers makes it out to be. It requires continuous reality testing and the process successfully actualizes itself only insofar as it reckons with this reality.

I also miss in Rogers' conception an appreciation for the positive, process supporting character of the reality that surrounds it. To me the process needs the support of this reality to function fully. Thus, there is more to reality than its function of being an obstacle to flow. The process functions of necessity within a supportive structure without which it would operate in a vacuum.

4. is the process autonomous?

Rogers' description of a dynamic, internally unified, self-actualizing, autonomous process is so hard to understand, because it is such an *abstract* picture of human functioning. To me, he describes concrete self-actualization with the help of a supportive structure, without acknowledging its dependence on this structure, either in man himself or his environment. To say with Angyal, as Rogers does, that the process of life "does not merely tend to preserve life but transcends the momentary status quo of the organism, expanding itself continually and imposing its autonomous determination upon an ever increasing realm of events'' (4,II,D,2) is to me an overstatement of what within the context of a concretely given reality is only relatively true. It reminds me of a person who orders the sun to go down just at the point when it is about to disappear beyond the horizon, or of a person who stands on the middle of a road ordering the traffic to go in opposite directions, when it already does so, and who then believes that these events obey his bidding.

D. Some Basic Inconsistencies in Rogers' Conception

Thus far I have argued that the dynamic character of the process cannot be the sole guarantee for its unity. The process is thus not autonomous. Rather, reality factors, other than the flow itself are needed to keep the process integrated. Support for this argument first of all comes from inconsistencies in Rogers' own overall conception of human functioning. There are elements in Rogers' theory, which are at variance with his basic intent, which point in that direction.

1. the organism as computer: who supplies the program?

My first example is taken from p. 189 of *On Becoming a Person*, where Rogers discusses the concept of the fully functioning person. There he compares this person, and later the person's organism, to a "giant electronic computing machine" into which all the data of the person's experience, internal and external, are fed. The machine thereupon computes that course of action to be followed which would be "the most economical vector of need satisfaction in this existential situation". The fully functioning person "would find his organism thoroughly trustworthy because all of the available data would be used and would be present in accurate rather than distorted form", p. 190.

What are we to make of this passage? Rogers first of all seems to identify the person with his organism since he compares them both to a computer. This would be in line with his overall intent that a person "become" his organism(ic process), and with his view that the fully functioning person "is" his organism. But in the same passage he also refers to the latter as "his" organism, or the organism "of" the person, which implies ownership. Since one can hardly "be" what he owns, the person and the organism must therefore be two different entities.

This latter interpretation seems to be more what Rogers has in mind in this passage. It is reinforced by the fact that he calls the organism a computer, thus a tool, presumably for the person to use. The organism as computer receives the data that it needs from experience. But it needs rules as well as data to operate. Who supplies the rules? Who programs the computer? A self-programming computer does not exist. So if the organism is a computer it can indeed be the evaluator of experience, but it cannot supply itself with the values, the rules, the program it needs to do its valuation. Someone other than the organism has to supply the values.

But this way of speaking is utterly at variance with Rogers' basic intent which views the organismic process as autonomous, self-valuing and purposefully directional. Nevertheless, it seems that Rogers does indeed need a *real* person who is more than and other than the process itself in order to describe the activity of the process.[10]

2. actualized potentials, the program of the process?

My next example is taken from my description of Rogers' anthropology in chapter four. It concerns the various levels of differentiation complexity which are said to exist potentially in the original unity and which are actualized via a process of differentiation/assimilation. These levels were described as being the levels of organic need fulfillment, of experience, of consciousness (including awareness, symbolization and perception), of self-conception, of regard and finally the level of communal functioning (4,II).

My question to Rogers is this: How can a process, the essential characteristic of which is growth, generate such qualitatively different activities as the ones mentioned above within itself, and still remain a unified process? Is Rogers not guilty here of uncritically uniting matters of an essentially different order under the one common denominator of dynamic growth? To this Rogers might reply that the organismic process does not generate or unite anything in the way that I have described. Instead, it only *actualizes* these diverse potentials, which it carries within its original unity right from the beginning. If this is so, then does this not tie the process to at least a *potential* program? And does this not entail, therefore, that the process itself is *not* autonomous? For, either the organism has only one potential, namely growth, or it has many diverse potentials other than growth in which case these potentials at least potentially co-determine *the way in which* the actualization process enfolds.

3. actualization as aid and threat to the process, a conceptual impasse

Now, Rogers may argue that, since these potentials are part of the process, and their actualization occurs principally within the process, they cannot possibly violate its autonomy. This the more so, since it is precisely their actualization that enhances the process. If this is so, however, then it seems inexplicable that under certain adverse social conditions these very same potentials in their actualized form could post such a threat for the process. In fact, as we shall see presently, this threat seems to increase with the number of potentials actualized. The more the process diversifies, the more complex it becomes, the more vulnerable it seems to become to disruption.

We seem to have arrived at the curious impasse where the actualization of these potentials is the very lifeblood of the process, where, furthermore, these potentials are needed in their actualized state as waystations, as levels, to keep the process going, but also, where these same actualized potentials pose a threat to the very existence of the process, which threat increases, it seems, the more of them are actualized. Perhaps it is time to ask just how sturdy and trustworthy this organismic actualization process really is when its own products can become a threat to its existence.

4. examples of the impasse

Several examples can be given of this impasse in Rogers' thought. These all have reference to the gestalt fashion in which the differentiation levels are said to relate to each other. I will first discuss the way this problem manifests itself on the level of consciousness. Then I will give an example of it on the level of conceptuality and finally one on the level of regard.

4.1 selective awareness, the occasion for defensiveness

It will be remembered that in order to maintain the unity of the process, the higher levels of differentiation complexity selectively assimilate only that material of the lower levels of differentiation which they need for their own actualization and further differentiation. On the level of consciousness, for example, this selectivity allows perception to be configurational. That is to say, it allows perception to function as figure with respect to experience once it has emerged out of experience (4,II,H,2).

This kind of selection is thus functional for the enhancement of the actualization process. It keeps the process unified. But under certain adverse social conditions it can also become dysfunctional when, in the interest of defensiveness, it turns into denial and distortion. Thus the very selective mechanism that serves to enhance the process also provides the occasion for its disruption.

In this connection it is important to note that Rogers never views experience as selective. Thus he also never speaks of the danger of experience leading one astray.[11] Rather, experience is seen as inherently meaningful and capable of guiding us in the right direction. For that reason awareness must also open itself up to the meaning of experience to function properly. But this notion of openness to experience seems to be at variance with the selective capacity of awareness with respect to experience. And yet, the notion that awareness is selective is surely also part of Rogers' conception of the process. For he says somewhere[12] that in order for the organism to actualize itself, it must first *clearly perceive* the choices available to itself. But this notion seems to be inconsistent with Rogers' intent that perceptive awareness should become a mere reflection of the activity of the organism.

Is it possible that Rogers has recognized that awareness is inherently selective, as Wexler has shown (see next section)? And is Rogers perhaps trying to reduce the activity of awareness because he perceives its selectivity as a threat to the naturally enfolding actualization process? If so, this would be another example of the impasse which I mentioned earlier, namely, that the products of the actualization process pose a threat to the actualization process.

4.2 the internally contradictory self-concept

This impasse is even more evident on the level of self-conception, where the very notion of self-concept appears to be inherently contradictory. That is to say, the 'self' part appears to be at variance with the 'concept' part (4,II,J).

The self-concept is a concept, and *as such* it is necessary for the further actualization of the organism. It must be a concept rather than a percept, that is to say, it must be less affected by experience than perception in order to become the most significant, most durable percept in perceptual awareness. It must be first among equals, the figure in terms of which perception can organize/actualize itself as ground. It must be a concept to exercise the necessary regulative control over perception. It is the central entity, the anchorage point within us, that allows us to "own" all our functioning. It gives us an awareness of ourselves as a separate gestalt. Finally, the organism enhances itself at the conceptual level of actualization via a process of self-consistency. For all these, the self-concept must be a concept.

But the self-concept is also a self. That is to say, it is the organism itself. It is a process which changes from moment to moment. It dictates that the self-concept may *not* be controlling or regulative. Rather, it requires that the self-concept must be open to experience, must float on experience, must diminish in importance and must relinquish its power. Because the self-concept is a self it must be a process. Thus, the self-concept is that actualized potential of the organism which simultaneously enhances the process and *by its very inner nature* also arrests the process. Again we see that the more potentials are actualized the more compelling the impasse becomes.

4.3 "under certain adverse social conditions"

On the level of regard this impasse reaches perhaps its fullest expression. Before I get into a discussion of the impasse on this level of actualization however, some preliminary remarks are in order. Rogers may argue that my description thus far on the impasse in his thought only applies to a person who is not fully functioning. He may further argue that no actualized potential ever poses a threat to the organismic actualization process, if that process remains dynamic, thus if it is allowed to differentiate and assimilate freely.

This is Rogers' usual way of explaining the problems that arise in his dynamic description of organismic functioning. The problems that arise at a given level of differentiation complexity are never described as originating there, but are always referred to as being "caused" by some activity or other at the next higher levels of differentiation complexity. Thus, for example, the reason why we are not in touch with our real organic needs or the forces of growth within us is because our awareness denies or distorts our experience. And the reason why awareness distorts or denies experience is because our self-concept is rigid and defensive. Finally, the reason why our self-concept is rigid and defensive is because others do not receive us. They regard us conditionally.

Thus Rogers may chide me for neglecting to mention more fully the negative impact of the adverse social conditions in the environment on the process. He may argue that man as an organismic process is fully trustworthy and constructive and that the problem lies in society, not in the individual. If a person were interpersonally received then he would be congruent, transparent and fully functioning. He would be unified. He would be autonomous.

If all this is so, then my next discussion on interpersonal regard should finally clear up all the inconsistencies that we have thusfar encountered in Rogers' thought.

4.4 the dependence of the process on interpersonal reception

In order to continue to actualize itself and thus to maintain and enhance itself dynamically the organism cannot stop at the (self) conceptual level, but must also differentiate to the level of regard and the communal level. Thus, Rogers does not restrict himself to a discussion of intrapersonal functioning only, but expressly links it to interpersonal functioning as well. Fully functioning is not possible outside of an interpersonal relation (4,II,K,L).

The link between intra- and interpersonal functioning is our need to be regarded unconditionally positive by others. It is our need to be received by others. The fulfillment of this need is necessary to actualize our own potential for regarding ourselves without conditions of worth. Other-regard must become other-reception, for self-regard to become self-reception. If this need is not met, we end up regarding ourselves conditionally. This will have the ultimate consequence that we end up distorting or denying those experiences which are related to the part of us we find unacceptable.

It is important to note that this need can only be met interpersonally. We are thus dependent on others for it, as others are likewise dependent on us. Because of this need we are vulnerable to others. We need to be received by others to become fully functioning. With this formulation Rogers clearly locates the source of both our intrapersonal wellbeing as well as malfunctioning in the other, or in society. The manner in which others regard us, or the manner in which we regard others, is what Rogers refers to as either the facilitative or adverse social conditions of the organism.

To receive the other is thus one of the two ways in which we can regard the other. It is our unconditionally positive regard for him. This regard implies that we do not only trust our own organism totally, but that we trust the organism of the other as well. Interpersonal reception is thus ultimately based on an active receptivity to the growth process that man is in others as well as in ourselves. *The organism is interpersonally trustworthy.*

The important question now is, if interpersonal unconditional positive regard is so beneficial for personal functioning what is it that causes people to regard each other conditionally rather than receptively?

4.5 mutual non-reception by trustworthy organisms, the ultimate impasse

The first answer that Rogers gave to this question was that it is our natural tendency to evaluate others, to judge others in terms of what enhances our own organism (3,IV,B,1.1).[13] This in effect means that our conditional regard for others is an expression of our trust in our organism as the locus of valuation. But if this is true, however, then it also implies that to receive others goes *against* our organismic enhancement, and that represents a form of distrust in our own organism. Thus, like self-conception, our receptivity toward others would involve us in blocking our own actualization process, this time at the interpersonal level. This in turn would mean that organismic enhancement is ultimately self-defeating since the very movement that actualizes the organism further, is also the cause of its cessation. Once again we have arrived at the impasse.

Rogers has seen this problem and has later reversed himself.[14] His revised conception now holds that reception of others and a non-judgmental attitude toward them are in fact expressions of fully functioning and interpersonal congruence. Thus, conditional regard is now no longer seen as the actualization of our organismic valuing capacity at the level of regard (3,IV, B,2). Rather it now becomes a sign of personal malfunctioning.

But that still leaves us with the question: If receiving others is now seen as a natural part of man as a process, what then causes people *not* to receive others?

Rogers' later answer to our question is that our culture makes us regard others conditionally rather than receptively.[15] But this is not a satisfactory answer since, and Rogers would agree, people make culture and not the reverse.

In the final analysis Rogers' answer to this question would be that people don't receive others because they are not received *by* others. This, of course, begs the question at hand and it does not explain how something that is so natural to organisms is not practiced by organisms. The question is pressing: How can people who are basically so constructive, so forward-directed, and so well meaning do this to each other? The answer that Rogers gives is hardly encouraging. Nevertheless, it allows him once again to push the explanation for the impasse back to one more higher level of differentiation complexity, namely to the communal level. By doing this, he says in effect that our negative way of relating to each other is the ultimate source of our interpersonal and intrapersonal troubles.

5. no conceptual basis for optimism

The implications of this formulation should not escape our notice. We have arrived at the terminus of Rogers' explanations of the cause of the disruption of the organismic actualization process. Beyond this he gives no further explanations. Having arrived there he states that when two or more positive, inherently constructive and forward-directional organisms meet they have within themselves the potential for arresting each others' growth process, and thus their own as well. It is not some defensive group of people that do this, which then must be changed, actualized by other, non-defensive people. No, we all have it within us and we do it to each other mutually. I do not receive you and thus I arrest your growth because you do not receive me. And you do not receive me and thus you arrest my growth because I do not receive you. Thereby we checkmate each other. On the basis of this view it is inconceivable that anyone should become fully functioning. It is a truly tragic view of what ails us. Rogers is too optimistic to draw this conclusion. Rather, he continues to believe in the inherent capacity of the forces of growth to positively reform us intra- and interpersonally. But he has no rational, conceptual basis for following through on his basic intent, it seems to me.

140

E. Conclusion

Thus far I attempted to show that Rogers' conception of man as an organismic actualizing process is inherently self-contradictory and that it ultimately leads to a conceptual impasse. As Truax has shown[16], Rogers' therapeutic practice is also in some respects at variance with his basic intent. This leads me to suggest that perhaps the growth process in man is not autonomous and that it does not guarantee the unity of man.

From that vantage point it is not necessarily bad that Rogers is inconsistent with his own basic intent. It may simply be a case of reality not allowing thought to distort itself.[17] One can only interpret what is already given. Rogers would be one of the first to recognize this. For him too, reality (which he then of course identifies with experience) is primary. For him theory is only "a net of gossamer threads over solid facts" (3,I,B). Nevertheless, the inconsistency in his conception is significant for us. It helps us decide what of his conception we can accept and what of it we can justifiably reject.

IV. EXTERNAL CRITIQUE OF ROGERS' CONCEPTION

In this section I will briefly discuss several other important critiques of Rogers' conception. These are admittedly external critiques. That is to say, they derive from a basic intent that is essentially alien to Rogers' view of man. But their discussion is important because they provide alternative explanations of the phenomenon under discussion.

A. The Thematization of Relational Systems by Kropf

Detlef Kropf (*Grundprobleme der Gesprächs-psychotherapie*, 1976) has analyzed Rogers' conception in detail, in what he calls "an epistemological critique of interview psychotherapy" (erkentnis-theoretische Kritik der Gesprächs-psychotherapie). In his critique he makes a number of assumptions, that need to be enumerated first of all.

One of them is that our thinking about anything always occurs in terms of "relational systems" (Bezugssystemen, BZS en). He calls his method of analysis the "thematization of relational systems". (Thematizierung der BZSe), p.17. Via this method we can discover these relational systems. He first of all argues that no concept has meaning, except in relation to other concepts. Thus the search for relational systems starts with the question which concept obtains meaning in relation to which other concept, or which concept is meaningless in relation to which other concept (p.19). A concept has meaning only in the context of a relational system (p.23). Those concepts, which give meaning to each other by reason of their relationship together make up a relational system. If two concepts do not obtain meaning when related to each other, they do not belong to the same relational system. Thus, this standing-in-relation character of concepts implies at the same time a certain ordering of concepts into relational systems (p.19). That is to say, the cosmos about which we think and which we experience allows itself to be conceptually analyzed into relational systems. Such systems are always related to an "I", because it is I that think them (p.106). Nevertheless, these relational systems represent only one thematization (or aspect) of the cosmos, and not the whole, since we always think from out of a certain viewpoint. Thus whenever we have a certain concept we can thematize the relational system to which it belongs via the above method of analysis. As examples of such relational systems Kropf mentions the biological, the anthropological, the mathematical or the metaphysical, etc. (p.24).

The other assumption that Kropf makes is that whatever man experiences, he experiences consciously or not at all (p.77). According to him we cannot say anything about the unconscious (p.33). Thus he states, against Rogers, that for this reason there can never be any conflict, nor for that matter a state of congruence *between* consciousness and experience, since experience, to be know-able, must necessarily be conscious. Via the same reasoning he also rejects the possibility of unconscious perception or subception (p.62).

Furthermore, Kropf states that an organism (understood by him as a physiological organism) cannot experience anything. Only man can experience and for that reason there can be no tension between the organism and the self-concept either. Neither can there be any inconsistency between the self-concept and experience but only between the self-concept and a *concept* of experience.

Kropf's major point is thus that relational systems are incommensurable. Therefore to relate a concept which belongs to one BZS to a concept that belongs to another BZS is to relate matters of a different order to each other as if they were the same. The result of this is meaninglessness.

Kropf himself does not view the qualitative differentiation levels of Rogers' system as products of actualization by the organism. Rather he sees them as differentiations by the "I" into different relational systems within *conceptual, conscious experience*. Thus unlike Rogers, he does not adhere to differentiation across qualitatively diverse relational systems. Rather he sees differentiation occurring within consciousness only. This process within consciousness moves from some sort of vague undifferentiated awareness toward a more clearly articulated conceptual awareness. Kropf's conclusion is therefore also the reverse of Rogers' position. For him it is undifferentiated, rather than differentiated consciousness that causes problems in man because it is less conceptually controlled than is desirable.

B. Wexler's Cognitive Theory of Experiencing

David Wexler[18] is another reviewer of Rogers' thought. He has especially criticized Rogers' view of awareness in relation to experience. Himself a client-centered therapist, he has attempted to give a cognitive theory of experiencing, self-actualization and the therapeutic process. In doing so he views man primarily as an information processor, whose information processing system is limited. He uses data from experiments based on information theory to support his argument.

He first of all criticizes Rogers' notion of "openness to experience" because it is at variance with the ability of the organism "to select relevant stimuli for processing while ignoring other, irrelevant stimuli". And he argues further that to "be open to, and to freely relay every stimulus through the nervous system without being distorted by any defense mechanism would in effect mean that the person would find himself overwhelmed by the multitude of stimuli impinging on him". Thus, "selection is not only necessary for adaptive behavioral functioning, but is also essential for sheer physical survival".

Next, he asks how this selection process in a person who is open to his experience differs from selection in the service of defense. To this Rogers would reply that his ability to trust his organism would make the difference. That is to say, for a person who is open to his experience, the locus of evaluation for the symbolization of experience is his own immediate bodily reaction (organismic valuing process) rather than conditions of worth introjected from others in the process of socialization. Wexler contends, however, that whether an immediate body reaction is "really" one's own, or the result of influence of others is basically unknowable. Hence there is no clear basis for distinguishing, in practice, conditions of worth from the organismic valuing process. Consequently, neither is it possible to distinguish defensive from nondefensive selection in the symbolization of experience on the basis of organismic valuing process (p.51).

The point implied in Wexler's criticism is worth making. The only way in which total openness to experience can be maintained by Rogers, without threat to the unity of the process is that experience is already prepackaged before it reaches awareness. But this implies a pre-experiential, preconscious, cognitively selective and distinguishing or valuing activity by the organism, which would indicate *to* awareness that *this* experience is organism-enhancing, and that *that* experience is not. In that case, however, awareness can only function registratively. But it does more than that. Considering that it can, and does, select defensively as well as nondefensively, some form of active selection over and above the preconscious selectivity of the organism must be accepted. As we saw earlier Rogers himself also states that the organism must be aware of its choices before it can value constructively. It seems therefore that by advocating total openness to experience Rogers involves himself in maintaining a pre-conscious consciousness and a pre-cognitive cognition.

Unlike Rogers, Wexler does not ascribe the valuing actualization process to the organism. Instead he ascribes it entirely to cognitive awareness, which he also invests with the capacity to differentiate and integrate experience. He further notes in passing that whenever Rogers talks in detail about actualization, he himself does so only in terms of experiencing and not in terms of the realization of inherent potentials (p.52). All the creative, actualizing, differentiating and integrating powers which Rogers ascribes to the organism Wexler ascribes to cognitive, conscious experiencing.

Thus he states that "experience is not something already existing to be open to, but is what is created by the functioning of cognitive processes," (p.59). And he adds, ". . . an optimal mode of experiencing is the activity of differentiating and integrating meaning so as to *create* a richness in experience. Experiencing is productive and optimal when the client's cognitive processes are functioning to their fullest capabilities (within the constraint of the information processing system) to create change and reorganization in experience through vigorous differentiation and integration of meaning" (pp.77-78).

C. The Anthropological Basis of Critique

Kropf's criticism of Rogers, to the effect that he is guilty of uncritically combining matters of a conceptually different order under the one common denominator of organismic actualization is noteworthy. So is Wexler's criticism that awareness cannot possibly be totally open to experience, as Rogers seems to advocate. The other critical reviews, which I discussed at the end of chapter four are also worthy of consideration in the context of the present discussion. Noteworthy in particular are Smit's criticism that Rogers' self lacks an ego, as well as the critique by Dijkhuis and Wijngaarden that Rogers' view is monological rather than dialogical, or that he fails to recognize the essential relational dependence of the individual on others.

The common thread running through all of these critical reviews seems to be the need to *anchor* the process in something/someone/some activity that itself is not (part of) the process. This motivation is entirely in line with my own argument that the process is necessarily embedded in a reality structure, either within man or his environment, which is not of the process' own making and with which it has to reckon to remain unified. In the main they add up to the conclusion that the dynamic character of the process is incapable, by itself, to guarantee the unity of the process, and that therefore the process is not autonomous.

To me, this seems to be a valid criticism of Rogers' conception of man. However, it is also an external criticism. That is to say, it does not share Rogers' basic intent for man. It is based on a view of man that differs from Rogers' anthropology. It is "up to something" that Rogers is not "up to". This leads to the question whether external criticism is anything more than a fight between anthropological preferences. Rogers appears to restrict it to just that, hence his reservations about judgment and external evaluation. However, in view of the foregoing discussion it seems highly doubtful to me that there should not be anything more to external criticism than that.

But if there is more to it, this raises the question of what function one's basic intent has for the way one thinks about man or the rest of reality. And it raises the question what function one's basic intent has for one's evaluation of the conceptions of others. If one can believe my analysis, then Rogers' basic intent seriously distorts the reality of human functioning. But if my own views were analyzed in terms of their basic intent the same might possibly be said for my anthropological intent as well. What is then the value of one's basic intent for one's thinking about man? Several things need to be said about this issue.

In the first place, it seems that no one can do without it. We never just think. Ever since Kuhn's discussion on the history of science[19], the notion of "pure thought" has become outdated. Our thoughts about anything are always "up to something". We cannot do without a basic intent. It orders our own thought and our critique of others. It is in terms of our basic intent that our thoughts and our critique make sense (to us *and* to others if they take the trouble to discover what we are up to).

Second, I believe this dissertation has demonstrated that one's basic intent need not distort the views of others. It is possible to give a Rogers-centered description of Rogers' conception without sharing his anthropology.

Third, I believe (and I think Rogers agrees), that my own view of man has been able to "light up" a number of positive implications in Rogers' thought that had escaped his notice. Thus, it would seem strange to me that on the same basis I should not also be able to bring to light the negative implications of his views. We ourselves can hardly be critical of our own intent, since for us it is basic. But others can, from out of *their* basic intent, bring to light[20] the positive features as well as the complications, the inconsistencies and the distortions which our thoughts exhibit by virtue of their relation to our basic intent. The value of differing anthropologies is that they make it possible for others to criticize us. And their criticism in turn allows us the privilege of changing our minds. Thus, in this respect also, we are not self-sufficient but need each other to be and become ourselves.

V. CONSEQUENCES OF ROGER'S BASIC INTENT FOR THERAPY, PERSONALITY AND INTERPERSONAL RELATIONS

Anthropological viewpoints are not just viewpoints. They tend to have concrete implications for the practice of living. Thus, this section will investigate some concrete effects of Rogers' viewpoint on therapy, personality and interpersonal relations.

A. Consequences of Rogers' Basic Intent for Therapy

1. consequences for the relation, the process and the involvement of the client

I believe it is fair to say, first of all, that in Rogers' view of therapy the therapeutic relation has its *raison d'être* wholly in the therapeutic process. The therapeutic relationship takes its cue from the process. It must be guided by it. It must be geared towards it. It has the process as its end in view. It may in no way interfere with it, and it focusses entirely on it. The therapeutic process determines the therapeutic relationship at all times.

Second, this therapeutic process is not created between the therapist and the client as a result of their relationship. It is not a function of the relationship.

It occurs entirely within the client. Therapy does not create it or even evoke it. Rather, it serves to "facilitate" the "release" of this ready-made, but dormant process in the client.

Third, it is not consciously brought about by the client. It does not occur from the top down but from the bottom up. The client's thinking must be wholly subservient to his experience of the process. The process changes the client therapeutically and that change *happens* to the client, spontaneously.

2. consequences for the behavior of the therapist and the client

This formulation of therapy has important consequences for the way in which the therapist and the client "behave" in relation to each other. The therapist, for example, may never interfere with the life of the client. He may not view him from his own frame of reference. He may not judge him or regard him critically. He may not diagnose or interpret in the traditional sense of the word. He may not take responsibility for the client and he may not direct him. Or, if he does any of these things his behavior is considered antitherapeutic.

The client in turn may not psychologically depend on the therapist. He may not take over any of his values. He may not see himself as the therapist sees him. He may not use the therapist as a role playing partner, or as a surrogate information processor or as a teacher, or as a reinforcer of his behavior. He may not engage in any of these except insofar as they would make him aware that he has the capacity within himself to change himself. The therapist has nothing to offer but his total trust in the client. The client must bring about the process himself. Not only that, but he must also bring it about *by* himself. If not, then the therapeutic process is considered to be still dormant.

It is clear from the foregoing that in Rogers' conception the therapist can never create the process. He can only facilitate its release. As he attempts to create process he will fail, since he is thereby "up to something" that the client is not "up to". But we must take this one step further. The same holds for the client as well. Not even the client can consciously bring this process about. No sooner does he deliberately plan to set the process in motion or he will thereby obstruct its occurrence. He must let the process happen spontaneously to him. Not even the client can do more than facilitate its release within him.

This facilitation of the process by the client within himself occurs when his self becomes disorganized, thus when the client starts to question his usual way of *thinking* about himself. Through this process of therapeutic self-doubt new, and reintegrative insights are said to occur inevitably to the client. And equally spontaneously the client finds himself exhibiting more mature and more creative behavior as a further outcome of this process. This process of therapeutic self-doubt is facilitated (but not created) by the non-directive client-centered attitude of the therapist. The facilitation of self-doubt thus appears to be the only function of the therapist's client-centered attitude. The rest of the therapeutic process occurs inevitably and is the result of the growth forces within the client himself, or such is Rogers' interpretation of his experience as a therapist.

146

3. trust in the client, or in the therapist?

I would first like to raise the question whether this non-directive, client-centered attitude by the therapist is actually interpreted by the client as "trust in himself". The client's behavior does not seem to bear this out. In the first place, in view of the confusion that occurs in the client as a result of this attitude, the client does not appear to interpret it as a trust in *his* capacity to *think*. On the contrary, while it does seem to communicate to him that the therapist accepts him and cares for him this does not initially result in a great deal of confidence on the part of the client in his cognitive ability. Rather, this attitude places him cognitively in a dependency relation with respect to the therapist, whose client-centered attitude is the only thing that maintains him as his self-concept is disintegrating. The attitude thus undermines rather than boosts his capacity to think for himself. Whatever thinking the client is doing at this point in therapy, one can imagine it to be something like this: "This person, to whom I came for help must really know what he is doing, for he deals with me in a way that I meet in no other life relationship. There, people tell me what they think (of me) and expect me to consider them right or wrong. This person does not even bother doing that. He must see me in a way that I cannot fathom. He must be up to something that is unknown to me. *I had better trust him* totally, for I myself, coming to him for help seem to know neither who I am nor what I should be doing." I suggest that what is built in the client during this part of therapy as a result of the therapist's attitude is not trust in himself but *trust in the therapist*.

Furthermore the *behavior* of the client-centered therapist has everything to do with the development of distrust that the client experiences with regard to his ability to think for himself. By focussing on the client's feelings the therapist ignores *what* the client is thinking or saying and thereby selectively centers him on *how* it is being said. This can hardly be viewed as a respect for the client's ability to think. It seems therefore that whatever trust the therapist communicates to the client it is not trust in his cognitive ability. To communicate *this* trust to the client the therapist would be better off to speak his mind clearly and tell the client exactly what *he* thinks (of him).

But perhaps this is not the task of the therapist in the initial stages of therapy. Quite possibly he must first bring the client in touch with his feelings. Perhaps his task is to create an emotional release, a catharsis by orienting the client affectively rather than cognitively. If this is so, then client-centeredness appears to be admirably suited to bring this about, on par perhaps with the psychoanalytic technique of free association. But it should then be noted that for this part of therapy the client is quite dependent on the selective attention of the therapist.

4. does insight inevitably follow open expression of feelings?

Furthermore, it is Rogers' view that once this openness to his feelings has been accomplished by the client he will inevitably gain new insights into himself and thus begin the process of self-integration spontaneously. In this connection I would like to raise the question whether this process really occurs spontaneously. My own experience as a therapist does not always bear out what apparently is Rogers' experience, namely, that insight follows catharsis inevitably. My experience is that it happens in some cases but by no means in all.

Now, it is entirely possible that in those cases where insight failed to materialize spontaneously, I was not as genuinely client-centered as I should have been. This seems all the more possible since I do not share Rogers' basic intent. This would mean then that in client-centered therapy insight does indeed follow openness to feelings spontaneously but that I have been unable to generate the client-centered conditions it apparently requires.

This in effect puts me in a situation Rogers was in many years ago, when he was faced with having to explain why his application of the psychoanalytic method did not produce the predicted therapeutic outcome (2,VI,A). In his explanation Rogers chose against dogmatic Freudianism rather than question his own therapeutic ability. In effect he said that the method did not work. Faced with what I perceive to be dogmatic client-centeredness on this point, I feel therefore justified to do the same. That is to say, it is my experience that as a result of client-centered therapy some of my clients claim to "feel better". But they also state that they still do not know what got them so upset in the first place, nor do they know what to do in the future to avoid it. Thus they obtained some emotional relief, but they gained no appreciable insight. Rather than question my own ability to be client-centered, my conclusion is that in some cases the method did not produce insight spontaneously.

How now to explain this discrepancy between Rogers' experience and my own? To do this, I will first argue that no insight occurs in the client without some sort of interpretation on the part of the therapist. Whether Rogers likes it or not, his client-centered approach is also an expression of his frame of reference. Without saying so, he also communicates to the client what he is "up to". In fact, I believe that it is precisely because Rogers' intent is tacit in his therapeutic approach that it is likely to command the greatest attention from the client. The stimulus value of Rogers' message to the client is heightened because it represents an *exception* to the way people usually relate to the client in other relationships.

The content of Rogers' message to a given client would seem to be something like this: "You are the only one that can know what is right for you. I cannot help you there. It is your own responsibility. Furthermore, this knowledge cannot be achieved. It is given to you. You cannot think it through. You can only intuit it. It is your experiencing, not your thinking that will show you the way. You must be open to the former and limit the influence of the latter. And when you do this, you will never know for sure, for very long, where you ought to go or what you ought to do. You will have to make your decisions on a moment by moment basis."

Now, I am suggesting that it was the critical thinkers among my clients, the people who are used to weighing the pro's and con's of everything, the "reality testers", the people with cognitive ability, with "ego strength" so to speak, who rejected the client-centered interpretation imbedded in Rogers' message. They did so, I suggest, because it asked them to relinquish the one thing they were good at, namely clear thinking, cognitive processing. Hence, they "felt better" but did not gain any "insight". At the same time it was the people who had already some trouble cognitively structuring their experience who found solace in the "insight" that to structure one's experience is an impossible task to begin with. Hence they "felt better" *and* gained the "insight" that client-centered therapy intends.

I conclude therefore that insight does not occur spontaneously in client-centered therapy but rather that it results from the interpretation of reality which the therapist intends. And secondly, whether such insight occurs in a given client depends on his conscious decision whether to accept or reject this interpretation.

5. does the client inevitably act upon his insights?

The next and final event which Rogers hypothesizes to happen inevitably in client-centered therapy, as part of, or the result of the therapeutic process, is that the client acts upon his insights in ways that others characterize as more mature, more creative, more confident, etc. This means therefore that the client has resolved whatever he initially presented as the problem, presumably by changing the way he experiences the problem. Thus just as renewed insight follows catharsis spontaneously, so more mature behavior also inevitably follows the attainment of insight. Once again this prediction is not always born out in my own experience as a therapist. In some cases my clients have actually come to feel better and gained a considerable amount of insight but appeared to be either unwilling or unable to act upon it.

So what to make of this? In the first place, if a person is to make changes of any kind, including those likely to occur in therapy, he must be motivated to do so. With this Rogers agrees and he identifies this motivation as a growth motive (see glossary A,1.) For him, however, this motivation to change or to grow, is a general rather than a specific motive. It can either be obstructed or facilitated. If it is facilitated then all sorts of *specific* changes follow inevitably. Rogers bases his view in this regard on his experience in therapy.

It may be asked, however, whether the motivation to change, which is evident in the client, is indeed a general rather than a specific motivation. It seems fairly safe to assume the when a client enters therapy he is motivated to make some changes. For one thing he is likely to labor under a lot of anxiety and thus would want to change from feeling anxious to feeling better. However, from this it does not necessarily follow that he is also motivated to change his view of himself and thus to gain insight into himself. Nor does it follow that he therefore is also motivated to change his behavior or to act upon his insights. Thus it may be that the motivation to change which the client exhibits is specific rather than general. My experience in therapy with some of my clients would seem to bear this out. Thus, if a given client does not appear to be motivated to change his view of himself nor to act upon his insights, it may be the task of a therapist to confront him with the need for change in this regard.

In the second place, it is possible that a client is indeed motivated to act upon his insight and thus ready to change his behavior but simply does not know how to go about this. And since the client receives precious little direction for changing his behavior in client-centered therapy this may be another reason why my clients failed to act upon their insight. At any rate, it can be argued that for this final step in the therapeutic process, the client needs to cooperation of the therapist as well.

6. the therapeutic process, in the client or in the relationship?

Thus far I have attempted to show that for each of its three aspects, catharsis, insight and action the therapeutic process seems to require the active participation of the therapist in the process. This implies that the three aspects of therapy do not follow each other spontaneously as Rogers suggests. Rather, it seems that the therapeutic process is dependent on the therapeutic relationship all the way.

This leads to the question whether the therapeutic process really occurs exclusively *in* the client. It seems much more accurate to say that it occurs *in the relationship between* the therapist and the client. This would mean that the therapeutic process is not a facilitative but rather a cooperative event. It would also mean that it is not released in the client but rather achieved by the client and the therapist working together. Therapy would thus be a cooperative event in which the therapeutic process is realized between two or more people when they are ''up to something'' together.

7. therapy as cooperation rather than facilitation

In the second place I have attempted to show that the therapeutic process is not an event that occurs spontaneously when the client becomes open to his experience but that it needs the thinking of both the therapist and the client to happen in the relationship. By all accounts the therapeutic event and the people that participate in it exhibit a structure, an order that can be studied and thought about. Both the event and the behavior of persons involved in it can be understood conceptually. Since the therapist can be expected to have made a special study of these phenomena he is likely to have a more competent understanding of both the intrapersonal and interpersonal dynamics of therapy than the client. Thus it seems entirely strange to me that he should not communicate this understanding to his client for the client to consider. And it also seems strange to me that this information, when presented as a possibility, should hamper rather than aid the achievement of insight in the client.

Naturally, if therapy is a cooperative event the therapist should tailor his remarks and behavior to fit the intent, the cognitive capacity and the problematics of the client. That is to say, he has to stay ''with'' the client. But, the client comes to the therapist for help and in my view he needs to receive more than the trust of the therapist if he is going to benefit from the therapeutic contact.

Finally, if therapy is indeed a cooperative rather than a facilitative event, then in the interest of achieving the therapeutic process the client also has the obligation to express himself in ways that are intelligible to the therapist. This is not merely for the benefit of the therapist's understanding. Much more importantly, in expressing himself cogently to the therapist the client can be expected to clarify his own thinking and thereby gain insight into himself.[21]

Client-centered therapy seems to place a predominantly greater emphasis on the input of the client in the therapeutic process. I have sought to stress the input of the therapist more fully. But the activity of both is necessary, for therapy remains a cooperative event between two or more people that are ''up to something.'' This event involves the feelings, but also the thinking and the behavior of both the therapist and the client. Moreover, it is successful to the extent that all the parties involved in therapy intend the same things.

By way of illustrating a cooperative approach to therapy I will discuss two ''syndromes'' which frequently occur in therapy, particularly when one is dealing with depressed clients. The first is a situation where the client has an unrealistically low image of himself. The other is a situation where the client has an unrealistically high view of what is expected of him.

The first client typically perceives himself to be a ''nothing'' or a ''nobody.'' This view is likely to be at variance with the view which the therapist has of his client. Quite possibly the perception of others is also at variance with the client's negative self-perception. Within a cooperative approach to therapy the therapist can confront his client with this discrepancy and ask him to explain it. Thereby the therapist in effect confronts the client with the reality of his (the therapist's) perception of the client in the relationship. As a result the client may gain insight into the functional value of his negative self-perception. Thus, he may come to see that for him it is apparently more tolerable to bear the misery of being a nobody, than to bear the responsibility of being at least a somebody.

In the second case the client perceives the life demands placed on him to be so high as to preclude his ever attaining them. Here again the therapist may ask his client to explain the discrepancy between the therapist's more attainable perception of the client's actual demand structure and the client's own perception of the same. And again, the resulting insight for the client may be that he holds such high expectations of himself in order to avoid having to try to attain them. Or he may come to some other insight.

At any rate, the method of confronting the client with such discrepancies in perception appears to be conducive to the development of further insight. The cooperative approach does not need to maintain that the therapist's perception is superior to that of the client. All it does is seek to constantly eliminate the discrepancy that arises between the perception of the therapist and that of the client. The aim is thus clearly that the therapist and the client should increasingly be up to the same thing together.

B. Consequences of Rogers' Basic Intent for Personality Development and Functioning

In this section and in the next I will argue that because of his basic intent, Rogers overemphasizes the importance of personalization and growth at the expense of other aspects of (inter)human development and functioning.

One of Rogers' main contentions is that only those who are fully functioning congruent *persons* can truly relate to each other, and that inter-human relations are at their best when they are interpersonal relations. Thus becoming a person, or personalization, has priority over interhuman relating in the order of human development, and by Rogers' account it would seem that the main business of child development is personalization, or the process of becoming more and more oneself.

While this formulation may fit Rogers' basic intent, it appears to be a one-sided account of what actually happens in human development.[22] Unlike his animal counterpart, the human infant appears to be born with very few instincts to guide his behavior. For these guidelines he appears to be dependant on the significant adults around him, his parents in particular. Thus, while right from birth on we can observe him to be preoccupied with being and becoming himself, we can also see him busy learning to walk, to talk, to eat by himself, and to relieve himself. In each of these activities his behavior looks sus-piciously like that of his significant adults around him, and this is hardly surprising since he learns these activities from them. Therefore, it seems necessary to state that next to, in conjunction with and in support of a per-sonalization process, the human infant also goes through a socialization pro-cess. In fact, it can be argued that the process of personalization, or the preoccupation with identity formation is developmentally speaking of a much later date than the socialization process. It is after all during adolescence rather than during infancy or childhood that the problems of identity are most pro-nounced, suggesting that Rogers' formulation may actually put the cart before the horse. In any case, a description of human development may not neglect the process of socialization. Now the unfortunate consequence of Rogers' formu-lation is, in my opinion, that it leads him to accent only the negative factors of this socialization process. My criticism of Rogers is therefore that he has insufficiently described the manner in which the social context *supports* the development of personality.

Does this now mean that what Rogers describes has no basis in fact at all? Not necessarily. It is conceivable that the growth process in therapy follows the pattern described by Rogers. That is to say, the problem of a given client may be that he is oversocialized and underpersonalized. In such instances personalization may be the first order of business in therapy. But this is then a therapeutic matter and not a developmental matter. That is to say, it pre-supposes that the socialization process has already occurred but that it needs to be readjusted. Developmentally speaking, however, it appears that socializa-tion occurs alongside of personalization. This is so, it seems, because as *human* beings we need the concrete support of others to become ourselves.

A second contention by Rogers regarding human development is that the more one becomes a fully functioning person, the more one becomes open to one's experience and the less one is guided by one's conceptual awareness. The process is thus one that moves from being cognitively oriented toward being affectively oriented, and presumably, human development moves in this direction.

This, too, seems to be a one-sided description of actual human development. Cognition and experiencing go hand in hand in human development if for no other reason than that the child must make some sort of sense out of his experience to experience anything at all. Human development is thus at all times a matter of development within cognitive experience. In this process thinking is equally important as feeling. A human infant must thus think as well as feel to develop. In that sense he functions as fully as an adult. Now, it may be that within this overall cognitive experiencing a person may at one time process his experience more conceptually than at another, but this is then a matter of degree, or differential emphasis within cognitive experiencing. With regard to this matter it is doubtful, to my mind, that the human child should first be guided by concepts and only later by affects. If anything, the reverse seems to be more the case.

Moving now from personal development to personal functioning, the main characteristic that Rogers ascribes to the fully functioning person is "changingness". Thus, as the end product of personal development, the fully functioning person is the epitome of man as a process. Here again I run into difficulty. It seems to be realistic to be open to the experience of the moment as Rogers' fully functioning person is. This safeguards a person from mistaking memories for present experiences. But does this not imply an identity, that is, a certain "sameness" over time, as anchorage point, in terms of which to distinguish here-and-now experiences from memories, and in terms of which to decide on realistic change? I believe that Rogers would not deny the need for an identity. The trouble is that in his stress on "changingness," he neglects to mention the role of this identity in this process. This creates the impression as if the self of a fully functioning person is wholly determined by the experience of the moment, and thus that the "good life" is one that is lived literally from moment to moment.

My final question about Rogers' view of personal functioning relates to his contention that the essential business of life is changing. Is it not possible that this ties man to a life of excessive change? Rogers' main preoccupation has been with eliminating those factors that *retard* or obstruct change. But is it not possible for human life to sin in the other direction? Is it not possible for man to change *too much?* This is of course the problem that faced Dewey many years ago (2,V,B,2.2). Rogers has indicated to me that he is aware of this problem and has stated that he always meant that rest should alternate with change if this should appear necessary. But this modification seems to be hard to reconcile with the major thrust of his writings.

Rogers might have answered that what he is after is not change, but growth. In that case the growth of the person would determine when he should change and when he would rest. Fully functioning could thus be restated as perpetual changingness in a positive direction, or perpetual growth. But this does not really resolve the issue, for now the problem returns in the form of excessive growth. Since by all appearances, life on this planet is finite, is it really realistic to expect a person to keep on growing? Is Rogers not guilty here of what Richard Farson has called "maximizing rather than optimizing"?[23] Is more always better and can there not be too much of a good thing? Concretely, is there any retirement from growth?

C. Consequences of Rogers' Basic Intent for Interpersonal Relations

Rogers' view of interpersonal relations was born in (client-centered) therapy and was later extrapolated to become the central characteristic of good interhuman relations everywhere. Relationships are interpersonal, in the Rogerian sense, when the parties involved respect each other as persons. The aim of such relationships is to promote the personal growth or fully functioning of the participants. Conversely, interpersonal relations are at their best when the people involved in these relationships are fully functioning persons.

It should be remembered first of all that what I am discussing here is the term "interpersonal relations" in the meaning that Rogers ascribes to it and that I am contrasting this notion with what I call "interhuman relations." One could argue, for example, that all human beings are persons (as it were by birthright) and that therefore all interhuman relations are necessarily interpersonal relations. But this is not what Rogers means by his term "(inter)personal". This is evident from the fact that he speaks of "becoming a person", which implies that at one time in one's life one is less of a person than at another time. By "person" Rogers means the goal, or end product of a process of becoming autonomous, self-sufficient, free, self-valuing and experientially oriented. By "interpersonal" he means by implication, that form of interhuman relating which does not direct, which rather respects that intra-individual movement toward autonomy, characterized by him as "personal". A "person" is thus a human being who works out his destiny, independent from any social support and free from any outside interference.

This view of the person differs markedly from a dialogical view of the person which stresses the inherent relatedness of individual human beings to other human beings (4,V,B). Wijngaarden, for example, stresses the inherently relational dependence of individual human beings. In his view of the person, therefore, being dependent on others and being a person are not mutually exclusive. Similarly, his notion of interpersonal respect entails rather than excludes, that in relation to the other, I should offer him the benefit of my person, which the other needs in order to be and become himself (4,V,B,2). For Wijngaarden, therefore, one cannot possibly be a person outside of a prior inherent relatedness to others. It is this inherent relatedness that I characterize as "interhuman relations". And this is what I contrast with Rogers' "interpersonal relations".

I chose the term "interhuman relations" rather than "interpersonal relations" to indicate that, for me our relational dependence on others is a more basic characteristic of human life than our individual autonomy, in the Rogerian sense. It implies that we can only achieve our individual autonomy, or self-governance in the context of this most basic relational dependence and thus also that the achievement of this self-governance is always limited, relative to our dependence on others. Human life is at best not autonomous but cooperative. For Rogers "interpersonal relations" appears to be an ideal construct. It is what all interhuman relations ought to be, to be good. It implies a freedom from society, a freedom from others (2,VII,A). This gets at the essential difference between my own, and Rogers' view of interhuman relations. I value positively my relational dependence on others and that of others on myself. Rogers, it seems, does not. At least, this is how I interpret his avowed lack of interest in teaching and his preference for facilitating learning instead.[24] I also get that impression from his reluctance to lead a group and his preference for making decisions via group consensus.[25] In both these social situations (teaching and leading), and also in the parent-child relation, there exists a certain relational dependence of some persons on others. Moreover, it is functional to the business transacted in these relationships that this dependence be respected.

My main criticism of Rogers' view of interpersonal relations is therefore that it sets up an unnecessary tension between our relational dependence and our need for relative individual autonomy. To me it is another example of how his basic intent distorts (inter)human functioning.

VI. CLOSING REFLECTIONS

As I reflect on this study of Rogers' thought I am first of all aware of how much I owe to him as a therapist. I dare say that I am not alone in this. Clearly the whole field of psychotherapy is greatly indebted to Rogers. His contributions to the field and to my own professional development are numerous. The problem is not what to say but where to begin and when to quit. I will restrict myself to selectively mentioning only those of Rogers' insights that have had the greatest impact on my life.

Chief among his contributions to my development is surely the fact that he taught me to listen. By now this is almost a commonplace, since everyone knows that Rogers and listening are synonymous. But it is true. I did not really know what empathy was, what it feels like to put it into practice, or what it can accomplish until I came in contact with Rogers' view. Coupled with this is the debt I owe him for teaching me "to welcome those that differ from me". He also taught me to wait with my response to the other until I *really* understood the other. In short, I could not have been as Rogers-centered as I was in this study, had it not been for the fact that Rogers himself has taught me in the first place how to understand another person from the inside out.

I also greatly appreciate his continual drive for personal wholeness and congruence. For me, too, man is an integral unity rather than a composite of "parts". Thus in my practice I have learned to deal with people rather than cases. I have learned from Rogers to listen to myself (thinking and feeling), particularly during those times when I run stuck in "what I am up to". I have learned from Rogers that life changes, that it moves and I have learned that this is normal. From him I have also learned to like growth.

At the same time, from the beginning of this study I have felt uneasy about some of the other elements of Rogers' views. I could never accept the way he seemed to set the individual over against society. I could not understand why a person's autonomy should be expressed as "freedom from society" (2,VII,A). I could not see that personality should have priority over communality. Not only is this self-others dilemma hard for me to accept but also those of process vs. structure, thought vs. experience, self vs. organism. While I agree that human life is changing, I cannot agree that it is changing*ness*, or that experience of the moment should have priority over past experience. Finally, while I see growth as an important aspect of life I cannot see it as being the essence of life. Nor do I believe that growth is autonomous because this would imply that nothing can set limits to it.

In summary, even though I have learned a great deal from Rogers, there is also much in his thinking that has disturbed me. Thus it was important for me to study Rogers in depth as I have done, if for no other reason than to make me aware that his intentions for human life differ considerably from my own. I have also come to understand that this leads us to differences in our therapeutic approach as well.

In closing, I should like to make a number of, what I now feel justified in calling, informed judgments about the subject matter of this study.

It appears that inherent in all one's descriptions of human functioning an anthropology, or view of man, or basic intent for man, is operative. This basic intent is not an unfortunate, subjective byproduct of our thinking, but rather a basic motive that integrates our thoughts and signals what our thoughts are "up to". It seems further that our basic intent for man is significantly influenced by the cultural-historical context in which our thinking occurs.

Second, one does not need to share a person's basic intent to be able to describe his views in depth from out of his basic intent. Furthermore, one's own basic intent for man, if it differs from that of the other, has the capacity to bring to light both the positive elements and the complications that are inherent to the conception of the other. External criticism, that is, critique across anthropological viewpoints, serves the positive function of illuminating our neighbour's conception of himself. External evaluation and empathy are therefore not opposed. Rather they serve the same illuminating purpose.

Finally, an anthropological study of the major approaches to psychotherapy is valuable in that it demonstrates that extra-therapeutic factors are operative within these therapeutic approaches. A study of such meta-therapeutic considerations has the additional benefit that it safeguards us from misrepresenting a given therapeutic approach, which apparently occurs all too frequently when the description restricts itself to therapeutic considerations only. A case in point is my own anthropological study of Rogers which demonstrates that Rogers is not a self-theorist, or a phenomenological theorist but rather a growth theorist. Such a conclusion can only be drawn if one studies a given therapeutic approach in terms of its basic intent.

SUMMARY

Chapter One: This dissertation raises the question, "How is it possible that there are so many diverse or even opposing views of the one unified event called psychotherapy?" In answer to this question it suggests that extra-therapeutic considerations play an important role in the so-called "school formation" in psychotherapy. In particular, it hypothesizes that, psychotherapy being a human event, a view of man, or anthropology underlies all major schools of psychotherapy. It suggests that this anthropological basis comes to expression within a given approach to therapy as the basic intent of that approach. It further suggests that knowledge of this basic anthropological intent will deepen our understanding of the approach in question. It also suggests that if such in-depth studies were undertaken for each major school of therapy, we would gain a better understanding of the unified character of psychotherapy, as well as of its nature.

As a beginning to this major undertaking this dissertation attempts to investigate the basic intent of the client-centered approach to therapy via an in-depth study of the writings of its founder, Carl R. Rogers. The temptation to apply premature cognitive closure is great in studies such as these. Thus one could characterize Rogers as adhering to a view of man which he does not in fact have. To offset this danger, this dissertation attempts to describe his views entirely from out of his "frame of reference." The central criterion of this work is therefore whether Rogers can recognize himself in its description of his views. The additional purpose of this empathic mode of investigation and description is to provide a practical test of the manner in which, according to Rogers, we come to significant knowledge.

Chapter Two: No therapeutic approach or view of man exists in a vacuum. It originates at one point in historical time and in response to some cultural context or other. This chapter biographically describes the origin of non-directive (later called client-centered) therapy within the context of early twentieth century American culture. It is shown that there exists a close affinity between some dominant cultural themes of that time and Rogers' non-directive approach to therapy. American culture has always cherished the notion that if individuals were left to themselves they would naturally exercise their capacity to realize their potentials. It thus insists on the primacy of the individual over society. However, during the early part of this century the cultural dilemma of "individualism versus conformity" or of the "individual versus society" became particularly acute. Dewey's pragmatism brought about a solution to this dilemma by giving both the individual and established social opinion their relative due, dynamically. It held that traditional views and existing cultural patterns were to be innovatively reconstructed by means of the scientific method with the individual being the agent of such reconstruction. For psychotherapy this entailed that existing therapeutic dogma were to be transformed into therapeutic techniques which were then to demonstrate their efficacy in actual experience or to be modified accordingly.

This pragmatistic experimentalism in therapy allowed Rogers, who was trained in the psychoanalytic approach to therapy, to repudiate dogmatic Freudianism in favour of a more eclectic approach to therapy. In later years, however, he moved from experimentalism to non-directivity as an approach to therapy, thereby positing the primacy of the client in the therapeutic relationship. In doing so he reaffirmed an old notion in American culture to the effect that the individual has primacy over society. Thereby Rogers in principle went beyond the pragmatistic solution to the cultural dilemma of his time. Whereas Dewey held that the individual could only free himself through freeing society, Rogers in effect called upon society to free the individual.

Chapter Three: This chapter gives a systematic-dynamic description of Rogers' views on therapy, personality and interpersonal relations. Rogers' views on therapy are first of all described in their development around the central theme of therapy as an "autonomous process toward personal autonomy". Three stages are distinguished in the development of this theme. The first is the non-directive phase. During this phase Rogers advocates a non-interfering approach to therapy. The aim of this approach is catharsis, and the resulting therapeutic process, which, according to Rogers occurs exclusively in the client, is described as the spontaneous achievement of perceptual, emotional, and personal insight.

The next specification of the central theme is client-centeredness, which is communicated by the therapist to the client through an attitude of basic trust in the client's capacity for self help. This attitude is said to facilitate, but not to induce the resolution of incongruence between the self and experience which is present in the client as he enters therapy. The resulting therapeutic process in the client is variously described as a change in his self-concept, in his perception, in his value system or in his experience of the relationship. The main outcome of this process is a reorganized self-concept which now is much more congruent with experience.

During this second phase two major issues come to the fore: that of "attitude versus technique", and that of "process versus outcome". With respect to the former Rogers asserts that therapeutic techniques must be exclusively expressive of and functional for the attitude of basic trust in the client. In this connection he also formulates a number of therapeutic conditions which he deems to be necessary and sufficient for therapy to occur. Chief among these conditions is the congruence of the therapist.

Rogers resolves the second issue by holding that the process of therapy is the outcome of therapy. This brings his views on therapy into their final process-oriented phase of development. Therapy is now viewed as becoming a process. Its aim is to become one's dynamic experience. Its process is seen as a movement from fixity to constructive changingness. Finally, its outcome or end product is the fully functioning person, that is to say, a person who is fully an experiential organismic process.

In Rogers' view of personality, three successive formulations are distinguishable. The first is a structural view of personality. It contains a description of the human organism, of the self and of the (in)congruence that can exist between the self and the experiential organism. His second formulation is a dynamic description of personality. It starts with a description of how the human infant actualizes himself, guided solely by the organism as the locus of his valuation. Next it describes how the human organism differentiates into a self, which in order to satisfy its need for positive social regard, introjects the valuation of others next to its own valuation process. In this way a person is said to develop conditions of worth in his self-regard. The resulting incongruence between self and organism threatens to disintegrate the self and to disorganize the organism, which causes a person's behavior to be guided alternately by the valuation of others and by his own organismic valuation. Via a process of reintegration, the conditions of worth are eliminated and congruence between the self and the organism is restored.

Rogers' third formulation is an ideal description of personality. It describes the fully functioning person as the end product of the disintegration-reintegration process. Such a person is maximally open to the experience of the moment. He lives existentially and considers his organism to be a trustworthy guide for living. Finally, the whole of him is characterized by changingness. Here, too, therefore Rogers increasingly stresses fluidity as a characteristic of optimal living. As in his views on therapy, he moves from structure-bound to process-oriented thinking.

With respect to his views on interpersonal relations, Rogers' writings show a number of shifts in emphasis. First of all, as time goes on his writings increasingly begin to stress the interpersonal rather than the intra-personal. Thus relationship questions come more and more to the fore. There is a concomitant shift discernible from an emphasis on the therapeutic relation to a concern about interhuman relations in general. Rogers calls them ''interpersonal'' relations. In his view of these relations he extrapolates from his experience in therapy. Finally, the therapeutic relation itself is now more and more described as a person to person relationship rather than a client-centered or non-directive relationship.

Central to Rogers' view of interpersonal relations is the facilitation or breakdown of communication. For him the major barrier to free communication is external evaluation. Conversely, personal expression facilitates communication. More precisely, defensiveness or incongruence in the relation disrupts communication. But transparency or congruence in the relationship enhances it. This transparency implies that at least one of the partners in the relationship is intrapersonally congruent. When he is, he does not only facilitate communication interpersonally, but he necessarily enhances the intrapersonal congruence of the other as well. Ideally speaking then, the goal of interpersonal relations is to promote free flowing communication within and between persons. Thus in his view of interpersonal relations Rogers also stresses process rather than structure.

Chapter Four: This chapter attempts to pull all the strands of Rogers' thought together into one unified conceptual whole. This is accomplished via a description of his views in terms of their basic anthropological intent. It is recognized that, since Rogers himself has never given us a systematically worked out view of man, this chapter can only be offered as an interpretation of his views.

According to this interpretation, Rogers' view of man as an on-going process of organismic actualization is central to the whole of his thought. It characterizes the human organism as a process of growth. This means first of all that the human organism is an activity rather than an entity and secondly, that it is always active rather than reactive. That is to say, in its origin and perpetually thereafter it is always "up to something", namely organismic actualization. Furthermore, the human organism is a dynamic unity. It maintains its organic unity only insofar as it continually actualizes itself, and it can only actualize itself insofar as it does so totally, as a whole.

Actualization is described next as a process of differentiating those potentials which are inherent in the original unity of the organism. Via this process the organism realizes itself at increasingly more complex levels of differentiation. These differentiation levels are described as the levels of organic need fulfillment, of experience, of awareness, of (self)-conception, of social regard and of communication.

This movement by the organism from relative homogeneity to relative diversity could conceivably stop when the organism becomes fully differentiated. This would be contrary to Rogers' dynamic intention. He avoids this first of all by making the process open-ended, such that the possibility of further differentiation always exists. In the second place, he avoids it by adding the process of assimilation to the process of differentiation. As the organism differentiates itself to a higher level of differentiation, it simultaneously assimilates material from a lower level of differentiation, thereby further safeguarding the ongoing character of the actualization process.

In this manner the levels of differentiation-assimilation perpetually interact with one another. This actualizing interaction of the levels is what Rogers means by behavior. Since it occurs internal to the organization of the organism, it characterizes Rogers' view of man as an internal interaction process which moves perpetually in the direction of increased differentiation. If this differentiating-assimilating activity were to cease, the unity of the organism would be threatened. For then the level at which the process stops would become an end in itself and it would begin to actualize itself against the overall actualizing activity of the organism. Rather than differentiation within the organism, this activity would represent a bifurcation or splitting off from the organism. When this occurs the organism exists in what is therapeutically called a state of incongruence. Congruence can again be restored when that level is relativized from an end in itself to a waystation in the total organismic actualization process. This occurs in therapy where the entire process is re-directed into a forward, that is, differentiating direction. Thus in his view of man also, Rogers' basic intent appears to be to maintain the dynamic character of the growth process.

In a schematic, summarizing description, Rogers' view of man is characterized as a monistic geneticism.

Thereafter the chapter discusses the interpretative implications of Rogers' basic intent for his views in the various areas of human endeavor on which he has written. With reference to the cultural dilemma of his time, it is concluded that, while Rogers gives primacy to the individual over society, ultimately his reverence for growth is deeper than his respect for the individual. With respect to therapy it is shown that his later interpersonal view of therapy, with its emphasis on genuineness as the primary therapeutic condition, is a continuation and a richer expression of, rather than a departure from, his earlier client-centered and non-directive views. With respect to the therapeutic process it is shown why Rogers rejects the inducement of insight by means of interpretation. For him insight is only a partial solution to the more basic problem in therapy of re-directing the entire growth process of the client. Finally, it is shown how the self can gain control by relinquishing it. With respect to the outcome of therapy, it is shown that Rogers differs from other therapists in that he sees the goal of therapy as being growth rather than self-consistency.

Lastly, the chapter reviews some interpretations of Rogers found in the literature and it shows how, from out of his basic intent, it is incorrect to call him a (phenomenological) self theorist or a dialogical theorist. Rather, it shows that Rogers must be called a growth theorist.

Chapter Five: This chapter offers both internal and external criticism of Rogers' view of man in relation to his views on therapy, personality and interpersonal relations. It asserts first of all that Rogers advocates an actively receptive attitude to life. This entails basically an inter- and intra-personal receptivity to the process of growth. This receptivity results into a totally dynamic style of living which, because of its totalitarian character is labeled as "monistic". Hence it is argued that Rogers' view of man espouses a "monistic dynamism". The question is raised whether this style of living, which entails interpersonally that one person flows freely into another person, does not pose a threat to the uniqueness of individual persons.

Next, some cultural-historical reasons for Rogers' adherence to monistic dynamism are discussed.

Then follows an internal critique of Rogers' conception of man. It is questioned first of all whether the organismic actualization process is really as autonomous as Rogers makes it out to be. A second question is posed whether the dynamic, ongoing character of the process can really guarantee its unity.

It is shown first of all that the growth process, which Rogers believes man to be, needs realities other than itself to be able to function. Therefore, it is concluded that the process is not autonomous. Secondly, via a discussion of some basic inconsistencies in Rogers' view it becomes clear that his thought results inescapably into a conceptual impasse. In this manner it is demonstrated that the dynamic character of the process does not guarantee its unity.

Rogers' view of man stands and falls with the ongoing actualization of the organism at increasingly more complex levels of differentiation. Yet it is these very same levels which in their actualized state threaten to undo the process. The danger of this happening increases as more levels are being differentiated. Thus the very activity which serves to enhance the organism is also that which threatens it with destruction.

This impasse is most evident at the level of social regard and communication. Rogers believes that each person is capable of, and inherently focussed on his own self-realization, provided that the social conditions are facilitative rather than adverse. Under adverse social conditions the individual person develops internal incongruence, which is tantamount to a disruption of the actualization process. Thus the danger of disruption is greatest when persons contact each other. In view of that formulation the question is valid how it is possible that two or more inherently forwardly-directed individuals can disrupt each others' actualization process when they meet. To this question Rogers gives no satisfactory answer. Thus, it is concluded that his optimistic faith in the positive directedness of individuals is conceptually unfounded.

Next, two external critiques of Rogers' thought are discussed. One of them argues that Rogers has uncritically combined matters of a conceptually different order under the one common denominator of organismic actualization. The other shows that awareness is inherently selective and that therefore it cannot possibly be totally open to experience as Rogers advocates. These two external critiques lead to a discussion about the value and validity of external critique or evaluation in addition to empathic understanding. External evaluation is defined as critique that crosses anthropological intents. It is concluded that such criticism has self-illuminating value for the author whose views are being evaluated.

The consequences of Rogers' basic intent for therapy, personality and interpersonal relations are subsequently discussed. As to therapy, it is noted that the whole of Rogers' non-directive or client-centered approach is geared toward communicating basic trust in the client. It is questioned, however, whether as a result of this approach, the client actually experiences an increased trust in himself. It is argued instead that as a result of this approach he is more likely to experience a greater trust in the therapist. Secondly, it is one of Rogers' main contentions that once the therapeutic process is facilitated it runs its course autonomously. Thus, once the client is focussed on the expression of feelings he will spontaneously gain insight into himself and equally spontaneously act upon his insight. It is questioned, however, whether this process can occur spontaneously within the client. Instead, it is argued that the process needs the aid of the therapist's intervention every step of the way. Thus, therapy is described as a cooperative, rather than a facilitative event.

With respect to personality, the question is raised whether Rogers' basic intent for personal development does not neglect the positive influence of socialization on personality development. Finally, the chapter raises the question whether by substituting the term "interpersonal relations" for "interhuman relations" Rogers has not incorrectly extrapolated from (client-centered) therapy to life.

The chapter closes with an expression of the author's debt to Rogers as well as with a succint description of his difference from Rogers.

APPENDIX: A ROGERS GLOSSARY

This appendix contains a series of definition clusters, which represent the main constructs of Rogers' system as defined by Rogers himself. I have abbreviated some of the definitions, leaving out non-essential material for the purpose of greater clarity.

Rogers himself describes how he came to the definitions presented below. They are by no means arm chair definitions. Rather, each of them originated in clinical experience and research. Their characteristic development included clinical observation, initial conceptualization, initial crude research to test some of the hypotheses involved, further clinical observation, more rigorous formulation of the construct, together with its functional relations, more refined operational definitions of the construct, and finally more conclusive research (Koch, pp.95-212, Rogers and Kinget, pp.185-206).

A. Actualizing Tendency and Related Constructs

1. *actualizing tendency:* This is the inherent tendency of the organism to develop all its capacities in ways which serve to maintain or enhance the organism. It involves development toward the differentiation of organs and of functions, expansion in terms of growth, expansion of effectiveness through the use of tools, expansion and enhancement through reproduction. It is the development toward autonomy and away from heteronomy or control by external forces. It is the only motive postulated in the theoretical system. Only the organism as a whole exhibits this tendency. The self, for example, does not "do" anything. It is only one expression of the general tendency of the organism to behave in those ways which maintain and enhance itself.

2. *tendency toward self-actualization:* Following the development of the self-structure this general tendency toward actualization expresses itself also in the actualization of that portion of the experience of the organism which is symbolized in the self. If the self and the total experience of the organism are relatively congruent, then the actualizating tendency remains relatively unified. If they are incongruent, then the general tendency to actualize the organism may work at cross purposes with the sub-system of that motive, the tendency to actualize the self.

B. Experience and Related Constructs

3. *experience* (noun): It includes all that is going on within the envelope of the organism at any given moment which is potentially available to awareness. It is a psychological, not a physiological matter. It does not include neuron discharges or changes in blood sugar because these are not available to awareness. Synomyms are "experiential field" or "phenomenal field" (Snyggs and Combs). It covers more than the phenomena in consciousness. Earlier descriptions by Rogers were "sensory and visceral experiences", "organic experiences". This construct refers to an experience, the experience of the given moment, not to some accumulation of past experience.

4. *experience* (verb): To experience means to receive in the organism the impact of the sensory or physiological events which are happening at the moment. It is a process term often used in the phrase "to experience in awareness". This means to symbolize in some accurate form these sensory and visceral events at the conscious level.

5. *feeling, experiencing a feeling:* It denotes an emotionally tinged experience together with its personal meaning. It includes both the emotional and the cognitive content of the meaning of that emotion in its experiential context. It refers to the unity of emotion and cognition as they are experienced inseparably in the moment. It is a brief theme of experience, carrying with it the emotional coloring and the perceived meaning to the individual. When an individual *"experiences a feeling fully"* in the immediate present, he is then congruent in his experience (of the feeling), his awareness (of it), and his expression (of it).

C. Awareness and Related Constructs

6. *awareness, symbolization, consciousness:* These three terms are synonymous. Consciousness (awareness) is the symbolization of some of our experience. Awareness is the symbolic representation of some portion of our experience.

7. *availability to awareness:* When an experience can be symbolized freely, without defensive denial or distortion, then it is available to awareness.

8. *accurate symbolization:* The symbols which constitute our awareness do not necessarily correspond to the "real" experience or to "reality". Therefore, a distinction between accurate and inaccurate awareness is necessary. All perception (and awareness), is transactional, that is, it is a construction from our past experience and a hypothesis or prognosis for the future. These hypotheses can be checked. When a hypothesis implicit in awareness is borne out when tested by acting on it, it is accurately symbolized in awareness.

9. *perceive, perception:* A perception is a hypothesis or prognosis for action which comes into being in awareness when stimuli impinge on the organism. Perception and awareness are synonyms, perception being the narrower term, usually used when we wish to emphasize the importance of the stimulus in the process, and awareness is the broader term, covering symbolizations and meanings which arise from such purely internal stimuli as memory traces, visceral changes and the like, as well as from external stimuli.

10. *subceive, subception:* Subception is "a discrimination without awareness" (McLeary and Lazarus). It appears that the organism can discriminate a stimulus and its meaning for the organism without utilizing the higher nerve centers involved in awareness. It is this capacity which permits the individual to discriminate an experience as threatening, without symbolization in awareness of this threat.

D. Self and Related Constructs

11. *self-experience:* It is any event or entity in the phenomenal field discriminated by the individual which is also discriminated as "self", "me", "I", or related thereto. In general, self-experiences are the raw materials of which the organized self-concept is formed.

12. *self, concept of self, self-structure:* These terms refer to the organized, consistent conceptual gestalt composed of perceptions of the characteristics of the "I" or "me" and the perceptions of the relationships of the "I" or "me" to others and to various aspects of life, together with the values attached to these perceptions. The gestalt is available to awareness though not necessarily in awareness. It is a fluid changing gestalt, a process, but at any given moment it is a specific entity, at least partially definable in operational terms. The term self or self-concept is more likely to be used when talking about the person's view of himself, the term self-structure is used when we are looking at this gestalt from an external frame of reference.

13. *ideal self:* This is a term used to denote the self-concept which the individual would most like to possess, upon which he places the highest value for himself. In all other respects it is defined in the same way as the self-concept.

E. Incongruence and Related Constructs

14. *incongruence between self and experience:* Discrepancy develops between the self as perceived and the actual experience of the organism when the individual perceives himself as having characteristics of one kind, experiences feelings of another, and when an accurate symbolization of his experience would seem to call for yet other kinds of characteristics and feelings. When such discrepancy exists, the state is one of incongruence between self and experience. The manner in which this discrepancy develops is discussed in the theory of personality.

Incongruence is a state of tension and internal confusion, where in some respects the individual's behavior will be regulated by the actualizing tendency, and in other respects by the self-actualizing tendency, thus producing discordant or incomprehensible behaviors, as exemplified in neurotic behavior.

15. *vulnerability:* It refers to the potentiality of incongruence for creating psychological disorganization. When incongruence exists, and the individual is unaware of it, then he is potentially vulnerable to anxiety, threat and disorganization.

16. *anxiety:* Phenomenologically it is a state of uneasiness or tension whose cause is unknown. From an external point of view it is a state in which the incongruence between the self-concept and total experience of the individual is approaching symbolization in awareness. It is the response of the organism to the "subception", that such a discrepancy may enter awareness and thus force a change in the self-concept.

17. *threat:* Exists when an experience is perceived or anticipated (subceived) as incongruent with the structure of the self. It is anxiety as viewed from an external point of view.

18. *psychological maladjustment:* It exists when the organism denies to awareness, or distorts in awareness, significant experiences, which consequently are not accurately symbolized and organized into the gestalt of the self-structure, thus creating an incongruence between self and experience.

summary of constructs 14 - 18: If an individual is in a state of incongruence between self and experience and we are looking at him from an external point of view we see him as vulnerable (if he is unaware of the discrepancy), or threatened (if he has some awareness of it). If we view him from a social point of view then this incongruence is psychological maladjustment. If the individual is viewing himself, he may even see himself as adjusted (if he has no awareness of the discrepancy) or anxious (if he dimly subceives it) or threatened or disorganized (if the discrepancy has forced itself upon his awareness).

F. Response to Threat

19. *defense, defensiveness:* This is the behavioral response of the organism to threat, the goal of which is the maintenance of the current structure of the self. This goal is achieved by the perceptual distortion of the experience in awareness, in such a way as to reduce the incongruency between the experience and the structure of the self, or by the denial to awareness of an experience, thus denying any threat to the self.

20. *distortion in awareness, denial to awareness:* Material which is significantly inconsistent with the concept of self cannot be directly and freely admitted to awareness. When such an experience is subceived as being incongruent with the self, the organism appears to react with a distortion of the meaning of the experience (making it consistent with the self) or with a denial of the experience, in order to preserve the self structure from threat.

21. *intensionality:* If a person is reacting or perceiving in an intensional fashion, he tends to see experience in absolute and unconditional terms, to overgeneralize, to be dominated by concept or belief, to fail to anchor his reactions in space and time, to confuse fact and evaluation, to rely upon abstractions rather than upon reality-testing. The term covers the frequently used concept of rigidity, but includes a wider variety of behaviors than are generally thought of as constituting rigidity.

summary of constructs 19 - 21: These deal with the organism's response to threat. Defense is the most general term; distortion and denial are the mechanisms of defense; intensionality is a term which covers the characteristics of the behavior of the individual who is in a defensive state.

G. Congruence and Related Constructs

22. *congruence, congruence of self and experience:* This is a basic concept grown out of therapeutic experience, in which the individual appears to be revising his self-concept to bring it into congruence with his experience, accurately symbolized. During therapy an individual reorganizes the concept he holds of himself to include newly discovered characteristics of himself, which would previously have been inconsistent with self. When self-experiences are accurately symbolized, and are included in the self-concept in this accurately symbolized form, then the state is one of congruence of self and experience. If this were completely true of all self-experiences the individual would be a fully functioning person. If true only for some specific aspect of experience, such as the individual's experience in a given relationship or at a given moment, he is to that degree in a state of congruence. Terms generally synonymous with congruence are integrated, whole, genuine.

23. *openness to experience:* When the individual is in no way threatened then he is open to his experience. It is the polar opposite of defensiveness. The term may be used in regard to some area of experience or in regard to the total experience of the organism. It signifies that every stimulus originating within the organism or in the environment, is freely relayed through the nervous system, without being distorted or channeled off by any defensive mechanism. In such a state there is no need of the mechanism of "subception". In the hypothetical person, who is completely open to his experience, his concept of self would be a symbolization in awareness which would be completely congruent with his experience. There would, therefore, be no possibility of threat.

24. *psychological adjustment:* It exists optimally when the concept of the self is such that all experiences are or may be assimilated on a symbolic level into a gestalt of the self structure. Optimal psychological adjustment is thus synonymous with complete congruence of self and experience, or complete openness to experience.

25. *extensionality:* If a person is reacting or perceiving in an extensional manner he tends to see experience in limited, differentiated terms, to be aware of the space-time anchorage of facts, to be dominated by facts, not by concepts, to evaluate in multiple ways, to be aware of different levels of abstraction, to test his inferences and abstraction against reality.

26. *mature, maturity:* An individual exhibits mature behavior when he perceives realistically and in an extensional manner, is not defensive, accepts the responsibility of being different from others, accepts responsibility for his own behavior, evaluates experience in terms of the evidence coming from his own senses, changes his evaluation of experience only on the basis of new evidence, accepts others as unique individuals different from himself, prizes himself, and prizes others. (If his behavior has these characteristics, then there will automatically follow all the types of behavior which are more popularly thought of as constituting psychological maturity.)

summary of constructs 22 - 26: These form a cluster which grows out of the concept of congruence. Congruence is the term that defines the state. Openness to experience is the way an internally congruent individual meets new experience. Psychological adjustment is congruence as viewed from a social point of view. Extensional is the term which describes specific types of behavior of a congruent individual. Maturity is a broader term describing the personality characteristics and behavior of a person who is, in general, congruent.

H. Unconditional Positive Regard and Related Constructs

27. *contact:* Two persons are in psychological contact when each makes a perceived or subceived difference in the experiential field of the other. This is the *least* or minimum experience which could be called a relationship.

28. *positive regard:* If the perception by me of some self-experience in another makes a positive difference in my experiential field, then I am experiencing positive regard for that individual. In general it is defined as including such attitudes as warmth, liking, respect, sympathy and acceptance. To perceive oneself as receiving positive regard is to experience oneself as making a positive difference in the experiential field of another.

29. *need for positive regard:* This is a secondary or learned need, commonly developed in early infancy.

30. *unconditional positive regard:* If the self-experiences of another are experienced by me in such a way that no self-experience can be discriminated as more or less worthy of positive regard than any other, then I am experiencing unconditional positive regard for this individual. To perceive oneself as receiving unconditional positive regard is to perceive that of one's self-experiences none can be discriminated by the other individual as more or less worthy of positive regard. Unconditional positive regard means to accept, to "prize" (Dewey), to value a person, irrespective of the differential values which one might place on his specific behaviors. In general, acceptance and prizing are synonymous with unconditional positive regard.

31. *regard complex:* It is all those self-experiences, together with their interrelationships, which the individual discriminates as being related to the positive regard of a particular social other. This construct is intended to emphasize the gestalt nature of transactions involving positive or negative regard, and their potency. Thus, if one person shows positive regard to another person in relationship to a specific behavior, this tends to strengthen the whole pattern of positive regard previously experienced as coming from that person. Likewise, specific negative regard from this person tends to weaken the whole configuration of positive regard.

32. *positive self-regard:* This term denotes a positive regard satisfaction which has become associated with a particular self experience or a group of self experiences, in which this satisfaction is independent of positive regard transactions with social others. Though it appears that positive regard must first be experienced from others, this results in a positive attitude toward self which is no longer directly dependent on the attitudes of others. The individual, in effect, becomes his own significant social other.

33. *need for self-regard:* This is a secondary or learned need, related to the satisfaction of the need for positive regard by others.

34. *unconditional self-regard:* When an individual perceives himself in such a way that no self-experience can be discriminated as more or less worthy of positive regard than any other, then he is experiencing unconditional positive self-regard.

I. Conditions of Worth

35. *conditions of worth:* The self-structure is characterized by a condition of worth when a self-experience or set of related self-experiences is either avoided or sought solely because the individual discriminates it as being less or more worthy of self-regard. An older name for this construct was "introjected value". A condition of worth arises when the positive regard of a significant other is conditional, when the individual feels that in some respects he is prized and in others not. Gradually this same attitude is assimilated into his own self-regard complex, and he values an experience positively or negatively solely because of these conditions of worth which he has taken over from others, not because of the experience enhances or fails to enhance his organism. When a value is "introjected" from a significant other, then a condition of worth is applied to an experience quite without reference to the extent in which it maintains or enhances the organism. This is a specific instance of inaccurate symbolization where the individual is valuing an experience positively or negatively, *as if* in relation to the criterion of the actualizing tendency, but not actually in relation to it. An experience may be perceived as organismically satisfying, when in fact this is not true. Thus a condition of worth, because it disturbs the valuing process, prevents the individual from functioning freely and with maximum effectiveness.

J. Constructs Related to Valuing

36. *locus of evaluation:* This term is used to indicate the source of evidence as to values. Thus an internal locus of evaluation, within the individual himself, means that he is the center of the valuing process, the evidence being supplied by his own senses. When the locus of evaluation resides in others, their judgment as to the value of an object or experience becomes the criterion of value for the individual.

37. *organismic valuing process:* This concept describes an ongoing process in which values are never fixed or rigid, but experiences are being accurately symbolized and continually and freshly valued in terms of the satisfactions organismically experienced; the organism experiences satisfaction in those stimuli or behaviors which maintain and enhance the organism and the self, both in the immediate present and in the long range. The actualizing tendency is thus the criterion.

K. Constructs Related to the Source of Knowledge

38. *internal frame of reference:* This is all of the realm of experience which is available to the awareness of the individual at a given moment. It includes the full range of sensations, perceptions, meanings and memories, which are available to consciousness. The internal frame of reference is the subjective world of the individual. Only he knows it fully. It can never be known to another except through empathic inference and then can never be perfectly known.

39. *empathy:* The state of empathy, or being empathic, is to perceive the internal frame of reference of another with accuracy, and with the emotional components and meanings which pertain thereto, as if one were the other person; but without ever losing the "as if" condition. Thus it means to sense the hurt or the pleasure of another as he senses it, and to perceive the causes thereof as he perceives them, but without ever losing the recognition that it is *as if* I were hurt or pleased, etc. If this "as if" quality is lost, then the state is one of identification.

40. *external frame of reference:* To perceive solely from one's own subjective internal frame of reference without empathizing with the observed person or object, is to perceive from an external frame of reference. We generally regard all "objects" (stones, trees, or abstractions) from this external frame of reference since we assume that they have no "experience" with which we can empathize. The other side of this coin is that anything perceived from an external frame of reference (whether an inanimate thing, an animal, or a person) becomes for us an "object" because no empathic inferences are made.

Notes on Chapter One

1. See "Some Issues Concerning the Control of Human Behavior: A Symposium", Carl R. Rogers and B.F. Skinner, in R.I. Evans, *Carl Rogers, The Man and His Ideas,* (1975), p.xliv. Certainly no two persons represent therapeutic viewpoints more opposed to each other than Rogers and Skinner.
2. C.R. Rogers, *On Becoming a Person,* (1961), p.26.
3. In that repect Rogers' reaction to my description of his views has been overwhelmingly positive.

Notes on Chapter Two

1. R.I. Evans (ed.), *Carl Rogers, The Man and His Ideas,* (1975), p.124 (emphasis added).
2. E.G. Boring, G. Lindzey, *A History of Psychology in Autobiography,* Vol. 5, (1967), pp.343-383. The bulk of the autobiographical data was taken from this article. In view of the fact that the events in this article are presented in a time sequence, and my account of them in this chapter utilizes the headings which Rogers uses in this article, I will not make page reference to the article, except when it involves quotes, or data not found under these headings. In the latter case, page reference will be given in the text, directly following the quote.
Other principal sources consulted for biographical data are the following: C.R. Rogers, *On Becoming a Person,* (1961), pp.3-27; C.R. Rogers, "My Philosophy of Interpersonal Relationships and How It Grew", *Journal of Humanistic Psychology,* Vol. 13, No.2, Spring 1973, pp.3-15; H.E. Rogers, "A Wife's View of Carl Rogers", *Voices,* Vol. 1, 1965, pp.93-98, and R.I. Evans, *op.cit.* Beyond these sources, there are the many

personal remarks made by Rogers throughout his writings. Specific references will be given for all data obtained from sources other than the above-mentioned article in Boring and Lindzey's book.

3. "Fundamentalism versus Liberalism" refers to a heated controversy which arose in American Protestantism towards the end of the nineteenth century regarding the nature and extent of biblical authority in human life. Liberalism sought to reinterpret the traditional Protestant interpretation of the biblical message, to make it more compatible with the intellectual climate of the day. The latter had become moulded by the discoveries of modern science, the theory of evolution and Pragmatism. Fundamentalism, on the other hand, made an issue of what as a matter of unconscious tradition had been the interpretation of Protestantism in the past, by insisting on the verbal inspiration and inerrancy of the entire bible. It furthermore sought to gauge the authenticity of a person's belief in the bible in terms of his adherence to a number of "fundamentals" which it had distilled from the bible as presumably its central doctrines. Such fundamentals included, among others, the creation as having occurred in six twenty-four-hour days, original sin, and the virgin birth of Christ. Each of these fundamentals were put forward in reaction to specific views that were dominant in the American culture at large, and which came to theological expression in the writings of Liberalists. In terms of life style, this controversy meant that the Fundamentalists were the conservatives of Protestantism who attempted to retain the evangelical style of life of the early nineteenth century, when Protestantism had its heyday. The Liberalists, in turn, so thoroughly adapted their life style to the existing cultural climate as to become practically indistinguishable from it by the early part of the twentieth century. W.S. Hudson, *American Protestantism*, (1961), pp.143-149.

4. C.R. Rogers, "My Philosophy of Interpersonal Relationships and How it Grew", *Journal of Humanistic Psychology*, Vol. 13, (1973), p.3.

5. R.I. Evans, *op.cit.*, p.142.

6. This simultaneous appreciation for and experimental tinkering with "nature", is a familiar theme in the American experience. Pragmatism, particularly in the person of John Dewey, was instrumental in making this pattern *a way of life for* Americans.

7. W.S. Hudson, *American Protestantism*, (1961), p.113.

8. *Ibid.*

9. *Ibid.*

10. *Ibid.*

11. *Ibid.*, p.117.

12. *Ibid.*, p.110, p.135.

13. *Ibid.*, p.109.

14. *Ibid.*, p.128.

15. *Ibid.*, p.114.

16. *Ibid.*, p.123.

17. *Ibid.*, p.118.

18. W.S. Hudson, *Religion in America*, (1965), p.359.
19. W.S. Hudson, *American Protestantism*, (1961), p.149.
20. R.I. Evans, *op.cit.*, p.73.
21. W.S. Hudson, *American Protestantism*, (1961), p.141.
22. *Ibid.*, p.138.
23. *Ibid.*, p.118.
24. R.I. Evans, *op.cit.*, p.XXX.
25. H. Hart, *Communal Certainty and Authorized Truth*, (1966), p.8ff.
26. For a full discussion on this problem see: R.L. Rapson, (ed.), *Individualism and Conformity in the American Character*, (1967).
27. W.S. Hudson, *American Protestantism*, (1961), p.18.
28. *Ibid.*, p.64ff., p.99.
29. *Ibid.*, p.95.
30. John Dewey, *Reconstruction in Philosophy*, Enlarged Edition, (1963), p.187.
31. See: D.M. Potter, "The Quest for the National Character", in R.L. Rapson (ed.), *Individualism and Conformity in the American Character*, (1967), p.69.
32. See S.M. Lipset, "The Unchanging American Character", *op. cit.*, pp. 87,90.
33. *Op.cit.*, pp.90,91.
34. See: D.M. Potter, *op.cit.*, p.71. See also S.M. Lipset, *op.cit.*, pp.92,93.
35. See: D.M. Potter, *op.cit.*, p.70.
36. *Ibid.*, p.63.
37. *Ibid.*, pp.60-62, p.67.
38. *Ibid.*, p. 73.
39. *Ibid.*, p.64, p.73.
40. A. de Tocqueville, *Democracy in America*, Vol. II, (1845), pp.104-108.
41. J. Bryce, *The American Commonwealth*, Vol. 2, (1893), pp.344-353.
42. D. Riesman, "From Morality to Morale", in H. Stanton and S. Perry, (eds.), *Personality and Political Crisis*, (1951), pp.81-89.
43. J. Bernstein (ed.), *On Experience Nature and Freedom, Representive Selections, John Dewey*, (1960), p.286. John Dewey, *Experience and Nature*, (1958), p.217.
44. R.J. Bernstein, *op.cit..*, p.242. John Dewey, *Reconstruction in Philosophy*, (1963), pp.114-116.
45. John Dewey, *ibid.*, Chapter 4. John Dewey, *Human Nature and Conduct, An Introduction to Social Psychology*, (1957), p.295ff.
46. John Dewey, *Experience and Nature*, (1958), p.262.
47. R.J. Bernstein, *op.cit.*, p.91.
48. John Dewey, *The Influence of Darwin on Philosophy, and other Essays in Contemporary Thought*, (1965), pp.1-19.
49. R.J. Bernstein, *op.cit.*, p.XII, p.237. John Dewey, *Experience and Nature*, (1958), p.275.
50. *Ibid.*, pp.252-262,271-272,277-278,285.
51. John Dewey, *Reconstruction in Philosophy*, (1963), p.186.

52. R.J. Bernstein, *op.cit.* See the discussion on Liberalism in chapter 13. R.L. Rapson, *op.cit.*, p.56.
53. R.J. Bernstein, *op.cit.*, chapter 11, also pp.236-240.
54. *Ibid.*, see introduction p.XIV.
55. That this is by no means an imaginary problem has recently been dramatically documented by Alvin Tofler in his book, *Future Shock*, (1970). The pervasiveness of this issue currently in the North American mind is indicated by the fact that in the relatively short time span of five years, the book went through close to 20 printings!
56. R.J. Bernstein, *op.cit.*, p.XXI.
57. In a letter to me Rogers has stated, ". . .personally I have read relatively little of Dewey's work and most of my knowledge of his thinking comes from my contact with Kilpatrick. I suspect that you were right, however, in saying that the whole cultural context was strongly influenced by Dewey and that, in that way, I did become acquainted with his views and his philosopy . . .my relation to pragmatism is almost entirely unconscious".
58. R.J. Bernstein, *op.cit.*, p.XXII.
59. W. Boyd, *The History of Western Education*, (1961), p.415.
60. L. Idomir, *An Analysis of the Philosophical Compatability of Carl Rogers' Client-Centered Counseling and John Dewey's Pragmatism*, (1967).
61. C.R. Rogers, *On Becoming a Person*, (1961), p.398.
62. J. Linschoten, *Op Weg Naar een Fenomenologische Psychologie*, (1959), p.232.
63. John Dewey, *Reconstruction in Philosophy*, (1963), pp.148,156.
64. There are other views of therapy possible. Richard Farson (in R.I. Evans, *op.cit.*, p.XXXIX) deplores the preoccupation with such a pragmatic, utilitarian question about therapy as "Does it work?". He claims that all brands of therapy "work", but that none "show much permanent change". Rather, he seems to suggest that therapy is worthwhile simply because it is an instance of a human relationship where two people relate to each other meaningfully, and that to ask therapy to be "effective" is to ask more of it than it can deliver. In the pragmatistic view, therapy is still a means to an end. In Farson's view, therapy *is* the end. It is an example of what all interpersonal relations ought to be.
65. R.A. Harper, *Psychoanalysis and Psychotherapy*, (1959), p.156.
66. Riverside Press, Cambridge, Mass., (1939).
67. Throughout his writings, Rogers always presents his views as tentative formulations that are subject to change. As we shall see more fully in chapter 2, this attitude toward his own position is fully consistent with his view of life as a fluid process, and his view of "ideal" man as a fully functioning person. It is characteristic of Rogers that he strives to practice what he preaches.
68. I am not suggesting that this change in his thinking, at this point in his career, represented a total rejection of therapeutic techniques in favor of "something" else (non-directivity or client-centeredness). Rogers' writings show that for quite some time after this turnabout, he referred to his

newly developed approach as a set of (non-directive) "techniques". Rather, this turnabout represented a change in the *direction* of his thinking, away from a pragmatistic approach to therapy and towards a non-directive (later client-centered) approach.

69. R.A. Harper, *op.cit.*, pp.53-54.
70. Houghton Mifflin publishers, U.S.A.
71. R.I. Evans, *op.cit.*, p.XXVIII.
The phrase was used by Richard Farson in the article quoted above. Apparently, Rogers himself first referred to himself as such during an encounter group which was filmed and is available under the title of "Because That's My Way". In speaking to a radical leftist in the group, who stressed the fact that he was a revolutionary, Rogers responded by saying that he too was a revolutionary, but then a quiet one. (Personal communication by Rogers).

Notes on Chapter Three

1. R.A. Harper, *Psychoanalysis and Psychotherapy,* (1959), p.84.
2. C.R. Rogers, " A Theory of Therapy, Personality and Interpersonal Relations", in S. Koch (ed.), *Psychology: A Study of a Science,* Vol. 3, (1959), p.191. See also C.R. Rogers, *Client-Centered Therapy,* (1951), p.17.
3. The following quotation illustrates just how "primary" experience is for Rogers:
   Experience is, for me, the highest authority. The touchstone of validity is my own experience. No other person's ideas, and none of my own ideas, are as authoritative as my experience. It is to experience that I must return again and again, to discover a closer approximation to truth as it is in the process of becoming in me. Neither the Bible nor the prophets — neither Freud nor research — neither the revelations of God nor man — can take precedence over my own direct experience. *On Becoming a Person,* (1961), p.23.
4. For a precise description of the meaning content of Rogers' terminology in all three areas discussed in this chapter, the reader is referred to the Rogers' glossary appended to the end of the book. Its content was obtained from S. Koch, *op.cit.,* pp.194-212, C.R. Rogers and G.M. Kinget, *Psychotherapie en Menselijke Verhoudingen,* (1974), pp. 185-206.
5. These were taken from *On Becoming A Person,* (1961), pp.37,66.
6. This term is taken from E.T. Gendlin, "A Theory of Personality Change", in P. Worschel and D. Byrne (eds.), *Personality Change,* (1964), p.129.
7. Taken from S. Koch, *op.cit.,* pp.221-234.
8. Taken from C.R. Rogers, *On Becoming A Person,* (1961), pp.279-297.
9. *Ibid.,* chapters 17 and 18.
10. Throughout the chapter I will use the general term "therapy" wherever possible rather than the more specific term "psychotherapy" or "counseling" to designate the helping, healing process under discussion. Related terms like "therapist", "client", "counselor", "counselee", must

likewise be understood to refer to the helper and the helpee first of all. The word "psychotherapy" has the connotation of "healing or helping the psyche", and I feel that this phrase is not broad enough to cover the changes that occur in client-centered therapy. Likewise, the term "counseling" seems to me to be a misnomer for client-centered therapy, since it popularly has the connotation of "advice giving", an activity that goes contrary to the very essence of client-centered therapy. Rogers himself is much less precise on this, and uses the terms "psychotherapy", "counseling", "client-centered therapy", or just "therapy" interchangeably throughout his writings.

11. The dictionary definition of this term of "self-governing", or "without outside control" in intended here. The autonomy of this process ultimately holds for the client as well as the therapist. See *Client-Centered Therapy,* p.117.

12. See *Counseling and Psychotherapy,* pp.127,128,216; *Client-Centered Therapy,* p.64. This therapeutic process is but one instance of a general organismic process of actualization found in every human being *(ibid.,* p.488). See also definition 1 in the Rogers glossary appended to this book.

13. Beginning here and throughout the rest of this chapter I will adopt the practice of making page references directly in the text whenever it is clear from the context to which of Rogers' publications I am referring as our source of evidence. The interpretation of these page references is as follows. Immediately following the notes on this chapter there is a list of all of Rogers' publications that were explicitly cited in this chapter. Each publication will be given a letter, depending on its place in the order of publications. The page references in the text will always cite both the publication letter and the page reference itself. Thus a citation referring to page 60 of *The Clinical Treatment of the Problem Child* will be recorded as (a, p.60) in the text. A reference to page 12 of *Counseling and Psychotherapy* will be recorded as (b, p.12), etc.

14. C.R. Rogers, "The Necessary and Sufficient Conditions of Therapeutic Personality Change", *Journal of Consulting Psychology,* 1957, Vol. 21, p.102.

15. S. Koch, *op.cit.,* p.221. See also *Client-Centered Therapy,* p.490.

16. C.R. Rogers, "Some Observations on the Organization of Personality", in A.E. Kuenzli (ed.), *The Phenomenological Problem,* (1959), pp.57-59.

17. D. Snyggs and A.W. Combs, *Individual Behavior: A New Frame of Reference for Psychology,* (1949).

18. *Ibid.,* pp.49-74. See also A.W. Combs, "Phenomenological Concepts in Non-Directive Therapy", *Journal of Consulting Psychology,* Vol. 12, No. 4, July-August, 1948, pp. 197-207.

19. S. Koch, *op.cit.,* pp.210-212.

20. *Ibid.,* p.218, p.236.

21. C.R. Rogers, "The Necessary and Sufficient Conditions of Therapeutic Personality Change".

22. C.R. Rogers, *On Becoming a Person,* (1961), pp.16,33,50,61.

23. C.R. Rogers, *Client-Centered Therapy,* (1951), p.97.
24. *Ibid.,* p.514.
25. C.R. Rogers, *Freedom to Learn,* (1959), p.285.
26. *Ibid.,* p.286.
27. *Ibid.,* pp.287-288.
28. S. Koch, *op.cit.,* pp.212-220.
29. C.R. Rogers, *On Becoming A Person,* (1961), pp.37-38.
30. *Ibid.,* p.66.
31. Rogers, *Client-Centered Therapy,* (1951), pp.483-524.
32. S. Koch, *op.cit.,* pp.221-231.
33. *Ibid.,* p.234.
34. *Ibid.,* p.235; *Freedom To Learn,* (1969), p.295.
35. C.R. Rogers, *Freedom To Learn,* (1969), p.295.
36. *Ibid.,* pp.279-297.
37. C.R. Rogers, *On Becoming A Person,* (1961), p.123.
38. *Ibid.,* pp.329-338.
39. *Ibid.,* pp.338-346.
40. It should be noted that Rogers makes these remarks regarding the personal perception of congruent persons in the context of a discussion on the relationship. We should not interpret him to be saying that congruent persons are generally incapable of expressing such common facts as ''it rains'', for this would mean that he adheres to a perceptual solipsism. Such a position is not in keeping with Rogers' overall view.

   Rogers does indeed hold that at best we can attain only a *perception* of reality (*Client-Centered Therapy,* p.484). Furthermore, lately he seems to be moving toward the view that there are as many realities as there are persons (personal communication by Rogers). At the same time, however, he also stresses the fact that there exists a high degree of commonality between many of the personal perceptions of various individuals (*Client-Centered Therapy,* p.485).
41. C.R. Rogers, *Counseling and Psychotherapy* (1942), p.84.
42. S. Koch, *op.cit.,* p.236.
43. See *On Becoming A Person,* pp.33-35, p.66, pp.39-40.
44. *Ibid.,* p.339.
45. S. Koch, *op.cit.,* p.240.
46. C.R. Rogers, *Carl Rogers on Encounter Groups,* (1970), p.118.
47. C.R. Rogers, *Client-Centered Therapy,* (1951), pp.208-209.
48. See note 22.
49. C.R. Rogers, *Freedom to Learn,* (1969), p.108, p.126.
50. C.R. Rogers, *The Clinical Treatment of The Problem Child,* (1939), pp.8,173,180,274,356.
51. C.R. Rogers, *Freedom to Learn,* (1969), p.230.
52. C.R. Rogers, *Client-Centered Therapy,* (1951), p.500.
53. C.R. Rogers, *On Becoming a Person,* (1961), p.26. Here Rogers argues that ''what is most personal is most general''.

Major Works by Rogers
(cited in chapter three by letter notations, see note 13)

a. *The Clinical Treatment of the Problem Child*
b. *Counseling and Psychotherapy*
c. *Client-Centered Therapy*
d. "The Necessary and Sufficient Conditions of Therapeutic Personality Change"
e. "A Theory of Therapy, Personality and Interpersonal Relations", in S. Koch, *Psychology: A Study of a Science*
f. *On Becoming a Person*
g. *Person to Person*
h. *Freedom to Learn*
i. *Carl Rogers on Encounter Groups*
j. *Carl Rogers The Man and His Ideas*
k. *Carl Rogers on Personal Power*

Notes on Chapter Four

1. "Understanding" as used in this context is obviously a loaded term, which, because of its centrality, is almost impossible to define. I thought of other terms such as "perspective", "focus" or "direction", none of which I feel is an improvement over "understanding". In the final analysis all of these terms do no more than point to the contents of this chapter. Their integrating function for human thought and action is a matter that is open to discussion, however, and serves as the central hypothesis on my part to be demonstrated by the contents of this chapter.

2. It may help to clarify my intention in this chapter if I briefly describe how I came to see the need for a "view of man". In studying Rogers' views on how individual persons relate to one another, and on how one individual person can both acquire and resolve his personal problems through contact with another, I keenly felt the need for a unifying perspective, in terms of which each of these could make sense in their interrelatedness. I could, of course, have argued that each has its own organization principle, since they all deal with uniquely different areas of experience. However, this would hardly do in Rogers' case, who, perhaps more than anyone, stresses the organic unity of life. My solution might, instead, have been to take his views in one area as determinitive and explain the others in terms of it. Thus, for example, I could have explained the whole of Rogers' thought in terms of his view of personality. The consequence of this approach, I felt was that not enough justice would have been done to the other aspects of his thought. Thus I came to treating his "view of man" as a separate category, which was understood to comprise, and be more than, his views on human functioning in the three areas mentioned above. Hence, the part-whole terminology.

3. C.R. Rogers, "The Nature of Man", in *Pastoral Psychology,* (1960), pp.23-26.
   C.R. Rogers, *On Becoming a Person,* (1961), p.105, p.194.
4. Michael Polanyi, *Personal Knowledge, Towards a Post-Critical Philosophy,* (1964), p.x.
5. By this I do not mean to suggest that one does best to refrain from explicating one's anthropology, as if anthropology loses some of its value if it can be clearly articulated. On the contrary, there are definite times when a preoccupation with, and a reflection on, our view of man is called for. These are the occasions when our own actions or our confrontations with others drive us to reflect on the view of man to which we adhere. All I am arguing here is that whenever one is preoccupied with something other than one's view of man, the latter is nevertheless supportively present, albeit tacitly so.
6. This raises the question as to which version of his view of man is described in this chapter. My answer would be that it is the latest view of which I am aware. This answer is not nearly as problematic as it may first seem to be, because it does not imply that his earlier views are therefore to be ignored. Rogers himself sees his later formulations as better descriptions of his basic intent than his earlier formulations. In that sense his earlier views are included in his later views. As we will see later, this inclusion is implied in his anthropology itself. That is to say, his later writings deal more comprehensively with human functioning than do his earlier writings. To give but one obvious example: interpersonal relations, which he discusses in his later writings, presuppose personal development which he discusses in his earlier writings.
7. To me this is a rather important point. It refers to what I stated earlier in II B of chapter one regarding a Rogerian description of Rogers' views. For that reason it was encouraging that Rogers has responded to an earlier version of this chapter by saying that, as far as he was concerned, I had been able to "indwell" in his work to the point where, in his words, "you understand a number of aspects of it better than I do". He further stated that he felt "edified" and "clarified" by it, rather than "dissected". As far as I can see, the important question in this chapter is not whether Rogers' anthropology shows an adequate understanding of man, but whether my description shows that I have adequately understood his anthropology. For the answer to that question I believe I do well to listen to Rogers himself, since it safeguards me from misrepresenting his intentions and allows me to learn more deeply from his insights.

   However, all this presupposes that Rogers' anthropology is understandable and describable. The extent to which it is depends on the integrative power of his anthropology, which, although it is considerable, is not total. For that reason it is equally important to me that I should also report the tensions and ambiguities that are genuinely attributable to his anthropology.
8. "Leading" as I understand it, is a term that originated in counseling,

where the counselor expresses a statement that slightly anticipates the client's train of thought. Its function is to explicate what is implied in the client's verbalizations. As such it involves the use of the counselor's own frame of reference, but is less directive than a direct interpretation, in that it means to stay within the client's frame of reference. See also A.F. Benjamin, *The Helping Interview*, (1969), Chapter 7; and L.M. Brammer, *The Helping Relationship*, (1973), p.87-90.

9. E.T. Gendlin, "A Theory of Personality Change", in Ph. Worchel and D. Byrne, (eds.), *Personality Change*, (1964), pp.100-148.

10. Behavior is active in the sense that the organism determines what in the environment is a stimulus for itself, and free in the sense that it only responds to the environment so perceived.

11. The inferential character of many of my conclusions in this chapter requires that I do more than refer to Rogers' writings as a source of evidence for my assertions. For this reason, I will adopt the practice of supplementing my quotation from his writings with explanations of how I came to my conclusions on the basis of these quotations, wherever the text itself does not already do so.

12. C.R. Rogers, *Client-Centered Therapy*, (1951), pp.487-488.

13. C.R. Rogers, "The Actualizing Tendency in Relation to Motives and to Consciousness", *Nebraska Symposium on Motivation*, (1963), p.3.

14. *Ibid.*, p.5. Here Rogers states ". . . the organism is an active *initiator*, and exhibits a directional tendency" (italics added). I take the term "initiator" to mean that the activity *originates* in the organism, and is not the product of, does not "emerge" out of physical processes, as Dewey has argued (J. Dewey, *Experience and Nature*, [1958], pp.253-256). Rather Rogers' thinking *starts* with the organism as an active process. Here, I believe, we have the basic source of difference between Rogers and Dewey, who in many other respects have so much in common. That Rogers starts with the organism, whereas Dewey does not, is the basic reason why Rogers sees man's interactive functioning (see later) as an event that is *internal* to the organism, whereas Dewey sees it as an event occuring between the organism and its environment *(op.cit.)* pp.272-273, 282-286).

15. See Glossary, definition 1, in the appendix. See also *On Becoming a Person*, p.27, where Rogers states: "Life, at its best, is a flowing, changing process in which nothing is fixed."

16. *Client-Centered Therapy*, p.486. See also Glossary definition 1. In a comment on this definition in S. Koch (ed.), *Psychology: A Study of A Science*, Vol. 3, (1959) (henceforth referred to as *Koch*) on p.196, Rogers states:

> The self does not "do" anything. It is only one expression of the general tendency of the organism to behave in those ways which maintain and enhance itself.

Thus the organism is the initiator, "originally" (see note 14), but also after it has differentiated into a "self".

17. My term "organismic actualizing process" needs further clarification. In using it I define man as an organized *activity*. This manner of speaking differs from Rogers' usual way of speaking about man as an active *organism*. The difference between Rogers' formulation and mine is merely a difference in mode of speech, however, and not one of meaning. Both formulations refer to the same organized event, or active entity. As far as I know Rogers never defines the term organism. This probably because it is nothing in itself. In itself it is "empty". The organism is an "x" that is wholly defined by "what it is up to", by its actualizing activity. If we define the organism as something in itself, apart from its actualizing activity, then with Wijngaarden *(Over Het Onbewuste,* [1958] p.7) we may be justifiably puzzled over what an organism, so defined, might possibly be. Thus I consider it more in line with Rogers' *intent* to refer to man as an organismic actualizing process, rather than an organism that actualizes itself.

18. At this point a long explanatory note is probably necessary or else the reader will, like myself, time and again find himself puzzled at what Rogers is saying. The key difficulty in understanding Rogers is that he views human life as an absolute flux or flow in which nothing is ever fixed. Time and again one wants to find a fixed point in terms of which to explain the flow, the changingness, or the process, but there is none. The only thing that is "fixed", if we can say this, is flow itself. *It* explains all its "fixed points" in terms of itself, negatively, as not-in-flux, and therefore not part of human life.

Or to put it another way: Time and again one wants to know who or what is responsible for all this changingness. Who or what is the integration point of all this activity? The Behaviorists have their stimulus, the Gestaltists their gestalts, the Freudians their id, ego, and superego, but what about Rogers? It seems at times that he provides us with an integrative point in the organism, the self, the relationship, or the direction of the flow. But the organism is itself a *dynamic* principle, itself always already *in flux.* The self does have some regulative power but it is an aspect of the organismic actualization process and functions best when it changes continually and relinquishes its regulative power to the organismic flow. The relationship is necessary for individual change to occur but then only insofar as it is an *inter-personal* relationship, thus only insofar as it throws the flow change back upon itself. Anything else is interference with, rather than facilitation of, individual change. Thus flow can only be negatively explained in terms of the relationship. Finally, the forward direction of the flow cannot be its point of integration either because it is a characteristic *of* the flow. The flow does not occur to keep the direction going forward (that is to say, man does not change to attain more and more complexity) but the direction is forward to guarantee perpetual flow. (That is to say, man keeps on differentiating to keep from becoming fixed into a structure). Behind every integration point flow or change, or process keeps cropping up as a more primary, more comprehensive or more central reality.

If an anthropology is a view of man then Rogers' view is that man *is* change, and if one's anthropology is the integrator of all one's diverse experiences then for Rogers change is that integrator. It is the point of unity in all intra- and inter-human diversity.

Such a view has vast implications. It means that man is not a structure but a process. It means, for example, that personality structure is an aspect or function of personality change. It means that human identity is an aspect or function of human change. It means that man is not a diversity but a process of diversification. It means that his parts or aspects are diversifications (ways of becoming different rather than ways of being different). It means that what we usually understand as being aspects or parts or dimensions of the structure of man, such as experience, consciousness, self, relationships, etc. are to be understood as levels of diversification, mere points marking the direction of the flow. When these become more than points they become disruptive of the flow that man is. The important factor in human life is rather the activity that occurs *between* them.

The physiological is not important, and experience is not important, but the *change,* the differentiation of the physiological *into* experience, the differentiation of experience into awareness, etc., that is the important factor of human life. Change, not structure, is of the essence of man. It is what unifies human life. Structure is what pulls it apart. If change or flow could do without these qualitatively different structural points, it would. But since it can't, it will tolerate them, but only as points, as levels of differentiation, and no more than that. If these points were, for example, to become established structures which would dictate the pace, the extent and the direction of the flow, then this would be a great cause for alarm, since it would represent a disruption of the free flow that man is and thus it would thereby attack his central unity. Change must go on continuously for the organism to remain unified.

Finally, if the primary aim is not greater complexity, but rather to keep the whole of man in perpetual flux, then perpetually new opportunities for change would also seem to be required. Differentiation in the direction of greater complexity is necessary for change to occur. However, it could conceivably arrive at a point where one was *fully differentiated and thus the need for change would be eliminated. To offset that possibility Rogers includes the perpetual assimilation of new opportunities for change into the flow. It makes human functioning interactive.* Thus in every way Rogers' anthropology seeks to guarantee the perpetuity of this process of change which is the central characteristic of man.

In the above description I have gone on at length to give the reader a "feel" for Rogers' anthropology. It does not eliminate the ambiguities and tensions that are part of Rogers' view, but I hope it has given the reader some added insight into the *basic intent* of Rogers.

19. In *Client-Centered Therapy*, p.486ff., Rogers argues that organic life has a "... tendency towards total, organized goal directed responses", and that

"This is true of those responses which are primarily physiological, as well as of those which we think of as psychological." Thus, he rejects atomistic explanations and states further that ". . . the organism is at all times a total organized system, in which *alteration* of any *part* may produce *changes in any other part*" (italics added). This suggests that *internal to* its organization, its parts change, or that as we prefer to say it, the change that occurs is always total, organized change. This "organized change" is characteristic for organismic functioning at the level of least complexity (physiological) and also at levels of greater complexity (psychological).

20. For Rogers, man *is* growth, process, and change. This is man's *nature*. What this means for the present discussion is rather complicated and I am not sure that I can completely follow Rogers here. However, given Rogers' view in this regard, I would have to say that anything "within" the original unity that does not show this fluid changing character comes from the outside and has been "added to" it (see C.R. Rogers, *Personal Power*, p.247). This holds for the potentials it contains and also for the "parts" or "aspects" that differentiate "out of" it. Potentials are only possibilities of further differentiation. Perhaps it is best to say that the organism has only *one* potential, i.e. to change perpetually (like it also has one motive). Likewise "parts" or "aspects" are not potentially or actually pre-existing entities in terms of which differentiation can run its course but rather potential or actual manifestations of man's changing nature. They are stages of growth, increasingly complex levels of differentiation. They are "bits of process", "way-stations", "stopovers" of the changing process that man is.

For example, the first differentiation to be made is experience. When it is made, the fact *that* it is made is important because it shows that the organism has realized its potential to differentiate, and because it allows the organism to realize its potential for differentiation further in awareness. However, the fact that this first differentiation happens to be *experience* is much less important. Its peculiar character is only important insofar as it aids man to further differentiate, and thus to further live out his nature.

Finally, differentiation, change, growth always enhances and maintains man's organism because it is the expression of man's nature. Man is an active principle of diversification and his "parts" are not diversities but diversifications. Hence by diversifying, man is becoming what he is.

21. This question has to do with the relation of the parts to the whole, and to each other. In *Client-Centered Therapy*, p.488, Rogers states: "The organism actualizes itself in the direction of greater differentiation of organs and of function. It moves in the direction of . . . expansion . . . of greater independence . . . of socialization . . ." This quotation suggests to me that the "parts" relate to the whole as differentiations (function) which are then assimilated by the organism *as* its "parts" (organs).

The key point here, however, is that if, as I argue, the organism is primarily an activity, a process rather than an entity then both "function" and "organs" must be taken as such as well. Thus "functions" must be taken as man's differentiating activity and "organs" as man's integrating, assimilating activity, which together make up the actualization process through which the organism "expands". The business of actualizing is thus a matter of ongoing differentiating and integrating at increasingly higher, that is more complex, levels of functioning, by which the organism expands its sphere of activity.

The matters of differentiation and assimilation are not restricted, in Rogers' view, to what we usually designate as the "biological" or "physiological" organism. To use my terminology: differentiation and assimilation do not only occur at the level of organic or physiological need fulfillment but are operative at other levels of differentiation as well. The development of the self for instance is described as "differentiation" (*Koch,* p.223), and assimilation is most explicitly described by Rogers with reference to the assimilation of "experience into awareness or the self-concept". (*Koch,* p.206).

22. Considering what I said in the above footnote it should be clear that the function of this assimilation is to keep the differentiating process going. The material actualized "earlier" is dynamic material. It is the actualized manifestation of man's changing nature. Hence its incorporation serves to make the latest level of differentiation complexity differentiate further, thereby enhancing the organism. It is when earlier differentiations are *not* assimilated (e.g. when experience is not assimilated in the self-concept), that the latest differentiation threatens to become the static final differentiation. Thereby man is not enhanced and he becomes what he is not, hence fragmented.

23. In a personal communication to me Rogers has questioned my description of bifurcations. Because of this, I will briefly recount the material on which my description was based. In his latest book, *Carl Rogers on Personal Power,* chapter 11, Rogers describes bifurcation as follows. Its occurrence, according to Rogers, represents a split in man's total organismic functioning. The origin of this split, however, he finds in the fact that a person makes too much of his awareness. Normally, awareness is simply a reflection of the flow of the organism at any given moment and it is only when its functioning is disrupted that a sharply self-conscious awareness arises in a person. At times a person may introject certain beliefs or constructs which, because they are taken in from the outside, are rigid and static. Because they are static, these constructs clash with that person's normal process of evaluating his experience in a fluid, changing way. When this occurs the person tends to lose confidence in his own non-conscious processes. He tends to disregard his own experience whenever it conflicts with his introjected constructs. As a result he cuts himself off from his own organic functioning and becomes dissociated. Consciously he begins to behave in terms of static rigid constructs. Unconsciously he behaves in terms of the actualizing tendency. As a result the satisfaction or

fulfillment of the actualizing tendency has thus become bifurcated into incompatible behavioral systems. This is the basis of all psychological and social pathology, according to Rogers.

The difference between Rogers and myself seems to be that he localizes the *source* of this bifurcation in human awareness, and thus describes it psychologically whereas I describe the same phenomenon *anthropologically*. But beyond that I fail to see how my description in the text differs in any essential way from his description as related above. More than likely I have not understood Rogers' view sufficiently at this point. However, since I presently see no way of resolving this difficulty I will have to restrict myself to bringing it to the readers' attention.

24. The notion of "direction" plays an important role in Rogers' thought. As I understand this term, it has the following signification: The actualization process is not a once-for-all movement toward some preconceived "end" or goal, in terms of which we can measure the man's progress, or in terms of which we can predict what he is going to do next. It must not be confused, for example, with the development from childhood into adult-hood toward a state where one has presumably "arrived" as an adult. For Rogers, man never arrives, is principally always "on the way". To arrive would mean the stagnation of the ongoing "becoming" process that man is. Actualization, or growth, is thus an ongoing, reoccurring process that calls for different behavior from moment to moment. The only thing we can say, need to say, is that however man acts, however he changes, he can always be counted on to do so in a forward, constructive, self-enhancing, "good" direction. Whatever that "good" direction might be, can never be determined beforehand, but is decided at all times by the situation as it exists at that moment.

25. *On Becoming A Person,* pp.26,194. "The Nature of Man", *Pastoral Psychology,* 1960, pp.23-26.

"Good" must of course be taken in the sense of self-enhancing and self-maintaining. Since man enhances himself by perpetual differentia-tion, he is always becoming "the best he can become" when he differen-tiates himself. Furthermore, since it belongs to his personal enhancement at the regard level that he should enhance the differentiation of others as well, his differentiation is also socially constructive. Only when he ceases to differentiate does man become destructive. But not to differentiate is foreign to man's nature, therefore man's nature is basically constructive.

26. *Nebraska Symposium on Motivation,* 1963, p.14.

27. The term "gestalt *relation*" is implied in Rogers' view that the organism maintains its organization dynamically, that it must continually be achieved with reference to its environment, and that it is continually re-established with reference to its earlier organizational achievements. The organization of the organism is originally given only as an active dynamic actualizing *principle* and can only be maintained insofar as it is continually being realized in a forward direction, that is to say, insofar as it is continually enhanced.

28. *Client-Centered Therapy*, p.489, or A. Angyal, *Foundations for a Science of Personality*, (1941) p.48.
29. The notion of gestalt relation is helpful for explaining Rogers' view of the
organism's "external" relation to its physical environment as also for explaining the "internal" relations between the various levels of differentiation complexity in the actualization process. As I understand the gestalt notion, it contains at least the following characteristics:

A gestal contains a number of elements which stand in an organized relation to each other of figure to ground. It can be said that these are interdependent in the sense that figure would not be figure without ground and vice versa. There is mobility possible between them. That is, whatever is figure can become ground and whatever is ground can become figure. It can further be said that the figure *emerges* out of the ground, thus that the ground gives some of its elements greater *significance* than others, but it can also be said that the figure organizes the ground as *that which is not* (yet) *figure*.

Thus in the external relation of the organism to its physical environment, some physical processes can be designated as *an-*organic. Further, with respect to this external gestalt relation, Rogers speaks of it from the point of view of the organism organizing its physical environment as ground, but will not hear of an emergence of the organism out of a physical environment. From his viewpoint the former is exclusively active and the latter passive. In this *limiting* case, therefore, the gestalt notion is only partially applicable.

However, it is admirably suited to explain the internal relations between the various levels of differentiation complexity. It helps us to understand the *emergent* direction of the actualization process from less to more complexity. Every new level of differentiation complexity emerges as a figure out of the ground of an earlier, less complex differentiation level. Whenever the former assimilates the latter, it is no longer a figure but becomes the ground out of which a new, more complex figure emerges ("inevitably") etc.

At the same time it explains the organization enhancing character of the actualization process as well. Once a new level of differentiation has been actualized as figure it has the *capacity* to determine what of the next lower level is to be assimilated, thus what of it is to be ground. (It should be noted that Rogers does not seem to ascribe this *selective* capacity to experience, but all the subsequent levels do have it. My model assumes however that experience has this capacity as well.) The next higher level therefore appears to have the capacity to selectively assimilate only that of the next lower level which it deems to be enhancing for the total organization of the actualization process. However, this capacity also offers the occasion for the organism *not* to assimilate matters that it should assimilate to remain whole and fluid. This is how incongruence, stagnation and fragmentation can occur in the growth process. Actualization is always the interaction of the upward emergence of new differentiation and the downward selective organization of earlier differentiation. Both are necessary and the ambivalence inherent in the (fluid) gestalt notion helps us to clarify the actualizing relations between the various levels. Finally, the way that Rogers prescribes for becoming fully functioning can be most succintly described by saying that fully functioning is most nearly attained when a man can let his downward selectively assimilating organization be guided by his upwardly emerging differentiation.

30. *Client-Centered Therapy*, pp.491-495.

31. At first glance, the formulation that experience is the goal of behavior seems odd, and that for the same reason as was explained in note 17. However, consider the alternative: One could consider Rogers to be saying no more than that the task of behavior is the enhancement maintenance of the physiological organism. And further, that in determining the needs to be fulfilled it does not take its cue from the physiological tensions themselves, but from its experience of these tensions. Finally, that in determining the possibility in the environment of reducing these tensions, it takes its cue from the organism's *perception of* the physical environment, rather than from the physical environment directly.

One problem with this formulation is *that it presupposes what* I am trying to explain at this point, namely how a *physiological* organism can obtain such *psychological functions as experience and perception. The quotation by Rogers to which the above formulation refers, holds as a description of behavior only,* when it is assumed that the organism has *already* differentiated to the level of experience and awareness. The *manner in which this differentiation* occurs is what I am now discussing.

Another problem with this formulation is that it assumes that the goal of behavior is the maintenance and enhancement of the *physiological* organism. This, I believe, goes contrary to Rogers' intent who also speaks of "organismic *experiencing" (Nebraska Symposium,* p.16) and of *self-actualization (Koch,* p.196). The organismic wholeness of which Rogers speaks is not the integration of biological organs or physiological part-processes, but the integration of successive differentiation levels. It is the integration of physiological processes at the level of experience, of experiential events into awareness and of perceptions into a self-concept, etc.

32. *Koch*, p.203

33. Thus the relation between experiences and their substratum sensory and visceral (physiological) events, the relation between experiences and their symbolizations in awareness, and the relation between the self-concept and the inter-personal relationships all differ descriptively from each other. Yet all of them are ways in which the organism actualizes itself.

34. *On Becoming A Person*, p.105.

35. *Ibid*, p.20,21.

36. *Ibid*, p.26, and *Freedom to Learn*, pp.252-256.

37. *Freedom to Learn*, p.247. Here Rogers states that the "one primary value". . . in the therapeutic relationship is. . ."that this person, this client, has worth. He as a person is valued in his separateness and

uniqueness''.
38. *Koch*, p.197.
39. It should be noted that the meaning of my term ''felt'' or ''affect'', used here as a substitute term for ''experience'', differs from the meaning which Rogers gives to the term ''feeling'' (see glossary definition 5), as referring to (an) emotion and its personal meaning. For me, ''feeling'' or ''being affected'' is defined by the phrase ''to receive the impact of''. Thus it includes sight, touch and audition as well as emotion. It means to indicate the link between physiological functioning and awareness. One cannot be aware of physiological events without being touched, affected by them, or without experiencing them.
40. The terms ''psychological'', ''experiential'' or ''experienced'' organism are my formulations, not those of Rogers. They mean to indicate that the organismic actualization process has differentiated itself at the level of experience.
41. Even though I am not aware of any place where Rogers refers in explicit detail to the organized character of experience, the fact that experience is a part of the organismic actualization process entails that it is configurational. This further seems to be suggested by his definition of ''an experience'' as a *''segment of the field* of experience''. (*Koch,* p.197, italics added).
42. Their commonality of meaning, I would hold, derives from the fact that they all refer to the awareness level of differentiation complexity.
43. *Koch*, p.198.
44. This accurate symbolization occurs when you ''. . .let your experience tell you its own meaning''. *Client-Centered Therapy,* p.97.
45. *Koch*, p.198.
46. See *Client-Centered Therapy,* pp.503-507, for a description of this process. Differentiation without assimilation occurs at the awareness level when experiences are barred from awareness *in their own meaning.* When this happens awareness of symbolization becomes specious rationalization, a conscious superstructure without reference to felt reality. See also p.515, where Rogers states: ''It is the organization of the concept of self *against* the symbolization of the certain experiences, contradictory to itself, which is the significant negative fact''.

This selectivity of awareness deserves further scrutiny. As part of the total organismic actualization process awareness functions as a spotlight symbolizing only those experiences which need to be symbolized and leaving others ''in the dark'', only *potentially* available to awareness until such time as when the need arises for them to be symbolized.

The positive value of its selectivity is presumably its economizing character. By making available only those experiences which are relevant to the self, awareness makes further differentiation at the conceptual level possible.

However, it would also seem to make awareness the first ''sore spot'' of the actualization process. For while selectivity is a characteristic of awareness, it is regulated by the self-concept. If therefore the self-concept is such that it cannot accept or recognize certain self experiences, it finds its occasion in the selective character to do so. It is interesting to note that Rogers never speaks of a lack of assimilation on the experiential level, even though his anthropology would allow him to do so. There is, in other words, never any mention in Rogers' writings about an incongruency between experience and organic need fulfillment. The latter are always assumed to become fully differentiated into the former. On the other hand, Rogers' writings abound with references regarding the incongruence between awareness and experience. This is probably due to the fact that he sees awareness as intrinsically selective whereas he does not view experience as such.

47. See especially *Client-Centered Therapy,* pp.503,504.
48. *Koch,* pp.197,198.
49. See for example *Client-Centered Therapy,* pp.190-196; *Koch,* pp.203, 205-206,213,216,218-219; *On Becoming a Person,* pp.64,157.
50. *Client-Centered Therapy,* pp.503-509.
51. *Ibid,* pp.497-503; *Koch,* pp.200-203.
52. It seems to me that the *dis*organization of the self which occurs in successful therapy means that the self-*concept* becomes a self *percept.* That is to say, it temporarily loses its status of *"primus inter pares",* with beneficial results for the reorganization of the perceptual field and the self itself.
53. *Koch,* p.202. *Client-Centered Therapy,* p.508.
54. A comment is in order at this point that applies specifically to my description above regarding the nature of concepts, but has application as well for the whole of this chapter. What I am attempting to give in this chapter is an anthropological account of the possibility of the occurrence of processes, which Rogers describes in his writings.

      Specifically in the context of the present discussion, my definition of a concept attempts to explain *why* the self-concept can become regnant in man to the detriment of man's total actualization process. Factually Rogers explains this in terms of our introjections of the regard of others. But this explanation begs the question now under discussion. Rogers states that the reason why a person can come to be ruled by the evaluations of others is that the part evaluations by the other are communicated to the total regard complex which we associate with the other. In short, when I introject, I unrealistically elaborate part evaluations into whole evaluations. My further explanation of *this* process is that it is of the nature of concepts to generalize, in order to maintain consistency.
55. *Client-Centered Therapy,* pp.497-503.
56. For an extensive discussion of the valuing process in man see: *Client-Centered Therapy,* pp.498-503, pp.522-524; *Koch,* p.210; and especially *Freedom to Learn,* Chapter 12, "A Modern Approach to the Valuing Process", pp.239-259.
57. This, according to Rogers, is particularly true for the way the infant values

his experience and behavior. See *Freedom to Learn*, pp.242-243.

58. "Other-regard" (negative or positive) precedes "self-regard" (negative or positive), *Koch*, p.209.
59. The term "received" is a later formulation by Rogers of what it means to "experience unconditional positive regard". The term includes the notions of "empathic understanding" and of "acceptance". See *On Becoming a Person*, pp.130-131.
60. *Nebraska Symposium on Motivation*, 1963, pp.19-22.
61. "Personally inevitable" in the sense that for our ongoing growth, the organism needs to actualize itself at the regard level in terms of unconditionally positive self-regard, and for that we are interpersonally dependent on the unconditional positive regard of others.
62. *Koch*, p.225.
63. *Client-Centered Therapy*, p.501.
64. This, I believe, is one of the basic intents of Rogers' work: *That society free the individual to grow.*
65. *Carl Rogers on Encounter Groups*, pp.53,117,127.
66. *Ibid*, pp.17-23, 134-136.
67. *Freedom to Learn*, pp.228,108,126,232.
68. *On Becoming a Person*, p.341.
69. For an extensive discussion on Rogers' view of communication and transparent, interpersonal sharing see: *Koch*, pp.235-240; *On Becoming A Person*, pp.329-346; *Freedom to Learn*, pp.221-237; *Carl Rogers on Encounter Groups*, especially pp.120,123,173,36,118; pp.23-26,123, 127,53,117; pp.17-23,134-136; pp.163,171.
70. In a recent interview Rogers calls growth the "key note of my work with people" and he adds ". . .I'm interested in growing people. This has been true in therapy, and it's been true with the staff groups I've worked with. I think the thing that I pride myself on most in working with students and patients is that frequently I've been able to help them to grow and develop." R.I. Evans, *Carl Rogers the Man and His Ideas*, (1975), p.72.
71. C.R. Rogers, B. Stevens, *Person to Person, The Problem of Being Human*, p.87.
72. *On Becoming A Person*, pp.33,37,16,50. *Person to Person*, pp.188-189.
73. Even though Rogers ultimately comes to endorse transparency as the most therapeutic element of a relationship, he himself repeatedly hedges on whether one ought to "say" all that one "thinks" or "feels". (See e.g. *Person to Person*, p.87). It seems to me that he is unnecessarily hesitant in this regard. If a therapist is *genuinely* non-directive or client-centered in his attitude towards the client (as all "Rogerians" are, per definition) then his expressions of what he is feeling cannot help but also be characterized by his attitude. Only when a (negative) feeling is expressed *evaluatively,* is it non-therapeutic, because evaluation implies directivity and directivity is per definition anti-therapeutic. But to voice a negative feeling as a *personal* expression can't be non-therapeutic because it is per definition non-evaluative and thus non-directive.

Furthermore, how could one better express one's trust in the growth capacity of the client (which is the core principle of client-centeredness) than by asking the client to deal with one's negative feeling about him? When expressing such feelings, the therapist in effect says to the client: "I trust your growth capacity so much that I'm not even going to hide my feelings from you". Apparently, O.H. Bown saw this point already early in the development of the client-centered movement. (See *Client-Centered Therapy,* pp.160-167).

74. See Glossary Definition 25.

75. Here we have the problematics of "individualism versus conformity" referred to in chapter one.

76. *Koch,* p.197.

77. *On Becoming a Person,* pp.122,153,171-172,176,188.

78. *Ibid,* chapter 7.

79. Rogers calls this movement, learning to "trust in your organism" (see *On Becoming a Person,* pp.102-105,122,189). It gets man living again "from the bottom up" rather than "from the top down" and is thus a change into a forward direction of growth.

80. James J. Dagenais, *Models of Man, a Phenomenological Critique of Some Paradigms in the Human Sciences,* (1972), chapter II.

81. In a letter to me Rogers has confirmed that there were no direct contacts with any existential or phenomenological thinking until he was teaching at the University of Chicago.

82. A.W. Combs, "Phenomenological Concepts in Nondirective Therapy". *Journal of Consulting Psychology,* vol. XII, no. 4, (1948), pp.197-208.

83. C.S. Hall and G. Lindzey (eds.), *Theories of Personality,* (1957), chapter 12.

84. C.H. Patterson, *Theories of Counseling and Psychotherapy,* pp.431-439.

85. A.W. Combs and D. Snyggs, *Individual Behavior, A Perceptual Approach to Behavior,* (1949).

86. *Ibid.,* p.20.

87. C.E. Beck, *Philosophical Foundations of Guidance,* (1963), pp.66-67.

88. R.I. Kellerman, "Themata in de Zelf-beoordeling", *Nederlands Tijdschrift voor de Psychologie en Haar Grensgebieden,* N.R. 12 (1957), pp.215-230.

89. W.A. Smit, *Mens En Persoonlikheid, 'n Antropologies-sielkundige studie,* (1975).

90. J.J. Dijkhuis, *De Process Theorie van C.R. Rogers, een Kritische en Methodologische Analyse van zijn Opvattingen over het Process van de Psychotherapie en de Interventies van de Therapeut,* (1964).

91. The term is hard to translate. The phrase, "standing on your own two feet" describes it best. Other translations could be "self-reliance", "autonomy" and "maturity" but these meanings come too close to the notion of independence to be suitable.

92. See C.R. Rogers, *On Becoming a Person,* chapter 10.

93. H.R. Wijngaarden, *Over Het Onbewuste,* (1958) and the following ar-

ticles in *Nederlands Tijdschrift voor de Psychologie:* "Gespreks-thera-
pie", (1961), pp.421-431; *"Nog Iets Over Gesprekstherapie"*, (1963),
pp.156-163; *"De Ontwikkeling in de Niet-directieve Therapie"*, (1965),
pp.577-591; and the article written with J.F. Petrie, *"Actuele Ontwikkelingen in de Psychotherapie"*, (1970), pp.205-250.

94. H.T. Upshaw, *The Interdependence of the Religious and the Psycholo-
    gical, Considered through a Comparison of the Views of Martin Buber and
    Carl Rogers on the Nature of Personal Meaning,* (1970).
95. Martin Buber, *The Knowledge of Man,* (1965), pp.166-184.
96. Martin Buber, *Between Man and Man,* (1947), p.244.
97. Toine Vossen, *Zichzelf Worden in Menselijke Relatie,* (1973).

Notes on Chapter Five

1. Whenever I refer in this chapter to matters discussed in earlier chapters I
   will adopt the following method of notations: The Arabic numeral will
   indicate the chapter number, the Roman numeral will indicate the section
   of that chapter, the capital letter will indicate the subsection, etc.
2. C.R. Rogers, *Carl Rogers on Personal Power,* (1977), p.244ff.
3. D.A. Wexler and L.N. Rice, (eds.), *Innovations in Client-Centered Therapy,* (1974), p.13.
4. C.R. Rogers, *On Becoming a Person,* (1961), p.27.
5. C.R. Rogers, "De Vormgevende Tendentie" in *Psychotherapie en Mensvisie,* (1978), pp.59-62. The contents of this article are a translation into
   Dutch by Prof. Cassee and Drs. Petrie of a short speech entitled "The
   Formative Tendency", given by Rogers at a recent 'Conference About
   Theory' by the Association for Humanistic Psychology held in Tucson,
   Arizona.
6. Howard Kirchenbaum, *On Becoming Carl Rogers,* (1979), p.432.
7. One of the best descriptions of this process by Rogers is found in chapter 11
   of his latest book, *Carl Rogers on Personal Power,* (1977). In this chapter
   he also struggles hard with the tensions inherent in his process conception
   of man.
8. Richard I. Evans, *Carl Rogers — The Man and His Ideas,* (1975),
   p.xxxvii.
9. Before moving onto the next section I should like to anticipate a possible
   criticism to the effect that I am unfair to Rogers when I compare his
   conception to an image which I have chosen and then proceed to criticize
   his conception for not living up to that image. To be fair, it may be argued,
   I should rather have utilized his own image of the growing plant.
       It must be remembered that my central aim in this section is to
   evaluate the coherence of Rogers' overall conception with his basic intent.
   And, as I have shown extensively in chapters three, four and in the present
   chapter, Rogers' basic intent is to promote the fluidity of human functioning. This fluidity is, in my opinion, better represented by the (hydro)-
   dynamic characteristics of a river than by the growth characteristics of a

plant. The river image was therefore chosen deliberately and is entirely in line with my interpretation, particularly in chapter four, of the central thrust of Rogers' thought. Thus, if my choice of the river image is unfair, then so is my interpretation of his view of man. However, to date Rogers has not found it necessary to contradict me in my understanding of his basic intent.

The issue at stake here, which was already discussed in detail in chapter four (see especially note 20), is the question of which is more primary in Rogers' thought, structure or process, fixity or changingness. It is my contention that Rogers consistently chooses for the latter, and at expense of the former. Thus the reason I chose the river image over that of a growing plant is that the latter puts too much emphasis on the structural, and not enough on the dynamic character of the process. This means that with regard to the basic intent of Rogers' *actual* conception of man the image of a growing plant is inadequate.

Admittedly, the plant image makes it easier to understand the other emphasis of Rogers, namely the autonomy of the process, since a plant seems to be a more active agency than a river in directing its (growth) movement. However, even with respect to the autonomy of the process, many of the criticisms leveled against Rogers' conception via the river image can also be leveled against him via his plant image. A plant, for instance, needs the right amount of rain to grow. Thus it does not grow autonomously either.

Moreover, in other respects the plant image is decidedly inferior to the river image. By way of example, for Rogers the process is inter-individual as well as intra-individual. This implies that at a given stage of growth, two or more individual processes meet, inter-mingle and augment one another. This fact is immediately evident through the image of a river, but not via the image of a plant.

The above discussion leads us to an interesting point regarding the comparison of Rogers' conception with that of other organistic thinkers. Rogers is not the first, nor the only person to think organistically. This kind of thinking has a venerable history that hails back all the way to Leibniz. By organistic thinking I mean the notion that a given organized system has the capacity to alter itself independent of outside help, thus autonomously, while all the while remaining an organized whole. For most organistic thinkers internal change is a function of the structure of the organism. For Rogers, however, the structure of the organism is a function of its capacity to change. Thus for most organistic thinkers the structure of the organism is primary. For Rogers changingness is primary.

10. Once again it may be asked whether it is fair to criticize Rogers on the basis of a (possibly unfortunate) choice of a metaphor. Yet, whether unfortunately chosen or not, the notion of a self-programming computer is exactly what Rogers has in mind for the human organism. His comparison between the computer and the human organism is by no means accidental. At the same time he writes about this comparison to real people who have

the freedom to choose. His intention is presumably to inform us about the course of action to be taken by us with respect to our organism. Presumably also, the course of action he wants us to take is to be receptive to this computing organism. Thus he is not just asking us to follow him in his manner of speaking about the organism. The analogy intended by him is not that there exists a one-to-one relation between the computer and the human organism. Rather, he means to convey that, like the (self-programming) computer the organism is a ready-made process within us which is influenced by no conscious decision on our part other than the one whether or not to yield completely to it. In the context of this appeal it seems legitimate to me to evaluate the validity of his metaphor.

11. Carl R. Rogers, *On Becoming a Person,* (1961), pp.23,24. On the basis of this passage it is more correct to say that experienc*ing* does not lead us astray.
12. Carl R. Rogers, *Client-Centered Therapy,* (1965), p.491.
13. Carl R. Rogers, *Carl Rogers on Personal Power,* (1977), p.247.
14. *Ibid.*
15. *Ibid.*
16. Ch. B. Truax, "Reinforcement and Non-Reinforcement in Rogerian Psychotherapy", *Journal of Abnormal Psychology,* (1966), Vol. 7, 1, p.1-9.
17. C. Sanders, L.K.A. Eisenga, J.F.H. van Rappard, *Inleiding in de Grondslagen van de Psychologie,* (1976), p.61.
18. D.A. Wexler, "A Cognitive Theory of Experiencing, Self-Actualization and Therapeutic Process," chapter 3 in D.A. Wexler and L.N. Rice, (eds.), *Innovations in Client Centered Therapy,* (1974).
19. T.S. Kuhn, *The Structure of Scientific Revolutions,* (1970).
20. For the notion of the illuminating function of one's anthropology I am indebted to Dr. Johan Vander Hoeven, professor of philosophy at the Free University of Amsterdam, the Netherlands.
21. I am indebted to Prof. Dr. H.R. Wijngaarden for this insight. To me, this is an important therapeutic insight. In the first place it is born out of a genuine desire on the part of the therapist to understand his client empathically. Thus it avoids appearing to be judgmental in a rejecting sense. Second, it challenges the client to think more clearly about his problems. This in itself can have a therapeutic effect. Finally, it allows the therapist to confront the client from out of his *own* person. By doing this the therapist in effect says to the client, "I think I understand what you are telling me but it does not make any sense *to me*. Please, try to convince me of the rightness of what you are saying." Wijngaarden gives an example, where he first attempts to fathom the depth of the client's feeling and then says to the client: "I know how you are feeling. I also understand the conclusion that you draw on the basis of this feeling, but I don't understand what it is that makes you feel the way you feel."

Via these kind of confrontative questions he can break open the onetrack, dead-end thought patterns of the client and give him room to consider alternative ways of responding to his feelings.

22. For an important and exhaustive treatment of human development see Theodore Lidz, *The Person, His and Her Development Throughout the Life Cycle*, revised edition, (1976). This book is important in my view. It never describes the person as an autonomous entity. Rather, it shows that personal development necessarily occurs in a supportive social context and it shows that the relation of the person to this social context is an important part of his development.
23. Richard I. Evans, *Carl Rogers—The Man and his Ideas*, (1975), p.xxxvii.
24. Carl R. Rogers, *On Becoming a Person*, (1961), chapter 13.
25. Howard Kirschenbaum in his biography of Rogers (*On Becoming Carl Rogers*, 1979) gives two examples of Rogers' reluctance in this regard. The first (p.175ff) was his way of dealing with the staff of the counseling centre at the Chicago University. This non-leadership style apparently had a very positive effect on the staff members. The second example (p.281ff.) occurred during his Wisconsin years and relates to the disappearance of research data, for which one of his fellow researchers was allegedly responsible. His other co-workers urged him repeatedly to take disciplinary action, which Rogers put off for so long that the situation deteriorated beyond repair.

BIBLIOGRAPHY

This bibliography refers to those of Rogers' writings which are cited in the text or consulted for its preparation. A detailed bibliography of Rogers' writings can be found in the following books: Carl R. Rogers, *On Becoming a Person*, (1961), pp.403-411 (publications 1930-1960 inclusive); Richard I. Evans, *Carl Rogers The Man and His Ideas*, (1975), pp.179-186 (publications 1957-1974 inclusive); Howard Kirschenbaum, *Carl Rogers: A Case Study of a Psychologist and Educator*, unpublished doctoral dissertation, Temple University, 1974, available through University Microfilms. A list covering his latest writings is available from the National Humanistic Education Center, 110 Spring St., Saratoga Springs, N.Y., 12866.

ANGYAL, A. *Foundations for a Science of Personality*. New York: Commonwealth Fund, 1941
BARRETT, WILLIAM. *Irrational Man, A Study in Existential Philosophy*. Garden City, New York: Doubleday & Co. Inc., 1958
BECK, C.E. *Philosophical Foundations of Guidance*. Englewood Cliffs, N.J.: Prentice-Hall, 1963
BECKER, ERNEST. *The Denial of Death*. New York: The Free Press, 1973
BENJAMIN, A.F. *The Helping Interview*. Boston: Houghton Mifflin Co., 1969

BERENSON, BERNARD G. and CARKHUFF, ROBERT R. (eds.). *Sources of Gain in Counseling and Psychotherapy*. New York: Holt, Rinehart and Winston, Inc., 1967

BERGIN, ALLEN E. and GARFIELD, SOL L. (eds.). *Handbook of Psychotherapy and Behavior Change: An Empirical Analysis*. New York: John Wiley & Sons Inc., 1971

BERNE, ERIC. *Games People Play*. New York: Grove Press Inc., 1964

BERNSTEIN, RICHARD J. (ed.) *On Experience, Nature and Freedom, Representative Selections, John Dewey*. New York: Liberal Arts Press, 1960

BORING, E.G. and LINDZEY, G. *A History of Psychology in Autobiography*. New York: Appleton-Century-Croft, 1967

BOYD, W. *The History of Western Education*. London: Adam and Charles Black, 1961

BRAMMER, L.M. *The Helping Relationship*. Englewood Cliffs, N.J.: Prentice-Hall, Inc., 1973

BRIL, K.A. *Tien Jaar Probleemhistorische Methode*. Bibliografie en overzichten over de jaren 1960-1970. Amsterdam: Free University, 1971

BRILL, A.A. (trans.) *The Basic Writings of Sigmund Freud*. New York: Random House, 1938

BRYCE, J. *The American Commonwealth*, Vol.2, 1893. New York: The Macmillan Co., 1893

BUBER, MARTIN. *Between Man and Man*. Translated by Robert Gregor Smith. London: Collins, 1947

— *Eclipse of God*. New York: Harper and Row, Inc., 1952

— *The Knowledge of Man, A Philosophy of the Interhuman*. Translated by M. Friedman and R.G. Smith. New York: Harper and Row, Inc., 1965

— *The Way of Response*. Edited by N.N. Glatzer. New York: Schocken Books, Inc., 1966

— *I and Thou*. Translated by Walter Kaufmann. New York: Charles Scribner's Sons, 1970

BÜRKI, HANS. *Tussen geloof en skepsis*. Amsterdam: Buijten & Schipperheijn, 1971

CASSEE, A.P., PETRIE, J.F., and SANDERS, C. (eds.) *Psychotherapie en Mensvisie*. Deventer: Van Loghum Slaterus, 1978

CARKHUFF, ROBERT R. and BERENSON, BERNARD G. *Beyond Counseling and Therapy*. New York: Holt, Rinehart and Winston, Inc., 1967

COMBS, A.W. "Phenomenological Concepts in Non-Directive Therapy", *Journal of Consulting Psychology*, XII, No. 4 (July-August, 1948)

COMBS, A.W. and SNYGGS, D. *Individual Behavior, A Perceptual Approach to Behavior*. New York: Harper and Row, 1949

DAGENAIS, JAMES J. *Models of Man, a Phenomenological Critique of Some Paradigms in the Human Sciences*. The Hague: Martinus Nijhoff, 1972

DE GRAAFF, ARNOLD (ed.). *Anthropology and Psychology in Christian Perspective*. Institute for Christian Studies, 229 College Street, Toronto, Ontario

DE GRAAFF, ARNOLD. *An Alternative to Our Traditional Anthropological Models.* Institute for Christian Studies, 229 College Street, Toronto, Ontario, 1976

DE TOCQUEVILLE. *Democracy in America,* Vol. II, 1845. New York: Henry G. Langley, 1845

DEWEY, JOHN. *Human Nature and Conduct, an Introduction to Social Psychology.* New York: The Modern Library, 1930

— *Experience and Nature.* New York: Dover Publications, 1958

— *Reconstruction in Philosophy* (enlarged edition). Boston: The Beacon Press, 1963

— *The Influence of Darwin on Philosophy, and Other Essays in Contemporary Thought.* Bloomington: Indiana University Press, 1965

DIJKHUIS, J.J. *De Process Theorie van C.R. Rogers, een Kritische en Methodologische Analyse van zijn Opvattingen over het Process van de Psychotherapie en de Interventies van de Therapeut.* Hilversum-Antwerpen: Paul Brand, 1964

DOOYEWEERD, H. *A New Critique of Theoretical Thought.* 4 volumes. Amsterdam: H.J. Paris; Philadelphia: The Presbyterian and Reformed Publishing Company, 1953-1958

— "De Analogische Grondbegrippen der Vakwetenschappen en Hun Betrekking tot de Structuur van den Menselijken Ervarings-horizon", *Mededelingen der Koninklijke Nederlandse Akademie van Wetenschappen, Afd. Letterkunde.* Nieuwe Reeks, Deel 17, No. 6. Amsterdam: N.V. Noord-Hollandsche Uitgevers Maatschappij, 1954

— *In the Twilight of Western Thought.* Nutley, N.J.: The Craig Press, 1975

EISENGA, L.K.A. *Structuralisme, Functionalisme en Behaviorisme, de gedachte van een behavioristische revolutie in de psychologie.* Amsterdam: Vrije Universiteit, 1973

EISENGA, L.K.A. and TAKENS, R.J. (eds.) *De Veranderbaarheid van de Mens De pretenties van de psychotherapeutische hulpverlening.* Dordrecht: Floris Publications, 1978

EVANS, R.I. (ed.) *Carl Rogers, the Man and His Ideas.* New York: E.P. Dutton, 1975

GENDLIN, E.T. "A Theory of Personality Change" in P. Worschel and D. Byrne (eds.). *Personality Change.* New York: John Wiley & Sons, 1964

GORDON, THOMAS. *P.E.T. Parent Effectiveness Training.* New York: Peter H. Wyden, Inc., 1970

HALL, CALVIN S. and LINDZEY, GARDNER. *Theories of Personality.* New York: John Wiley & Sons, Inc., 1957

HARPER, ROBERT A. *The New Psychotherapies.* Englewood Cliffs, N.J.: Prentice-Hall, Inc., 1975

HART, HENDRIK *Communal Certainty and Authorized Truth.* Amsterdam: Swets and Zeitlinger, 1966

— *The Challenge of Our Age.* Toronto: The Association for the Advancement of Christian Studies, 1968

HUDSON, W.S. *American Protestantism*. Chicago: University of Chicago Press, 1961
— *Religion in America*. New York: Charles Scribner's Sons, 1965
HUSSERL, EDMUND. *Die Krisis der Europäischen Wissenschaften und die Transzendentale Phanomenologie*. Den Haag: Martinus Nijhoff, 1969
IDOMIR, L. *An Analysis of the Philosophical Compatability of Carl Rogers' Clientcentered Counseling and John Dewey's Pragmatism*. Tulsa: University of Tulsa, 1967
JAMES, WILLIAM. *Principles of Psychology*. 2 volumes. New York: Dover Publications, 1950
JASPERS, KARL. *Reason and Existenz*. Translated by William Earle. Noonday Press, 1955
KALSBEEK, L. *Contours of a Christian Philosophy*. Translated by B. and J. Zijlstra. Toronto: Wedge Publishing Foundation, 1976
KELLERMAN, R.I. "Themata in de Zelf-beoordeling", *Nederlands Tijdschrift voor de Psychologie en Haar Grensgebieden*, N.R. 12, 1957
KIERKEGAARD, S. *Fear and Trembling and the Sickness Unto Death*. Translated by Walter Lowrie. Princeton: Princeton University Press, 1941
— *Concluding Unscientific Postscript*. Translated by D.F. Swenson and Walter Lowrie. Princeton: Princeton University Press, 1941
KIRSCHENBAUM, HOWARD. *On Becoming Carl Rogers*. New York: Delacorte Press, 1979
KOCH, S. (ed.). *Psychology: A Study of Science, III*. New York: McGraw-Hill, 1959
KROPF, DETLEF. *Grundprobleme der Gesprächspsychotherapie*. Gottingen: Verlag fur Psychologie, 1976
KÜBLER-ROSS, ELISABETH. *Death The Final Stage of Growth*. Englewood Cliffs, N.J.: Prentice-Hall, Inc., 1975
KUENZLI, A.E. (ed.). *The Phenomenological Problem*. New York: Harper, 1959
KUHN, THOMAS S. *The Structure of Scientific Revolutions*. Chicago: The University of Chicago Press, 1970
KUIPER, P.C. *Neurosenleer*. Arnhem: Van Loghum Slaterus, 1968
LAING, R.D. *The Politics of Experience*. New York: Ballantine Books, Inc., 1967
LASCH, CHRISTOPHER. *The Culture of Narcissism*. New York: W.W. Norton & Co. Inc., 1978
LIDZ, THEODORE. *The Person His and Her Development Throughout the Life Cycle* (Revised Edition). New York: Basic Books, Inc., 1976
LIEBERMAN, M.A., YALOM, I.D., MILES, M.B. *Encounter Groups: First Facts*. New York: Basic Books, Inc., 1973
LINSCHOTEN, J. *Op Weg Naar een Fenomenologische Psychologie*. Utrecht: Erven J. Bijleveld, 1959
— *Idolen van de Psycholoog*. Utrecht: Erven J. Bijleveld, 1964
LIPSET, S.M. "The Unchanging American Character", in R.L. Rapson,

(ed.). *Individualism and Conformity in the American Character*. Lexington, Mass.: D.C. Heath and Co., 1967

MATSON, FLOYD W. and MONTAGU, ASHLEY (eds.). *The Human Dialogue, Perspectives on Communication*. New York: The Free Press, 1967

MAY, ROLLO (ed.). *Existential Psychology*. New York: Random House, 1960

Mc INTIRE, C.T. *The Ongoing Task of Christian Historiography*. Toronto: Institute for Christian Studies, 1974

MERLEAU-PONTY, M. *Phenomenology of Perception*. Translated by Colin Smith. London: Routledge & Kegan Paul, Ltd., 1962

OLTHUIS, JAMES H. "The Unique Certitudinal Focus of the Scriptures: Towards a Certitudinal Hermeneutic", Institute for Christian Studies, Toronto, Ontario

PATTERSON, C.H. *Theories of Counseling and Psychotherapy*. New York: Harper and Row, 1965

PERLS, FREDERICK S. *Gestalt Therapy Verbatim*. Toronto: Bantam Books, 1969

POLANY, MICHAEL. *Personal Knowledge, Towards a Post-Critical Philosophy*. New York: Harper Torch Books, 1964

POTTER, D.M. "The Quest for the National Character", in R.L. Rapson (ed.). *Individualism and Conformity in the American Character*. Lexington, Mass.: D.C. Heath and Co., 1967

RAPSON, R.L. (ed.). *Individualism and Conformity in the American Character*. Lexington, Mass.: D.C. Heath and Co., 1967

RIESMAN, D. "From Morality to Morale", in H. Stanton and S. Perry (eds.) *Personality and Political Crisis*. New York: The Free Press, 1951

ROGERS, C.R. *The Clinical Treatment of the Problem Child*. Cambridge, Mass.: The Riverside Press, 1939

— *Counseling and Psychotherapy*, Boston: Houghton Mifflin Co., 1942

— *Client-Centered Therapy*. Boston: Houghton Mifflin Co., 1951

— "The Necessary and Sufficient Conditions of Therapeutic Personality Change", *Journal of Consulting Psychology*, XXI, 1957

— "Some Observations on the Organization of Personality", in A.E. Kuenzli (ed.). *The Phenomenological Problem*. New York: Harper, 1959

— "A Theory of Therapy, Personality and Interpersonal Relations" in S. Koch (ed.). *Psychology: A Study of a Science*, Vol. 3. New York: McGraw-Hill, 1959

— "The Nature of Man", *Pastoral Psychology*, 1960, 23-26

— *On Becoming a Person*. Boston: Houghton Mifflin Co., 1961

— "The Actualizing Tendency in Relation to Motives and to Consciousness", *Nebraska Symposium on Motivation*, 1963

— *Freedom to Learn*. Columbus, Ohio: Charles E. Merrill, 1969

— *Carl Rogers on Encounter Groups*. New York: Harper and Row, 1970

— *Becoming Partners: Marriage and Its Alternatives*. New York: Dell Publishing Co., 1972

— "My Philosophy of Interpersonal Relationships and How It Grew", *Jour-*

nal of Humanistic Psychology, XIII, No. 2 (Spring, 1973), 3-15
— Carl Rogers on Personal Power, Inner Strength, and Its Revolutionary Impact. New York: Delacorte Press, 1977
ROGERS, CARL R. and COULSON, WILLIAM R. Man and the Science of Man. Columbus, Ohio: Charles E. Merrill Publishing Co., 1968
ROGERS, C.R. and KINGET, G. Psychotherapie en Menselijke Verhoudingen. Den Haag: Bert Bakker, 1974
ROGERS, C.R. and STEVENS, B. Person to Person, the Problem of Being Human. New York: Real People Press, 1967
ROGERS, H.E. "A Wife's View of Carl Rogers", Voices, Vol. 1, 1965
RUNNER, H.E. Syllabus for Philosophy 220 The History of Ancient Philosophy. Grand Rapids, Mich.: Calvin College, 1958-1959
— The Relation of the Bible to Learning. Toronto: The Association for the Advancement of Christian Studies, 1959-1960
SAHAKIAN, WILLIAM S. (ed.). Psychotherapy and Counseling Studies in Technique. Chicago: Rand McNally & Co., 1969
SANDERS, C., EISENGA, L.K.A. and VAN RAPPARD, J.F.H. Inleiding in de grondslagen van de psychologie. Deventer: Van Loghum Slaterus, 1976
SANDERS, C. De behavioristische revolutie in de psychologie. Deventer: Van Loghum Slaterus, 1972.
SCHEFFLER, ISRAEL. Four Pragmatists A Critical Introduction to Peirce, James, Mead, and Dewey. New York: Humanities Press, 1974
SCHOULS, PETER. Man in Communication. Toronto: The Association for the Advancement of Christian Studies, 1968
SCHUMACHER, E.F. Small is Beautiful. London: Blond & Briggs Ltd., 1973
SEERVELD, CALVIN. "A Turnabout in Aesthetics to Understanding", The Institute for Christian Studies, 229 College St., Toronto, Ontario
— "An Obedient Aesthetic Life", The Institute for Christian Studies, Toronto, Ontario
— Aesthetic Life and Artistic Task. Toronto: Wedge Publishing, 1977 (in print)
SKILLEN, JAMES W. (ed.). Christian Politics: Falso Hope or Biblical Demand. Indiana, Pennsylvania: Jubilee Enterprises Ltd., 1976
SKINNER, B.F. Walden Two. New York: The Macmillan Co., 1948
— Beyond Freedom & Dignity. Toronto: Bantam Books, 1971
SMIT, W.A. Pastoraal-Psigologiese Verkenning van die Client-Centered Terapie van Carl R. Rogers. Kampen: J.H. Kok, 1960
— Mens en Persoonlikheid, 'n Antropologies-sielkundige studie. Bloemfontein: Sacum Beperk, 1975
SOUTHWELL, EUGENE A. and MERBAUM, MICHAEL (eds.). Personality: Readings in Theory and Research. Belmont, California: Brooks/Cole Publishing Co., 1971
SPIEGELBERG, H. The Phenomenological Movement, 2 volumes. The Hague: Martinus Nijhoff, 1971
STRASSER, S. Fenomenologie en empirische menskunde. Arnhem: Van Loghum Slaterus, 1962

SZASZ, THOMAS S. *Ideology and Insanity*. New York: Doubleday, 1970

THORNE, F.C. "The Great Clinical Hangup", *Journal of Clinical Psychology*, XXVII, No. 3 (July, 1971)

TOFLER, ALVIN. *Future Shock*. New York: Random House, 1970

TRUAX, CH. B. "Reinforcement and Non-Reinforcement in Rogerian Psychotherapy", *Journal of Abnormal Psychology*, 1966, Vol.7, 1

UPSHAW, H.T. *The Interdependence of the Religious and the Psychological, Considered Through a Comparison of the Views of Martin Buber and Carl Rogers on the Nature of Personal Meaning*. Unpublished dissertation, University of Chicago, 1970

VAN DEN BERG, J.H. *Psychologie en Theologische Anthropologie*. Nijkerk: G.F. Callenbach N.V., 1952

— *Leven in Meervoud*. Nijkerk: G.F. Callenbach N.V., 1963

— *De Psychiatrische Patient*. Nijkerk: G.F. Callenbach N.V., 1969

VANDER HOEVEN, JOHAN. *The Rise and Development of the Phenomenological Movement*. Toronto: The Association for the Advancement of Christian Studies, 1965

— *Op de bres voor de open discussie*. Amsterdam: N.V. Buijten & Schipperheijn, 1968

VARIOUS AUTHORS. *What, Then, Is Man? A Symposium of Theology, Psychology, and Psychiatry*. Saint Louis, Missouri: Concordia Publishing House, 1958

VITZ, PAUL C. *Psychology as Religion: The Cult of Self-Worship*. Grand Rapids, Mich.: William B. Eerdmans Publishing Co., 1977

VOSSEN, TOINE. *Zichzelf Worden in Menselijke Relatie*. Haarlem: Uitgeverij De Toorts, 1973

WANN, T.W. (ed.). *Behaviorism and Phenomonology Contrasting Bases for Modern Psychology*. Chicago: The University of Chicago Press, 1964

WATERINK, J. *Man as Religious Being and Modern Psychology*. Separate from *Free University Quarterly*, Vol. VI, No. 1 (February) 1959

WEXLER, D.A. and RICE, L. (eds.). *Innovations in Client-Centered Therapy*. New York: John Wiley & Sons, 1974

WHITAKER, DOROTHY STOCK and LIEBERMAN, MORTON A. *Psychotherapy Through the Group Process*. New York: Atherton Press, 1970

WIJNGAARDEN, H.R. *Over Het Onbewuste*. Utrecht: J. Bijleveld, 1958

— *Hoofdproblemen der Volwassenheid*. Utrecht: J. Bijleveld, 1959

— "Gesprekstherapie", *Nederlands Tijdschrift voor de Psychologie*, 1961

— "Nog Iets Over Gesprekstherapie", *Nederlands Tijdschrift voor de Psychologie*, 1963

— "De Ontwikkeling in de Niet-Directieve Therapy", *Nederlands Tijdschrift voor de Psychologie*, 1965

WIJNGAARDEN, H.R. and PETRIE, J.F. "Actuele Ontwikkelingen in de Psychotherapie", *Nederlands Tijdschrift voor de Psychologie*, 1970

WINCH, PETER, *The Idea of a Social Science and Its Relation to Philosophy*. London: Routledge & Kegan Paul, 1958

WOLTERS, ALBERT. *On Vollenhoven's Problem-Historical Method.* Thesis, Centrale Interfaculteit, Free University, Amsterdam, 1975

WORCHEL P. and BYRNE, D. (eds.) *Personality Change.* New York: John Wiley & Sons, 1964

ZUIDEMA, S.U. *Kierkegaard.* Translated by David H. Freeman. Philadelphia, Penn.; Presbyterian and Reformed Publishing Co., 1960

— *Communication and Confrontation.* Toronto: Wedge Publishing Foundation, 1972

INDEX

DATE DUE

NOV. 1 0 1993 NOV 10 '93			
NOV. 2 9 1993 NOV 29 '93			

DEMCO 38-297